*This book is dedicated to
the children of the Philadelphia public schools*

THREE TO GET READY

THREE TO GET READY

The Education of a White Family in Inner City Schools

Lois Mark Stalvey

The University of Wisconsin Press

The University of Wisconsin Press
114 North Murray Street
Madison, Wisconsin 53715

3 Henrietta Street
London WC2E 8LU, England

Three to Get Ready: The Education of a White Family in Inner City Schools was first published in 1974 as *Getting Ready: The Education of a White Family in Inner City Schools* by William Morrow & Company, Inc.

Grateful acknowledgment is made for permission to quote from the song "We've Only Just Begun," lyrics by Paul Williams, music by Roger Nichols. Copyright 1970, Irving Music, Inc. (BMI). All rights reserved. Used by permission.

Library of Congress Cataloging-in-Publication Data
Stalvey, Lois Mark.
[Getting ready]
Three to get ready: the education of a white family in inner city schools /
Lois Mark Stalvey.
328 pp.   cm.
Originally published: New York: Morrow, 1974. With new afterword.
Includes bibliographical references and index.
ISBN 0-299-15394-0 (paper: alk. paper)
1. Education, Urban—United States. I. Title.
LC5131.G655   1997
370.19'348'0973—dc20   96-44854

ACKNOWLEDGMENTS

NO BOOK IS THE WORK OF ONLY ONE PERSON, NO EDUCATION IS EITHER. So many children and adults made a contribution; some, brief but unforgettable; some over long periods of patience and honesty.

Those to whom I owe most are: Irene Randleman, Vernell and Leslie Pernsley, Sonia Waters, Corinthia Williams, Sandy Leonard, Tom Deahl, Robin Houston, Roderick Purdy, Albert Letson, Sam Barnett, Fred Boneparte, Michael Myers, Charles Manns, Clayton McGill, Preston Johnson, Claudia Cuyler, Angelina Redmon, Oscar Murphy, Gerald Harris, Perry Wright, Stephen Grant, Agnes Tate, Othello Greene, Carol Williams, David Speller, Dorothy and Cronyn Matthews, Jacqueline Evans, Genevieve Cammerotte, Michael Bridges, Kenneth Brown, Edward Bibbs, Gerald Revello, Clifford Lilly, Donald Ellis, George Coleman, Sally Smith, and Ann Schoonmaker.

And most particularly I owe thanks to Edna Lee Smalls and to Joan McGuinn Jenkins who listened and helped me understand.

AUTHOR TO READER—1997

WHEN THIS BOOK WAS PUBLISHED IN 1974, I HOPED—EVEN EXPECTED— that by now the problems in America's public schools would at least have been lessened. I truly believed the quotation (whose source I have never been able to find) that "men and nations act wisely only when all other alternatives have been exhausted."

America has now had over twenty years to exhaust the alternatives. Yet in a newspaper article I read *yesterday* and a television show I saw *this week* it is obvious that the same problems exist.

As you will read, my own children learned valuable lessons in a big city public school system. So did I. But the children who needed most from the schools did not get it then. They are obviously not getting it now.

And I must wonder how many more alternatives we have.

LOIS MARK STALVEY

January, 1997

AUTHOR TO READER

WHETHER YOU ALREADY KNOW OUR FAMILY THROUGH READING *The Education of a WASP* (William Morrow, 1970) or whether we are strangers to you, there are a few things you might like to know.

This book is not a continuation. *The Education of a WASP* told only of what my husband, Ben, and I learned as people. This book tells what we learned as parents. Some of the same years are covered here, but there are now four extra years during which we saw what happened to our three children who grew to teen-agers in their mostly black schools.

To those who have not read my first book, it may seem that I pass too quickly over several crucial incidents—our first black friendships, and the events that led to our leaving Omaha. Omitted entirely are our relationships with black militants and blue-collar workers. The details of these events that affected—but did not involve—our children can be found in *The Education of a WASP.*

The people you will meet in this book are real. I have changed their names, physical descriptions and the names of the schools where they are teachers, pupils or principals. I have not done this to protect them or myself. Identifying them would, I believe, make the reader feel they exist in only one school. I am afraid they exist in too many.

LOIS MARK STALVEY

Philadelphia
March 8, 1974

one

ON A BRIGHT JUNE DAY IN 1972, I STOOD AT THE EDGE OF a crowded school yard watching my three children come toward me. They were easy to spot in the swirling mass of youngsters—my children were white and nearly all the other students in this inner-city Philadelphia public school were black.

During the ten years since our oldest child "Spike" began first grade here at the Willis Elementary School, I had often stood in the same spot near the black iron fence feeling many different emotions: apprehension, satisfaction, joy and anger. During the year I was a volunteer teacher, I had leaned against this fence, exhausted but fulfilled. This day I felt nothing but a bleak hopelessness.

Noah, our middle child, just thirteen, had graduated from the eighth grade an hour before. His father, my husband Ben, was away in Washington, D.C., for the week, and I had sat alone during the ceremonies, trying unsuccessfully to hold back tears. When the graduates began to sing, "We've Only Just Begun," I could hold tears back no longer. Noah, his streaked-blond head above most of his classmates, saw my wet cheeks, looked concerned and then benign. But I was not weeping out of sentiment. I was mourning the death of a hope and crying for two children who were not there.

Now, as I looked across the cracked pavement of the school

yard, smaller now with two ugly portable classrooms taking up a third of its space, I caught glimpses of Sarah, twelve years old, when her long bright-yellow hair caught the sunlight. Spike had stopped off on his way home from high school and his six-foot-two frame loomed up from the crowd. Noah's pink face glowed with a broad smile as he came toward me in a knot of brown-faced friends.

Noah and his friends reached the fence first. "Hey, Mom, is it okay if I hang around here a little longer?" Sure.

Noah's friends, "T.D.," "Fish" and Jimmy, all said, "Hi," and I asked T.D. how his brother was. His brother and I had once had a fistfight in our street, but we had ended up friends.

T.D.'s usually open face closed. "He's fine, Mrs. Stalvey." But T.D. looked at the sidewalk.

Noah, T.D. and Jimmy left. Fish lingered.

"Guess we won't be seeing you so much anymore," he said. His brown eyes looked up at me out of a broad brown face, his wide forehead wrinkling slightly. With graduation, there would be no more lunchtime basket ball games in our drive-way or boxing matches in our basement.

I said, "But you'll come over after school, won't you?"

Fish nodded, but his brown eyes were saying good-bye.

Impulsively, I put my hand on his arm and said, using his real name, "Richard, you're going to do real good things in high school. You're a good person and you're smart. You're going to have a lot of good luck." I repeated, "A *lot* of good luck," because luck was just about all that could change things for Fish.

"That's right, Mrs. Stalvey," Fish said soberly. He did not believe what I said either. He said, "You take care now, y'hear?" and walked away.

Spike was standing at our car with Sarah. I walked toward them, passing a young white mother bending down to admire the drawing her small son held up. I wondered how long she would keep her child in the public school and I hoped she would learn more quickly than I had.

When Ben and I met and married in Chicago in 1955, a predominantly black school in a big Eastern city was an unthinkable possibility for our future children. Until Spike's sixth birthday in the all-white Protestant Omaha suburb where he spent the first five years of his life, Ben and I had carefully followed one conventional step after another, trying to give our children what we saw as "the best" education, environment and family life.

Ben and I were, perhaps, even more conservative than many couples who had reached adulthood during the late 1940's, each of us for different reasons. Ben's parents, who had left South Carolina in the 1930's, had suffered in Detroit when the Depression followed them. Ben remembers holes in his shoes and moving from house to smaller house when money was scarce. He had decided not to marry until he felt as sure as possible of protecting his family from being poor.

My conservatism was emotional rather than material. I was born in Milwaukee and when I was three, my parents were divorced. Mother went home to her parents and had to go to work. I missed her and vowed I would never work when I had children and that I would try hard to see that my children never felt the pain of a divorce.

Ben and I had both moved to Chicago because of our jobs in advertising; mine with McCann-Erickson, the advertising agency; his, as advertising manager for Peter Pan peanut butter. We met in our apartment building, and it took a year before he proposed. It took me two cautious months to decide to say yes. Ben's rugged good looks were almost a handicap. (He looked—and still does—like someone on the cover of *Field and Stream*.) I had dated so many good-looking young advertising men who were absorbed only in their careers; I

(3)

wanted to be sure the man I married would put his family ahead of a corporate climb. Of all the men I knew, Ben was the only one I could picture bathing a baby and mowing the lawn. We were married in June, 1955. Whether by dumb luck or logic, everything I guessed about Ben has turned out to be right.

"Spike" (Bennett Odom Stalvey, III) was conceived two weeks after our wedding. The very day the doctor confirmed this, we began to look for a house-in-the-suburbs-with-good-schools. Chicago's Near North Side, the fascinating neighborhood where we had met, was never even considered as a place in which to raise children.

We chose Park Forest, Illinois, *because* all the houses looked alike. We felt safer buying among identical houses than risking a bad investment elsewhere. I needed the security of being among other couples our age and income. Because my mother had been gone all day and I was raised largely by my German immigrant grandmother, I had no models for motherhood that I wanted to follow. I hoped to learn from my neighbors and to be as much like them as possible. On April 6, 1956, a long, lean, lusty baby who was Spike was born at Chicago Lying-In Hospital and was put into a sterile glass cart so his father and I could look him over together minutes after he was born. Spike was red, squalling and actively flinging his arms and legs around. And we were parents.

While I learned to care for Spike, Ben planted trees and built a big wooden fence around our yard. We planned to have two more children, the conventional two years apart—another boy to play with Spike and then a girl who would be named Sarah Lois after Ben's great-grandmother and me. I could see our three children—first, protected by the fence, then climbing the trees and, someday, returning with children of their own.

Meanwhile, we happily lived the typical life of the suburbs. Ben took the train every morning in his Brooks Brothers suit.

I stayed home, trying to learn my job from Dr. Spock, assorted cookbooks and my neighbors. I had given up my advertising career without regret. Ben had offered to help if I wanted to work, but staying home with my baby seemed much more challenging and rewarding than writing any more television commercials.

In those busy days of learning to be a mother, I took little notice of what went on in the world outside our house on Shabbona Drive. The Supreme Court decision that ruled school segregation unconstitutional had come before we were married and I thought it was nice. Somewhere I had learned that the black population of America was a mere 10 percent. Since I had met exactly three black people to talk to—Duke Ellington whom I had interviewed for my high school paper, a stock girl where I clerked and the fraternity brother of a boy I once dated—this figure seemed about right. Integrating 10 percent of them with 90 percent of us should be easy, I decided before dismissing the subject from my mind.

I did, however, take notice of the white riots in Little Rock over the proposed integration of their Central High School. By then Spike was seventeen months old and bouncing beside me on the sofa as I paged through *Life* magazine. Nine Negro children had been prevented from entering the high school by big, armed National Guardsmen. They had walked away through a mob of screaming, spitting whites.

Spike, who had become a small hurricane of joyful, curious activity, wanted to go outside, and so I finished the article from a chair in the yard. I wondered how the mothers of those six black girls and three boys could send them into that threatening mob no matter how important the issue. I looked across to where Spike was trying to climb our one mature tree. If we were black, could I send him—or the baby I had just learned I was carrying—into the cursing mass of contorted white faces in these pictures? For the first time in my life, I was grateful that he was white and Protestant and that there were no nasty names he could ever be called. And I wondered what those black mothers were feeling. In September, 1957, I believed I would never know.

Questions about school integration were pushed from my mind by a major family event: Ben had just accepted a new job with a larger salary and we were moving to Omaha, Nebraska.

We made several house-hunting trips to Omaha and had been shown nothing but suburban areas. According to Ben's new co-workers, the best schools were in District 66 in the suburb of Rockbrook. When we saw a lovely, sprawling four-bedroom house on a hillside there, we bought it. The elementary school was two blocks away and reputedly the "best" in Rockbrook.

Noah Wolf Stalvey was born in Omaha on May 24, 1958, and, a bit ahead of our schedule, Sarah Lois Stalvey came along just seventeen months later. If I had been too preoccupied with my family to notice the world outside my house before, I was now lucky if I had time to read even the newspaper headlines.

Whatever outside news reached me came mostly through Ben or through Betty Cohen, a new friend I had made in Omaha when I shopped for the children's toys. Betty, a former schoolteacher, owned a small toy store in the city, and my shopping trips soon became social visits.

It was Betty who gently teased me about our all-WASP neighborhood. I said, "Nonsense." The realtor, Jewish herself, had assured us that it was merely a coincidence that no Jewish families had bought in Rockbrook. I told Betty I had never heard a bigoted remark from any of my neighborhood friends. They were all lovely people, well-educated and too secure to be prejudiced.

When Betty Cohen deplored the closing of Prince Edward County schools in Virginia to avoid integration, I joined her in agreement. When Ben mentioned the bombing of a

Clinton, Tenn., high school by outraged whites, I was shocked. Never once did I notice that our neighborhood school was exactly the kind of all-white, middle-class school that white Southerners were fighting *openly* to preserve.

During our first four years in Omaha, Ben and I were far too preoccupied with our own parenthood to question our choice of a neighborhood and a school for our children. We watched them develop into delightfully different types.

Spike had never lost his pell-mell curiosity and energy. He was obviously going to be as tall and lean as Ben. Noah was an affectionate, chubby clown with arms and legs that felt like good-quality foam rubber. It looked as if Sarah had inherited my handily average proportions. When I lost the ten pounds I was constantly fighting, I was 36-26-36 and 5 feet 5 inches; I could sew from patterns without alterations and walk out wearing dresses from a store. Sarah had my blond hair and, with luck, might *not* inherit my nearsighted gray eyes. Hers were a green-blue that changed with the color of the dresses I sewed for her.

The temperaments of our children, we noticed, were as different as their physical characteristics. Home movies from 1960 show Spike as a blur, Noah taking pratfalls for the camera and Sarah regally observing the action, her hands gracefully arranged.

When Spike started nursery school in the fall of 1960, he immediately displayed the incautious independence of a test pilot. I had read several books on how to handle tearful fears of separation, but when the car-pool mother arrived the first day, Spike raced happily to her car. "Hey, say good-bye," I called after him. He gave me a grin, a "Bye" and went off, leaving *me* tearful. When Ben and I discussed his future, Ben predicted he would be an astronaut: "With his energy, he won't even need a rocket!"

While Spike met the world head on, Noah cuddled up to it. He immediately occupied any available lap and was already a wheeler-dealer in the matter of cookies. Given one, his blue eyes would light and he would bargain for two. And get them. I told Ben, "I think law or politics for Noah."

Sarah reacted to being the smallest in a fast-moving world of boisterous brothers by watching, waiting and then determinedly competing. I watched in awe from the kitchen window the day she decided to swing across the rungs of the playladder in the yard. After watching her brothers for most of her nearly two years, she had climbed up, swung, fallen to the soft grass, then climbed up again. After a dozen times, she finally made it across. She looked for a moment at the ladder, smiled and walked away. Ben said, "Corporation executive?" I said, "First lady president of the United States!"

Ben and I enjoyed our long, late-night discussions about our children and their futures. By the summer of 1961, when Spike was five, Noah, three, and Sarah almost two, I had read many books on child psychology. Some of them confused me, but Ben helped sort out what might work. We both agreed that our job was to help our children prepare for real life: no loading them with luxuries we had missed, no demands they fulfill our unrealized dreams.

I remember Ben's smiling at me, raising one shaggy eyebrow and saying, "And no overprotecting." Yes, I did worry too much about their safety. I particularly worried whether Spike's active little mind would remind him to stay out of the road when he walked to kindergarten in a few months. Our children had to learn to cope with the world as it really was. Neither Ben nor I noticed that the "real world" was as different from our suburb as a playpen from a busy street.

During those first four years in Omaha, however, the world that was real to us was a secure and satisfying one. Ben was given frequent praise for the job he was doing as advertising director for the food corporation. I was proud of Ben and proud of myself for finally organizing my days to allow more free time now that the children were less dependent.

Ben had teased me the year before for volunteering my time to the school parents' group a year before Spike was to start kindergarten.

"Aren't you starting awfully early, honey?" he said.

I remember telling him, "Well, I want to do something in the community and the school is the most important. It will have our three children for eight years and my time is a good investment."

I had been assigned to write the monthly newsletter. At the board meetings, I noticed that the talk centered mainly around election of officers, fund drives and speakers for the programs. Speakers on golf, gardening and tax matters drew the largest audiences. I wondered why education was never mentioned, but felt too timid and inexperienced to ask.

When I asked friends in the neighborhood what made our "fine suburban schools" good, some looked at me as if I had questioned the roundness of the earth. Some pointed out that our Westside High School had a larger percentage of college-bound students than any other district. I stopped asking. If the parents' group was involved mainly in fund-raising (and debating how to spend the funds), it was probably because no educational problems existed in our district.

There was only one small "educational problem" that bothered me and I felt I had taken care of it. That spring Spike had been with me in our suburban shopping center when a smartly dressed Negro woman dropped a parcel. Spike piped up loudly, "Mommie, that *cleaning lady* dropped her package!" The woman had given me a contemptuous glare and had taken the package Spike handed her with a chilly "Thank you." Red-faced, I explained later to Spike that all brown-skinned people were *not* cleaning women; "Some are doctors, lawyers and teachers."

Spike asked reasonably, "Who?" He had seen the Negro cleaning women who came to our neighborhood; all the doctors and teachers he had ever seen were white. He also added,

"But they don't have children. If they did, they'd stay home with them." I explained that "some Mommies *can't* stay home —mine couldn't," but I realized suddenly that Spike had never seen a black child.

Because of this incident and prodded by a Brotherhood Week program at Betty Cohen's synagogue, I felt our school should have a Negro teacher. I pointed out to the parents' group board members that children should learn to know all people. As I expected, they enthusiastically agreed. The district superintendent was also enthusiastic and asked if I would help find a qualified black teacher. I had visited the Urban League and through my contacts there we had made friends with a black doctor and his wife. Their four little boys had become frequent playmates to our children. We had not as yet found a teacher willing to be the first at our school, but I believed one would be found. Meanwhile, Spike at least had filled a deplorable gap in his education.

I firmly suppressed any other doubts about the quality of suburban education. If we had bought the "best schools" with the same mindlessness as television commercials sold us "the whitest wash" and "the brightest smile," it was four years too late to do anything about it. Selling the house we loved and moving to another neighborhood was unthinkable. I reassured myself that I knew nothing about education; how could I judge what was good, bad or important?

On September 5, 1961, Spike began kindergarten. It was not until September 12 that I got a closer look at the school and felt the first serious qualms. Ben and I had gone to the first parents' group meeting of the year. The new young woman principal introduced the teachers. I looked at Ben, astonished. Nearly all of them were young and looked as if they were frightened of us, the parents. I whispered to Ben, "My gosh, they look like high school kids!" Ben nodded.

At home, we settled down for a discussion of what "education" meant to us. We had both been suppressing our doubts. Ben, however, knew more about education than I. He had stayed an extra year in college to earn a teaching certificate "just in case I couldn't get a job in advertising." That evening neither of us realized how typical and unfortunate that job insurance could be; we were concerned solely with our own children's education.

In our much-loved living room with its picture windows overlooking the valley, Ben began to give me a history of education that was both sobering and reassuring.

"From the conversation I hear down at the office," he said, "I think that middle-class people expect too much from the schools. They forget that free public schools weren't set up for middle-class kids anyway. They were set up for the children of immigrants *to protect the middle class*."

According to Ben, the well-to-do had tutors and the middle class educated their children in private church-sponsored schools. The poor could not educate their children at all. "Then, people like Horace Mann sold free public education . . . not as a generous gift to the poor . . . but as a way of taking *unemployed* children off the streets. Remember, in those days, children worked—if they could get jobs. But those who couldn't were running around beating up citizens and wrecking property. So Horace Mann convinced the establishment that free public schools would teach the children of immigrants to behave and that teaching them to read and write would make them better employees."

When the child-labor laws were passed in 1916, Ben said, the public school system had to expand. And by then, a new generation of immigrant children was passing through the schools and being taught middle-class values.

Everything Ben said checked with the experience in my family. My mother, my aunt and my uncles had literally been taught to speak English in the public schools and had brought it back home to my German-speaking grandparents. My mother had gone to work after completing the eighth grade; my oldest uncle had gone to a trade school. Only the two youngest children in the family had learned to aspire to the highest kind of education thinkable to my grandparents: teachers' college. The public schools had indeed pulled my immigrant family into the lower rung of the middle class.

"The only problem," Ben said, "is that middle-class people seem to expect the same *proportion* of improvement for their children. Those first public schools did accomplish miracles but I think it was only because those immigrant kids got so little at home. The schools gave them what they needed to succeed in America and lots of them succeeded. But it's different now. Some middle-class parents seem to think that the school can take an average child and make him into a genius or solve his emotional problems or teach him manners. It just can't happen."

All right. That made sense. I could see that if you watered and fertilized a neglected plant, you would get a remarkable change. A well-cared-for plant would not respond that dramatically.

But I had never expected a school to make geniuses out of our children. According to everything I had read, the first five years of a child's life are the crucial ones. Scary as the thought was, I knew that our children would learn most of their attitudes from us. If they saw us succeed by working hard, this is what they would expect to do; if they saw us take joy in new knowledge and learn from our mistakes, they would do the same. I knew I had absorbed the perfectionism of my German grandfather. Spike watched Ben and me reading books and was already trying to imitate what he saw.

I asked Ben, "All right, then, what can we expect our children to get in school besides learning to read and do math? I could teach them to read at home, though someone else would have to teach them math."

Ben said, "I guess there are two important things they've

got to learn in school that they can't learn at home. School is where they'll learn to work with an authority who is *not* a parent and, also, they'll learn how to work with a group. And this is what they've got to know for later—how to get along with a boss and with their co-workers."

Neither Ben nor I thought that evening about the one important experience their "superior" suburban school could not give them. Nor would we until Spike shocked us into awareness. We ended our discussion by agreeing that perhaps the youth of the teachers was not a handicap at all. Ben said, "Maybe it's a plus. They must be training teachers better than they did in my day."

On the first Parents' Visiting Day, I went to school, expecting to see new methods. Spike's kindergarten teacher was pleasant, pretty and pregnant. The children sat at the same little tables I remembered and gathered in the same kind of circle as the teacher read stories. When she played a march on the piano, the children tramped around the room—except for Spike who detoured to investigate the back of the piano. The teacher assured me that Spike was doing well. "He's very active, but he's cooperative and responsible. He does a good job of giving out and collecting the scissors." I had been good at collecting the nap mats. I decided that perhaps kindergarten was not a likely place for innovations.

By then, however, I had a school problem on my mind that had nothing to do with the teacher. The week before, Spike had come racing home from school, full of news of his day. I had listened while mixing a batch of bread, my mind mostly on measuring ingredients.

Spike climbed around a chair as he said, "And Richard says that Jews are bad. They only love money and they killed Jesus," Spike said proudly.

"That's nice, honey. . . . WHAT DID YOU SAY?"

Spike repeated what he had said, but it was now a question. Could Richard, his idol and a whole year older, be wrong?

I squatted down, my hands full of bread dough. "Honey, the Roman soldiers killed Jesus. Jesus was Jewish. So is Mrs. Cohen. Do you think she's a bad person who loves only money?"

Spike's high broad little forehead wrinkled from an inner struggle. Richard, fountainhead of all wisdom, said Jews were bad; Betty Cohen was his favorite adult; she talked to him as if he were grown up; he loved her.

"You mean Richard is wrong, Mommie?"

I said, "I'm afraid he is. Very wrong."

That evening when I told Ben about the episode, he only added to my concern. "Spike takes our word for things *now*, but I wonder how long it will be before his friends' opinions mean more to him than ours. He could also decide that Betty Cohen is an exception. Do you realize, honey, that there isn't even one Jewish family at our suburban school and that none of the teachers have Jewish names?"

Ben pulled his heavy eyebrows together and said, "I don't suppose there's much we can do about it, but I got a shock when I drove past Westside High School the other day. It kind of shook me that all those youngsters look alike . . . light hair and blue eyes and well-dressed. Our kids will be through college before they get to know anyone much different from the people they've grown up with."

All during dinner and while we put the children to bed, I had been thinking along the same lines. We could introduce non-WASP people into our children's lives, but that was no sure antidote for twelve years of working, playing and learning with youngsters who were of the same income, ethnic group and home background as theirs. Even my own school days had provided more variety. I had learned to cope with both envy and pity from kindergarten on. I could remember loathing Beverly who lived in a big house, had a new dress for every school day and naturally curly hair to boot. I had worked to get better grades than she did and realized, finally, that pretty clothes, curly hair and big house aside, she had the shyness and timidity of the overprotected child. I did not analyze it that maturely; I just knew I would rather be me. In Shirley, I found a friend beneath two patched dresses she wore alternately to school. In high school, my close friends were a mixture of girls from the big houses overlooking Lake Michigan and girls who lived over taverns and stores. In their homes, I had heard Polish, Yiddish, Greek and Italian spoken. Along with the foreign foods I ate, I had absorbed cultures and customs in a way no trip to Europe could provide. My children would have Coke and Pop-Tarts in kitchens much the same as their own.

Ben had experienced his own kind of variety. Until the age of eight, he attended a two-room school house in South Carolina. (When he asked why his Negro playmates went to a different school, he was told he was too young to understand.) He went to school with the children of farmers and—later, in Wyandotte, Michigan, just outside Detroit—with the children of steel-mill supervisors and laborers. When the G.I. Bill made it possible for him to go to college, his mother encouraged him to try. At the University of Michigan, the dorm adviser was a black man. Ben liked him and assumed this kind of Northern equality existed in most places.

So did I. The neighborhood in which I had been raised was at the opposite end of Milwaukee from the Negro neighborhood; no dayworkers came into our low income area. When I occasionally went through all-black neighborhoods in Milwaukee—and later in Chicago—I simply assumed that black people wanted to live together as the Polish, Italians and Germans I knew did.

The evening after Spike's brush with anti-Semitism we were still more concerned with mixture than with color. But what could we do? The questions we were now asking ourselves should have been asked four years earlier, before we bought our house.

I doubt if we would ever have sold the house and moved to another Omaha neighborhood. We were concerned, but we were not crusaders. It took a small, seemingly harmless impulse of mine to change our home and our lives.

Paul and Joan Benson, the black doctor and his wife, told us they were looking for a bigger, better house. I suggested our neighborhood, assuring them that our neighbors were "too intelligent to be bigoted." A few days later, I saw a "For Sale" sign two blocks away and stopped on impulse to speak to the owner, a pleasant but timid woman. Two days later, I learned that the neighbors had held a meeting in protest and threatened to get Ben's job. By January, he was told he must take a transfer to Philadelphia or resign.

two

BEN AND I ARE STILL EXPLAINING—BUT ONLY TO JEWISH, Black or Catholic friends—how we could have underestimated our neighbors' panic at the thought of a black doctor's living among them. Most fellow WASPs understand. They had surprises of their own when integration moved North. Minority groups, apparently, have always been aware of discrimination toward others; white Protestants who never met discrimination in jobs, clubs or housing could believe, in the early sixties, that it did not exist in the North. Because my neighbors were willing to accept a black teacher in our school—a portable human relations lesson—I believed they would accept a neighbor as enthusiastically.

Neither Ben nor I knew anything about the myths of property values. We had both grown up in neighborhoods so far from black communities that this issue was never discussed. My grandfather would have been upset if a *Polish* family had moved next door, but Negroes were only mythical figures in my grandmother's clichés. "Who was your nigger last year?" and "nigger in the woodpile" were phrases I had heard all my life. But the likelihood of a black family's hopscotching through the Italian and Polish neighborhoods that surrounded us in Milwaukee was so remote that it was never mentioned.

By high school, Ben and I had both learned that the word

"nigger" was not "polite" and I have recently come to believe that this "not polite" attitude toward racism helped hide it in the North. To our generation, racism is what sex was to our parents—"nice people" did not discuss it. I had never heard a bigoted phrase from my neighbors, and I feel sure they would have been as embarrassed if their children said "nigger" as my mother would have been if I had said "masturbate" or "intercourse." For both generations, sex and racism existed—but suppressed and secret.

Ben had been less sure than I that our neighbors would welcome a black family but had laughed at the threat to his job. His only worry was that I might be made uncomfortable in our neighborhood or that Spike might be treated unpleasantly at school. When the doctor and his wife heard my description of the house, they decided it was too small. I felt the episode was over. There were no more houses for sale on our block. My neighbors, I believed, would come to their senses and realize their reaction was wrong.

Ben felt I should continue to help the Bensons find a house in whatever way I could; looking at houses that realtors would not show to black people, trying to find an ethical realtor. The Bensons had asked us to stop. "It's not worth what it might cost you," Paul Benson said. But Ben and I both believed that if we quit in fear, our guilt would somehow affect our children. How could we tell them they must do what they knew was right—in matters of drugs or drinking or morals—when we knew we had not?

On the first working day in January, 1962, Ben was told he must accept the transfer to Philadelphia—to a job he knew was to be eliminated in two years—or resign.

We made two decisions rapidly: one, to accept the transfer to the East where the job market was bigger and two, to find a better kind of neighborhood there in which to raise our children. We were not interested in living *among* Negro families

(18)

as much as we were determined to avoid another neighborhood where black people were kept out.

We offered our house to the Bensons. They refused, graciously but firmly. Either they believed this could hurt us further with Ben's employers or they did not like the house. While I waited in Omaha for it to sell, Ben found that buying a house in an integrated neighborhood was not easy.

One realtor told Ben, "I wouldn't put my worst enemy in a changing neighborhood. Where would your kids go to school?" Another realtor told Ben it would be hard to get mortgage money: "Banks don't go for this integration!" Others ignored Ben's request and showed him only suburban properties. One woman realtor finally, after Ben's firm insistence, began to show him houses in West Mt. Airy, an area of Philadelphia we learned was well integrated. Ben liked several he saw and I flew from Omaha to see them.

When the woman realtor brought us to a big, three-story stone Colonial, I felt there was some mistake. This beautiful house could not be in our price range. But it was. The inside was even more welcoming. We were to learn later that the house had been built in 1912 by a father as a wedding gift to his daughter. The house and the yard had been lovingly planned as a place in which to raise children. There were fireplaces for popping popcorn and hanging stockings at Christmas. The stairways were broad with wide treads for little feet and the yard had enormous trees to climb, with heavy limbs from which to hang swings.

The low price and the fact that Ben had been shown three other houses for sale on the same block did not alarm us. I fell in love with the big stone house on Westview Street at first sight.

I asked the realtor about schools. "Oh, you have a fabulous choice!" she said. "Penn Charter, Chestnut Hill Academy, Springside . . . and if you don't mind a few Jews, there's also Germantown Friends!" I ignored her remark about Jews to

(19)

ask whether these were public schools. Oh, heavens, no, she said. There was a public elementary school around here somewhere, but of course, one could *hardly* use Germantown High School.

Germantown High School was so far in our future that we never did ask why one could "hardly use it." We did ask her to drive past the elementary school. I now understand her reluctance. In the three blocks between what was soon to be our house and the school, the houses decreased in size, block by block. Across from the big dark red brick building that was the Lillian B. Willis School, there were rows of shabby wooden row houses with peeling paint.

The school was closed for Easter vacation, but the neighborhood looked more and more like what we wanted. Between the big houses on our block and these small row houses, our children would certainly have a variety of playmates of different income groups. The black family who owned the house across our street was obviously affluent. I had noticed a swimming pool behind a louvered fence at the back of their large property. Now, near the school, I saw black children going into the small row houses. There were white children living in those row houses too and as we drove around the corner, I saw a small white boy wearing a yarmulke. trudging along, perhaps to the nearby synagogue for Hebrew lessons. The mixture of people we wanted our children to know existed right here.

As the realtor continued to talk about private schools, I listened with a prejudice of my own. In Omaha, I had talked with Betty Cohen who had taught in both. In her toy store, Betty leaned against an unopened carton, folded her arms and said, "Listen, kiddo, a school is as good as the teacher your child has *that year*. Good teachers in both, but you're obviously not the private-school type. Save all that dough for college. Private schools are mostly for kids who have problems or parents with social ambitions. And then there are some people who think a school has to be better if it costs. Your kids will do fine in the public school. Anyway, they pay the teachers more." While the realtor chattered on about the "fabulous" merits of Chestnut Hill Academy, I listened with a slammed-shut mind.

We moved in to our new house on June 18, 1962, after the schools had closed. As soon as our phone was connected, it rang. A resonant voice said briskly, "Give me Mrs. Stalvey." When I identified myself, the voice changed to a soothing melodiousness. "My dear, this is Evangeline Peters. Principal of the marvelous Lillian B. Willis School. I understand you have purchased the Schuster house. You know, he was president of the Philadelphia Board of Education and all the Schuster children went to our school."

As Vangie Peters went on to describe the virtues of the school, I listened intently. "Dedicated teachers," "the most advanced techniques," "professors' children," "best-known parents' group in the city" sounded fine. I was also impressed with a principal who used her vacation time to welcome all the new parents in the area. Vangie finally paused and asked what else she could tell me.

I said the only question I had was when could I register Spike for first grade?

There was a brief silence. "Oh. Then you *are* sending your children to our *public* school?" Oh, yes. She told me the registration date was September 10 and she would be waiting for me. If I had any further questions during the summer, please call her at home. I thanked her, hung up the phone and mused that any school with a principal who kept tabs on all new residents must be remarkable.

Before school started in September, there would be two events that became an important part of our personal history: Sarah and I would begin our deep, lasting friendship with Barbara Hamilton and her daughter, Paula; I would enroll Spike (inadvertently) in a summer day camp where his color

(21)

and middle-class background made him a minority of one.

My friendship with Barbara Hamilton had begun through the mail before we left the Middle West. Barbara, whose husband, Leland, was a minister, had been a childhood friend of black friends in Omaha. Barbara and I exchanged letters for months. When I telephoned her after we had signed the papers for the house—a house three blocks from hers—she said, "But I thought they didn't sell to us that side of Wayne Avenue!" All during our correspondence Barbara believed I was black.

Barbara agreed to come to visit. Though her open friendliness was temporarily closed, we had too many interests and personality traits in common for color to interfere. We both felt raising children was creative; we were both gregarious, inquisitive and quick to laugh. We even look alike. Except for Barbara's sable brown skin and my slightly florid pink one, Barbara and I have the same high broad foreheads, the same broad chins; we are the same height and, depending on which of us is dieting, often the same weight. But most important, Barbara is direct and, as she describes it, "suicidally honest." Her uncompromising candor was to be my lifeline through the complex decade ahead.

Barbara's daughter, Paula, and Sarah forged their friendship with immediate no-nonsense simplicity. They were almost exactly the same age. On their first meeting, they sat together on the living-room sofa while Barbara and I talked. Paula ran a dark-brown finger down Sarah's straight yellow locks; Sarah poked a pink finger into Paula's fluffy, springy hair. Sarah tried to pull Paula toward the playroom; Paula pulled toward the yard. Two strong personalities finally compromised and they played on the center-hall stairs. (A year later, Paula demonstrated the same emotional honesty as her mother. The girls were to model in a fashion show at Leland's church. At the last minute, Paula got stage fright. Not Sarah. While she strolled happily across the stage to loud applause, Paula sat on Ben's lap in the audience. She looked up at him. "That Sarah Stalvey," she said, "she makes me SICK!")

Leland Hamilton, Barbara's husband, was to become Ben's close friend, his fast-talking geniality a perfect match for Ben's quiet reflective nature. Jimmy Hamilton, midway in age between Noah and Spike, was a precocious personality image of his father.

The Hamiltons, however, were on their summer vacation when we decided to enroll our children in a day camp. One neighborhood camp had room for Sarah and Noah's age group, but none for Spike's. From a list of recommended day camps, I chose Germantown Settlement House Camp, visited the director and enrolled Spike for their program which was to start the following week.

It took two weeks before I learned that Spike was the only white—and only middle-class—child in his camp. To my Middlewestern mind, the term "settlement house" did not mean "underprivileged children." Because of Noah and Sarah's camp schedule, I had been dropping Spike off early and picking him up late. Then, one day, I was early. Spike's was the only white face. The director thought I knew this and also that most of the other children came from the low-income urban renewal projects around the corner.

As quickly as my fears—of the poor and of my child in a minority position—welled up, I realized they had already been disproved. Spike loved his camp. He had brought home none of the bad language, bad habits or whatever "contamination" the poor were supposed to spread.

The last week of Spike's camp, we moved one step closer. Spike was invited to spend Saturday at the home of one of his day-camp friends. I phoned the mother for confirmation. She said, "Davie would sure like to have Spike come if you let him. Don't worry none. I watches my kids."

With qualms I felt ashamed of, I drove Spike to the red

brick row house project. A stout woman invited me in. The bare living room with its lumpy sofa and two wooden chairs was neat and clean. I did not recognize that the woman's starch-swollen stomach and sticklike arms were symptoms of extreme poverty. But as we chatted over instant coffee and canned milk, I noted that her standards of behavior for her children were the same as mine. She reminded her three children of the boundaries within which they could play. Spike's friend Davie said, "Yes, ma'am." So did Spike. They went out to play stickball on a vacant lot. The woman led me to the front steps where we sat to finish our coffee. When I rose to leave, she assured me she would stay on the steps to watch. I intended to tell Ben that I found a mother more protective than I was. I drove away, feeling comfortable. Only years later did I realize I had left my son in the territory—the "turf"—of a notorious juvenile gang.

When I picked Spike up later, we drove back home down High Street and around the big yellow brick building that was Germantown High School. For nine years Spike's day-camp experience would free me from concern over "racial balance"; my visit to an urban renewal project would adjust my attitudes toward poor people. But nine years later I would drive these same streets, overcome by fear and unable to snatch Spike back from danger.

That late August day in 1962, however, I drove away from Germantown High School and back to the house on Westview Street, feeling strangely fulfilled. Our troubles were far from over; Ben's job would last a maximum of two years. He had not allowed me to feel guilty about precipitating his transfer, but now I felt that in spite of the insecurity and upheaval in our lives, we had gained much. Our Omaha suburb now seemed even more sterile, unreal and isolated than we had begun to suspect. Here, in the contrasts of Philadelphia, our children would learn what the world was really like.

And so would I.

three

In September, 1962, when I registered Spike for first grade, it was as easy to be naïve about big city public schools as I had been about integration in the suburbs. The national media concentrated on school desegregation in the South. During Spike's first months in Willis School and while Sarah and Noah were in Trinity Church Nursery School, national attention was focused on the University of Mississippi, and on the ugly white riots there when James Meredith became a student. Segregation in the schools of New York, Chicago and Philadelphia was ignored.

On September 10, the day Vangie Peters told me was registration day, I telephoned the school. An impersonal voice instructed me to bring Spike's records that morning. He could begin in the afternoon.

By then, I had learned that none of the children on our block went to the Willis School; the white children went to private schools and the only child of the black couple across the street went to a junior high somewhere else in the district. (Our black neighbors had proved to be polite, but distant. I decided they either did not like white people in general or, for some reason, me in particular. Several of the white families were equally unsociable, but we were otherwise surrounded by friendly people; a gracious Old Philadelphia dowager to our left, a childless couple our age to our right and across the street a pleasant family from Chicago with two teen-age sons in private school.)

During the summer I had met two women with children in public school who were to become close friends—Celia Spears, the redheaded vivacious wife of the minister of Trinity Church, and Abby Goldman, blonde and petite, whose two children had been with Sarah and Noah at their day camp. Both Celia and Abby had sons entering first grade at Willis School and they both talked enthusiastically about Vangie Peters, her interest in each child and the "fantastic way" in which she ran the school. They were both passionately partisan about public schools.

Celia had said, "How could Cal preach sermons on Brotherhood and then send his kids to a private school?" She paused, laughed and then added, "Anyway, God knows we couldn't afford it on a minister's pay!"

Abby Goldman, I learned, had been raised in a liberal family in New York. Her parents had been members of the NAACP for decades as had the family of her accountant husband, Sam. Abby had told me one day, "Anyone who thinks Jews are rich should know my family and Sam's! If they had to choose between shoes and books, it was books. And they worked themselves sick getting rights for Negroes when they weren't getting all the rights they should have had themselves."

It was Abby who had said, "Be sure to tell Vangie Peters you want Spike in Mrs. Schmidt's class. She's got the advanced grouping."

I listened to Abby and Celia, pleased at their enthusiasm for the school, but Ben and I were not sure we ought to ask that Spike be placed in an advanced class.

Ben said, "I'm not so sure that intellectual segregation is any better than color segregation. Anyway, how do they know kids are 'advanced' so early? Maybe some are slow starters."

I laughed and reminded Ben that we were both assuming

that Spike *was* advanced. I said, "Maybe he inherited my 'genius' in math." Ben knew that I had never been able to memorize the multiplication tables past the sixes.

We joked about my inability to keep a checkbook straight. But we were joking; we never doubted for a minute that Spike's active, curiosity-filled little mind was anything but superior.

That first morning in September, I walked through the bright red doors of Willis School for the first time. A wave of nostalgia hit me as I smelled the special odor of cleaning compound, chalk and freshly washed blackboards that had always meant First Day of School for me. This school was almost identical to the Fernwood Elementary School in Milwaukee where I had spent the first nine years of my school life. I learned later it had been built in 1908, making it older than Fernwood, but the wide doors were the same, the handles felt familiar to my hand and the click of my heels on the hard terrazzo floor brought back the special mixture of anticipation and anxiety with which I always began the new school year. Would my new teacher be nice or cross? Would the work be too difficult? I had never fooled myself with fantasies of "carefree childhood"; as I remembered it, it was a scary time when I measured myself against my mother's expectations, my teacher's demands and my own sense of worth. The sounds and smells and the feeling of my hand on the railing brought it back in a rush.

As I walked up the stairs to the main floor, I felt tremendously grateful that my children would never feel the special hurt that followed me through school. I was the only child in my class whose parents were divorced. When my classmates made gifts for Father's Day, I never admitted that I did not know my father's address and that the gift would go to my grandfather. When we read from Dick and Jane readers, I looked wistfully at the mother in an apron, welcoming a father at the door. My children would never feel this wistfulness. They would see themselves and Ben and me in their school books; they would never, as I had, feel frighteningly different and somehow inferior.

At the top of the stairs, I turned and walked down the wide corridor past classrooms already filled with children. Through the glass doors, I saw glimpses of the same charts from which I had learned to read. I had carefully refrained from trying to teach Spike to read at home. The methods at school might be different. Now I glimpsed the charts and remembered the thrill of the day I looked at those mysterious markings and suddenly I could read a word. I had told Spike that when he learned to read this year, "It will be like a special key. It will unlock the door to all kinds of things you want to know." Poor as I was at numbers, I had devoured books—those at school and then finally every book in the big bookcase my grandfather had built himself. With my children, I had tried to pass on the excitement in books by reading to them every night as I had been read to. Soon Spike would be among the children whose faces I saw through the door. Together they would all learn how to make those mysterious markings make sense and, I hoped, feel the same triumph.

When I stopped sneaking peeks into the classrooms I passed, I noticed that there was a long line of women seated in small chairs along the wall of the hallway. I sat down in the last chair.

Here again, the difference between this school and the school we had left behind in the suburbs was remarkable. In Omaha, registration day was a social occasion. Coffee and cookies were served in the gym. There all of us had looked alike and we were certainly of the same age. Here, some of the women looked more like grandmothers than mothers; some were shabbily dressed, some almost elegant in dresses, hose and high heels. There were only two white women in the line; one, a stout woman in a faded cotton dress and chopped-off light brown hair and the other, a thin woman with her hair fastened back in a bun. The other women were all different shades of brown—from blue-brown to the toasted shade I try to achieve in the summer. There was little conversation. I tried to chat with the gray-haired woman next to me. She gave brief answers with a gentle smile on her lined face, but her eyes were focused on some other thoughts.

I had no way of knowing that day that, while registration day in Omaha was a time for neighbors to get together, in Philadelphia, it was a tense and expensive day for some of the women there. Undoubtedly, many of them were grandmothers; others had taken a day off from work. Under Philadelphia's "open enrollment" system, many of these women were here to try to get their children into a "better" school than the school in their neighborhood. It was up to the principal to decide whether or not there was room for out-of-district students. The woman next to me may well have been thinking of how to persuade Vangie Peters to accept her grandchild or how her own grammar would sound when she tried.

Suddenly, a short, black-haired white woman in a brilliant yellow suit strode out of the office. She was followed by two other white women, holding papers and talking to her. "In a minute," I heard her say, then "Is Mrs. Bennett Stalvey here?"

I recognized her deep, resounding voice, surprised it came from such a small person. She was Evangeline Peters, the principal.

I raised my hand, which happened to be holding Spike's records. With one movement, she took his birth certificate and his kindergarten report card, handed them to one of the women who had followed her out of the office, took my other hand and propelled me out of the small chair.

"I want to show you our wonderful school," she said.

As I trotted along behind her small, quick steps, I was too busy trying to keep up with her to form more than a quick impression of the person in charge of our children's education. She appeared to be in her late fifties. Her jet-black hair showed no gray and her translucent white skin with its slightly lavender undertones looked young. There were no lines around the eyes or on her straight, flat forehead. Only her hands and the lines around her mouth hinted at her age. Her yellow suit was beautifully tailored and fit her small plump figure perfectly. Her black alligator pumps clicked down the corridor like a metronome, out of rhythm with my longer, flat-heeled steps.

I now understand the special tour I was given. We visited only the lower-grade classrooms. At the time, this seemed logical. It would be years before our children reached the seventh and eighth grades. Vangie swooped me in and out of classrooms, sometimes introducing me to the teacher, sometimes not. She asked questions of one or two children. Between classes, she told me that this child was the son of a university professor, that child of a doctor. She said, "Have you noticed how our school is rebalancing itself racially? Fifty percent of the *younger* students are white."

In the hallway, she introduced me to a tall, slim teacher with light hair and bright blue eyes. "This is our Miss Arnold— a veteran English teacher in our seventh and eighth grade." To Miss Arnold, Vangie Peters said, "Mrs. Stalvey is one of our new parents—with three marvelous children. She left the suburbs to bring her children into our school."

Miss Arnold looked at me somewhat closely, I thought, and moved on. I told Vangie Peters we had not left the Omaha suburbs entirely by choice. I explained.

She said she did not know "such things ever happened to WASPs." As an Irish Catholic, she had felt discrimination— in college and in jobs. "But whatever the reason you're here, we're so glad to have you! You look so Chestnut Hill," she said.

Her smile told me this was a compliment. The realtor who sold us our house had been from Chestnut Hill and I thought she looked rather disheveled. I was wearing a dark cotton shirt-dress and a cardigan sweater. Vangie had looked from my collar to my loafers, pronounced me "Chestnut Hill" with a wide, pleased smile.

"Now," she said, "would you like to meet the first-grade teachers and decide which one you want for Spike?"

I had no idea I would be offered a choice and even less idea of how I would be able to judge. However, when Vangie took me into the first first-grade class, I was sure this teacher was not one I would want for Spike! She was gray-haired, stout and was shaking her finger at a little brown-faced boy, holding him by the arm, while the rest of the class ran around the room. When she saw us, her manner changed abruptly. She dropped the child's arm and fluttered over to us. The other children quieted down when they saw their principal. The teacher chattered at us in a series of unfinished sentences, her pink face flushed and her voice high and nasal. I could not wait to leave.

The room across the hall was decorated with brightly colored pictures. A group of children was clustered around the teacher's desk and in the middle, I saw the round, brown face of a smiling woman in her thirties. She came toward us, a child holding each of her hands. Vangie introduced her as Mrs. Grant. She asked how old Spike was, what his interests were and then said she was sure he would enjoy "our school." She spoke loudly enough for the other children to hear. "We have some wonderful children at Willis School," she said. The class tittered in pleasure.

The last classroom we visited was that of Mrs. Schmidt, the teacher Abby and Celia had talked about. Her room was orderly and absolutely quiet. I was glad Ben and I had discussed the pros and cons of "advanced classes." I did not like Mrs. Schmidt at all.

Vangie's attitude with Mrs. Schmidt was smiling and friendly. She had shown impatience with the fluttery teacher, had been silent while I talked with Mrs. Grant. In Mrs. Schmidt's room, Vangie waited until Mrs. Schmidt told the class to "sit quietly while I speak with Mrs. Peters." Mrs. Schmidt was white-haired, elderly and unsmiling. She too looked closely at me as Vangie told her we had left the suburbs. Mrs. Schmidt had a nervous twitch in the corner of her mouth. Mrs. Schmidt said, crisply, "I believe I can accept one more student." As she dismissed us with a nod, I quickly examined myself for reverse prejudice, but color aside, Mrs. Grant, the Negro teacher, was both warm and calm. And she was the only teacher of the three who had asked me anything about my child.

I said to Vangie in the hallway, "Could Spike have Mrs. Grant?"

"Oh—may I call you Lois?—Lois, you're so right. She's the best choice you could have made. She's new this year, but the reports I have had on her are simply marvelous."

We were now back near the office. The line was still long and I felt Vangie Peters had been generous with her time. I thanked her and was told Spike should report to her after lunch. She said, "Lois, I can't *tell* you how happy I am that you'll be with us." I was happy too. Any school with a principal as dynamic and interested as Vangie Peters would be exciting for Spike; and Mrs. Grant's warm sensitivity to children would give him a wonderful first year.

Spike was unalterably opposed to my taking him to school his first afternoon. "I want to go by myself," he said, wiggling in his chair and gulping his lunch. Why not? We had already taken several walks to school during the summer. I was delighted that Spike would no longer have to cross a highway as he had in Omaha and I was intrigued with the sights he would see on his way to school. No more sidewalkless streets that wound past split-level after split-level. He would have broad, safe sidewalks now and he would walk past large and small houses, an auto repair shop and, across from the school, there was a tailor shop, a lawyer's office, a grocery, a drug store and a luncheonette with a glass case full of penny candy. If I started Spike to school early, he would have time to look at all the fascinating sights and still get to school on time.

He was off in a streak of short-cropped blond hair and glowing pink cheeks. At 3:40, he returned, grabbed an apple and casually tossed off a statement I have cherished for years: "Hey, Mom, that school's nice. They like everybody—just like you."

Two days later, Noah and Sarah began attending Trinity Church Cooperative Nursery School and I began a year of hearing questions about our public school and trying to answer them for my questioners and myself.

Trinity was a cooperative nursery school which meant we mothers were required to contribute time as Teacher-Helpers and Housekeeping-Helpers. With two children at the school, I had many days to put in and to talk with nearly all the other mothers. Like us, they could not afford the expensive nursery schools and they had a difficult choice to make. If they sent their children on to kindergarten in public school, there was no problem, but private school meant they would have to take a job outside the home. I realize now what a debt I owe these women. They discussed their qualms with candor, raising questions Ben and I had not considered. They forced me to dig deeply into my feelings and to answer out of Spike's day-to-day experiences during his first year at school.

Considering the color proportions of Willis School (Vangie Peters told me, "Averaging in the upper grades, our school is seventy percent Negro right now, but more white families are enrolling every day!"), I was surprised to find that Trinity Nursery School was all white. Celia Spears, the minister's wife, sounded apologetic. She explained she hoped to have some Negro children. Did I know any?

Barbara's daughter, Paula, went to nursery school at her father's church and her son, Jimmy, was in kindergarten at Willis School. The other black families we had met all had older or much younger children.

Celia shook her bright red head. "Gee, that's too bad. We've just started getting Negroes as members in the church, but I can't talk any of them into nursery school."

Barbara was not surprised. "Not too many people want to have their child be the only one." I pointed out that Spike had been "the only one" at his day camp. She smiled, "Friend, he has three hundred years of security in this society behind him. That's a whole different thing."

Sarah and Noah blended almost imperceptibly into the nursery school group. Noah went immediately into the center of a pile-up of boys, wrestling over a ball. Sarah sat in a small chair, watching to see how one played *this* new game. When he pell-melled into the next room, she daintily slid down from her chair and followed. I was Teacher-Helper the first day and, with another mother, poured the juice and put out the cookies.

The mother with whom I poured juice that morning was a medium-sized woman with no makeup and short-cropped curly hair. She told me she had married after getting her master's degree in chemistry. She looked very intellectual, and I decided she probably kept Plato in the bathroom instead of the *Reader's Digest*.

"To what schools have you applied?" she asked me.

I told her that we planned to send our children to the public school.

"Oh? But aren't you concerned? I understand that the Negro children there are terribly aggressive."

Just then there was an ear-splitting shriek. We both ran out of the kitchen area. The woman ran to a scarlet-faced little girl who was still shrieking. Noah stood next to her, looking as astonished as if a siren had gone off in his hand. One of the two nursery-school teachers asked, above the din, what had happened.

Noah said, "I just kissed her. Sarah doesn't yell when I kiss her."

I smiled weakly at my kitchen companion who was standing

over her daughter, explaining, "The boy did not *mean* to hurt you." Someday we would have to explain to Noah about the age of consent. Meanwhile, I wondered if this answered her question. Little white boys could be aggressive too.

Her question was still in my mind when we met Spike at school to walk home together. It was the first time I had seen the crowd of children outside the school. Some were, to me, enormous and looked hard-eyed. Could these be eighth graders? Some of the youths looked as if they shaved! But Spike came toward us, darting between the long legs of the older students, grinning happily and pulling the hand of a round, sober-faced Negro child who he told us was "Neal. He lives on the corner." (Neal's father, one of the first black graduates of a well-known medical school, was to become our family doctor. We would begin the amusing incidents of having white specialists, to whom Dr. Brent sent us, invariably look astonished to see we were white.)

The five of us walked home together, Spike, Noah, Sarah, Neal and I. In the middle of the second block, a tall, dark-brown young man lounged against a tree and my stomach clenched. He looked exactly like the photographs in the newspapers under headlines reading: YOUTH ARRESTED IN SHOOTING. The street was deserted. I slowed my steps. Maybe he would go away before we reached him.

Suddenly Spike broke away and ran toward the young man up ahead.

"Hey, Sonny! Here's my Mom."

Sonny's face that had looked so hostile to me as we approached broke into soft curves of shy friendliness. Spike said this was Sonny Saxon; he lived around the corner and they had walked to school together at noontime. Close up, I could see that Sonny's mahogany-colored face had the rounded lines of childhood, but he was a big child for his age. Eleven and a half and taller than I. Big, shy, gentle Sonny was to be a patient playmate for all our children during the next two years before he graduated. The young man who had been the focus of all my stereotypes about big, black youths was, in reality, not a tough gang member, but the only child of a social worker and a teacher. His mother, Ilka Saxon, was to give Spike a special sensitive understanding almost exactly ten years from the day I cringed from her son.

Other mothers at the nursery school asked me questions about the aggressiveness and hostility they expected from the Negro students at the public school. By then, I had met other white parents in addition to Celia and Abby who had chosen the public school. One of them, a woman who taught anthropology at a local university, smiled when I told her of the frequent questions. In her opinion, it was "paranoia based on guilt."

"Those whites who smashed windows and shot at the troopers in Oxford, Mississippi, during James Meredith's first weeks were pretty scary. I think a lot of whites *expect* Negroes to feel resentment. So they're afraid of the hostility they believe Negroes *must* feel . . . the hostility whites *would* feel if things were reversed."

At the time, this seemed a bit complex for me, but the fact was that Spike had reported no problems at school—in his classroom or on the playground. However, Spike was tall for his age, nearly the biggest in his class; on the playground, his friendliness and quick, darting activity may have kept him out of trouble. I admitted to some of the mothers who asked that this might be a factor in Spike's happy, easy adjustment to the crowded playground.

It was Abby Goldman who brought up another question. "Are you ever worried that Spike might pick up bad grammar or a funny accent from Mrs. Grant?" Abby had been surprised when I did not request Mrs. Schmidt as Spike's teacher. But Mrs. Grant had grammar at least as good as mine and she had grown up in Boston and sounded like President Kennedy.

The next question that would come, "Aren't you afraid your child will be held back by slow learners?" would have an unexpected answer in a few months, but during Spike's first month at school, there seemed to be no problems. Spike came home, full of pride, displaying papers of wobbly handwriting on which Mrs. Grant had drawn a smiling face. On October 11, Ben and I attended the first Parents' Night at Willis School where we were to talk with the teachers in our child's classroom.

While we waited our turn to speak to Mrs. Grant, we looked at the folder of papers on Spike's classroom desk. Ben said, "Well, it looks like he's inherited my handwriting, poor kid!"

Mrs. Grant was talking to two shabbily dressed black parents, who were frowning and shaking their heads. I heard Mrs. Grant say, "Please don't worry. She's a bright child and will do well. It takes some children a little longer to begin, that's all." The mother and father seemed suddenly to stand straighter and their smiles now shone with unadulterated gratitude.

To us, Mrs. Grant said, "Spike is a very good friend to his classmates . . . and his teacher. He has a little trouble sitting still, but we're working on that." I wished her luck. Since babyhood, Spike's long thin body had been in constant motion. Occasionally, I had felt a pang of envy when I saw quiet, placid children. Mrs. Grant said that Spike's bright little mind and his curiosity was more important than sitting still. His handwriting? She believed beautiful handwriting was an inborn talent, like a singing voice. Ben grinned. Mrs. Grant said they were working to make Spike's writing legible. More important, she said, Spike was an eager reader, now well into the second primer. "I'll bet he sees his parents read a lot," she said. "I only wish that were true with all our children."

When we emerged from Mrs. Grant's room, Vangie Peters appeared, moving through the parents in the hallways, a vivid spot in a bright green dress. I introduced her to Ben. "Ah, Lois, I should have known you would have a handsome husband! Come, I want you to meet Dr. Steel and Dr. Chambers."

The Steels and the Chambers (both white) had *voluntarily* moved from the suburbs, each for different reasons, and were happy to tell us why.

Dr. Steel taught in an all-white high school in the Northeast. He had seen, he said, too much competition among the students for material things; too much rejection of the children who were not good-looking or well-to-do. "Everybody out there was walking in lockstep—afraid to be themselves. It's healthier here." His shy quiet wife nodded agreement.

The Chambers, it developed, had moved from a fashionable suburb of New York when Dr. Chambers joined the university in Philadelphia. He had found a lot of disillusionment among his students when their families "*talked* liberality and *lived* conservatively." "These kids were hurt by the hypocrisy they saw in their parents—the people they believed in and loved most. Mama and Daddy would be out, raising funds for SNCC or demonstrating in the South—and yet they lived in all-WASP neighborhoods and didn't even know the last name of their maid. Some of those young people rejected *all* the values of the parents." His wife, smiling and gregarious, added that they decided that if they believed in integration, they ought to live it. "It's a lot simpler for whites to do the integrating," she said. "And I think it'll give us a better relationship with our children."

It was good to hear reasons for what had been, for Ben and me, largely instinct. I needed the reassurance that we were not alone in our choice of a school for our children. People who had dug more deeply into the issue had given me reasons I had not even considered.

The questions of the nursery-school mothers continued. Some sent me to other experts for an answer. One woman asked, "Aren't you afraid of . . . well, you know . . . lice and other things?" At the next checkup at our pediatrician's, a relaxed, elderly man who always had time to chat, I asked about "diseases of poor people." By now, I had seen a number of children on the playground who had the look of poverty—the gaunt faces, the faded too-large or too-small clothing. When Vangie saw me looking woefully at a little girl who was literally bursting from her dress, she said, "You don't know what I go through in winter, Lois, trying to find warm clothing for some of these children."

Our doctor approved heartily of the school we had chosen. "Too many misguided parents try to protect their children from the facts of life. And it's like trying to protect them from chicken pox or mumps—if they run into these things for the first time as adults, it's rougher."

But could children pick up something other than chicken pox from children whose parents were poor?

"Nothing that you can't pick up in any public place—the zoo, the museums, any bus or trolley or in a store. Anyway, if this is a mostly black school, you're safe from lice. For some reason, lice only attack white people's heads. We're not sure why."

The problem of "bad words" that one nursery-school mother brought up was hilariously dispelled when Spike returned after playing with a private-school child on our block.

"Mom, is 'shut' a bad word in Philadelphia?" he asked.

No, why?

"Well, Roddy's mother said she'd wash his mouth out with soap if he ever said it again."

I whooped with laughter, suddenly realizing that Roddy's family had come from Georgia and the word might sound like "shut" from him.

In the interests of accuracy, I corrected Spike's mispronunciation, spelled the word and explained it was not "polite" to use it. It was like talking with your mouth full of food or picking at your nose—"not good manners."

Spike asked, with what looked like a gleam of mischief in his eyes, "Would you wash my mouth out with soap if I used it?"

I was not going to play that particular game. My theory was that children could learn to enjoy upsetting powerful grown-ups with four-letter words. I said casually that I didn't like hearing the word any more than I liked seeing someone eat with his fingers. I would appreciate it, I said, if he did not use that word in front of me, but I didn't think, I said, it was worth getting *that* upset. To myself, I noted that private schools obviously did not preclude "bad" words.

Celia Spears, the minister's wife, was also being quizzed about private versus public schools. She said, bitterly, "I can't tell this to our church members, but I think it's just plain social climbing with some." Perhaps it was, but with others it was, to me, real concern over the future of their children.

I was now digging into my memory when I discussed private schools with some of the women. Two nearly forgotten incidents returned now. In my advertising days, I had been hired to produce a charity fashion show using socially prominent woman as models. It had been interesting to find that these women, all graduates of the "best" private schools, were no more poised or confident or well-mannered than my own friends. I recalled too that a co-worker in Chicago had once confided to me that her parents sacrificed to send her to an expensive private school. "But I couldn't keep up with the rich girls. It gave me a 'poor' feeling I have never lost."

At least Spike was learning that he was in the middle of the middle class. He asked if we could have a swimming pool like the Negro family across our street and he had accepted the fact that we could not afford it; he brought home a bedraggled, thin little boy named Cephas Simpson who "forgot" to bring his lunch several times a week. Spike told me later, "He shouldn't forget. He's so thin. Even when he brings his lunch, there's not much of it. I think he's poor."

The crucial question of whether "slow" children held "gifted" children back was answered in segments. At first, I would point out that Barbara Hamilton's son, Jimmy, was only in kindergarten but had taught himself to read. He was allowed to come to Spike's first-grade classroom for several periods each day. When I was a child, I had been skipped a grade. These methods, I felt, were available for children who outstripped their classmates. Spike's first report card showed average progress; his friend, Neal Brent, the doctor's son, got *A*'s to Spike's *B*'s and *C*'s. Spike was doing well in reading and liked school. He was not, that we could see, being held back.

Shortly after his first report card, Spike brought home a note that said he was being transferred to the "advanced class." He would now have Mrs. Schmidt. I phoned Vangie Peters. Did he have to leave Mrs. Grant?

"You're so right, Lois, she is a marvelous teacher, but I'm giving her the slower children this year. Spike's IQ tested in the Superior range, so he belongs in Mrs. Schmidt's class," she said.

There is no use going back and wondering how much difference it might have made if I had followed my instincts. I meekly accepted the change, believing that Vangie Peters knew best.

In a short time, Spike brought home a note from Mrs. Schmidt. Would I come in to talk with her about Spike?

When I appeared at the appointed time, she took me into the corridor.

"You simply must make Spike sit still in class," she said, her thin mouth twitching at one corner.

I asked if he misbehaved or bothered the other children. Spike had always been active but cheerful and cooperative. Perhaps I was seeing him only through my maternal bias.

Mrs. Schmidt's mouth twitched again and she said, crossly, "No, he doesn't bother the other children, but he bothers *me*. He wiggles and plays with the buttons on his clothes. Makes me nervous. And his handwriting is atrocious. Look, here's Spike's messy paper and here's Archer Spears!"

I was glad Celia's son had such neat handwriting, but what did that have to do with Spike? I could try to work with him at home to improve his handwriting, but I could not imagine how I could "make him" sit still in school. I promised Mrs. Schmidt I would try. She frowned, nodded and dismissed me.

Asking Spike to sit still was like asking the rain drops not to splash. But I had got used to his constant motion. I explained to him that Mrs. Schmidt would like him to wiggle less. He said he would try.

From then on, any questions about children being held back by "underprivileged" children had to be answered by admitting that this was not Spike's problem. On his report card, his reading level rose one step and stayed there. It was hard to understand why. At home, he was reading on his own. His handwriting never improved. I sat with him, trying to keep him at the task of printing his letters. (The Palmer Method of exercising small muscles with those endless loops and circles was considered outdated). I felt alternately sorry for him, struggling so hard to control his pencil, and frantic when he used every possible excuse to leave his chair and move about. I had had several more requests from Mrs. Schmidt to talk with her. Her complaints were always about Spike's "wiggling in his seat" and "not paying attention." "He brings down the average achievement level of my class," she said during one visit. I suggested he might be sent back to Mrs. Grant. Heavens, no, said Mrs. Schmidt, Spike read too well for *that* class. "I think you ought to take him to a psychiatrist to see what makes him so distractable," she said, her mouth twitch punctuating her words.

Our pediatrician said angrily, "Don't you do it. Spike is a happy, normal boy. Very bright. I think that woman can't reach him and is angry at Spike because of it."

By then, the year was almost over. If there was something neurotic about our family, Sarah and Noah did not show it. The nursery-school director reported that Noah was affection- ate and sensitive to others' needs, cooperative and indepen- dent. Sarah, she said, gave Noah a few problems by following him around, depending on him. But Sarah had "a strong per- sonality" and would develop her own independence when she was on her own as she would be when Noah entered kinder- garten. I asked if either child was unusually or distractingly active. Not a bit, she said, very calm children.

I told Ben about Sarah's dependence on Noah right after I had handed him a jar to open for me. "Fancy that," he said, grinning. "Wonder where she learned that from?" According to Ben, Sarah and I were exactly alike. I was not sure how I felt about that, but perhaps I could help her learn to avoid the characteristics that had got me into trouble—the impulsiveness I counted on Ben to temper, the perfectionism that tensed me up over sewing or cooking. Meanwhile, it was a pleasure to watch her with Ben. In school, she would make Father's Day presents for a real father.

On my last visit to Mrs. Schmidt when I heard the same complaints that Spike "was not living up to his potential. He *must* sit still," I finally told her that he had been exceedingly active *before* he was born and probably always would be. She glared and turned away.

On the last day of school, I began the tradition of meeting my children at school so that the year's accumulation of draw- ings and papers could be put into the car. I had carefully hidden my dislike of Mrs. Schmidt from Spike, fearing it would undermine their relationship if he knew I saw her as a teacher far past her prime and even felt a pity for her in what must certainly be her last years of teaching. Now, as we drove home, with Spike looking crushed by a report card full of C's and an E in Work Habits, I let out my honest feelings.

"Honey, I did not like Mrs. Schmidt. I'm glad you'll be in another class next year. I know you'll do better."

Spike looked up at me. "You didn't like her either? Gee, am I glad! It hurt when she used to pinch me."

In the car in our garage, I heard for the first time that she had pinched the tender skin underneath Spike's chin when he would not sit still or if he got an answer wrong.

"She used to do it all the time, Mom. And it *hurt*."

"But why didn't you tell me?"

Spike shrugged, still looking at me questioningly. I had forgot that he was as inexperienced a student as I was a parent. Perhaps he believed teachers were supposed to act that way; that I would or could do nothing to help him.

There was nothing I could do that day. School was over for the summer and Mrs. Schmidt was, by now, on her way home. I instructed Spike to tell me . . . always . . . if a teacher hurt him. I could report the pinches to Vangie Peters in the fall (I would hear her appropriate disapproval and her assurances that she had never *dreamed* Mrs. Schmidt would hurt a child), but I could not overcome my own sense of guilt. All those questions I had answered for the mothers at the nursery school! I had assured them that Spike was not being terrorized by the black students. Why had I failed to notice he was being terrorized by a white teacher?

Mrs. Schmidt was the only teacher to hurt or frighten any of my children. It is impossible to be sure how much she affected the next five confusing years of Spike's education. But, just as I had looked in the wrong places during that first year at Willis School, I would continue to wear special blinders for several years to come.

four

THE NEXT THREE YEARS—FROM AUGUST, 1963, TO THE FALL
of 1966—are compressed in my memory. These were the years
when terrible events shook America, and our family faced a
calamity of its own. These were also years of learning and adjustment for me: first, as a parent of three children who displayed widely different learning styles in school and second,
as a white middle-class mother meeting the unexpected, but
inevitable adjustments to a mostly black urban public school.

Often the violent civil rights fight outside our neighborhood
made us feel that we were living in a rare oasis of sanity. The
murder of Medgar Evers, the assassination of John Kennedy
and Malcolm X, the whips, dogs and gas at the bridge in Selma,
the thirty black Americans killed in the streets of Watts, James
Meredith wounded on a highway in Mississippi—all these
bloody events occurred while our children were growing up
in an area where black and white Americans lived, learned
and worked together. What I saw as harmony in our school
made the television newscasts seem even more tragic.

I sentimentalized over the "bridges of understanding" being
built between my children and their friends. Neal Brent's
mother told me that on the day of the inspiring March on
Washington in August, 1963, her son was watching the March
on TV. He had said to her, "Spike's there." She told him, no,
Spike was home with a cold the same as he was.

She said to me, "He turned back to the set and said, very quietly, 'Well, Spike *wants* to be there!' "

The day after the March on Washington, Spike had watched television when news broke in nearby Folcroft, Pa. A young Negro medical technician, his wife and small daughter had tried to move into all-white Folcroft. An angry mob of neighbors set fire to the moving van, threw rocks, ripped out plumbing connections and gathered in the streets shouting threats. Telecasts showed jeering white faces, ugly with hate.

Spike watched with growing concern. "Mom, will they do that to Neal?"

I assured him that Neal was safe in our neighborhood. Spike wanted to know why those people in Folcroft were acting "so mean." I could only explain that it was like a foolish superstition. "Long ago, people believed in witches. Some people today believe that dark-skinned people are bad."

Spike shook his short-cropped blond head in disbelief. How could anyone think Neal and his parents were bad! "Can I go over to Neal's house just to be *sure* he's okay?" Spike asked. Of course.

As he sprinted from the house, I remember being glad that Spike would never be vulnerable to the superstitions that were costing our country so much agony. It would be a while before I learned that our children's adjustments to their two-color world were much easier than mine.

When school began in September, my attention was focused solely on Spike's second year and on Noah's entry into kindergarten. Spike was to have another elderly white teacher for second grade, but I had met her and was relieved to find she displayed none of the characteristics of Mrs. Schmidt. Mrs. Bothwell had the sweet expression of Cinderella's fairy godmother; she was plump, calm and, as I was to learn, devoutly concerned with her students.

It was Noah's kindergarten teacher about whom I had

qualms. Abby, Celia and a number of other mothers rolled their eyes when Mrs. Katie Greene was mentioned. She was called "over-strict," "old-fashioned," "unreasonable." But since these same women believed Mrs. Schmidt was a "wonderful teacher," I took Noah to school the first day determined to keep an open mind.

In the kindergarten room, Noah and I waited while another white mother talked with Mrs. Greene. Mrs. Greene's appearance told me nothing. She was apparently in her fifties, buxom, short and very slightly Negroid-featured. Her eyes looked glazed as she listened to the mother, patted a sober-faced child, handed paper to several others, balanced a roll book and sent admonitory glances to two scuffling boys.

The woman ahead of me was trying to free her hand from the grasp of her child. She said to Mrs. Greene, "I do hope Roger will be sufficiently stimulated. He's unusually bright and could regress out of boredom. He already knows his numbers and his alphabet. He's quite gifted."

Mrs. Greene's taffy-colored face was expressionless as she said, "Very interesting. Can he tie his shoes? He'll trip. Next?"

The mother bent to tie her son's shoes, sending a glare at Mrs. Greene's back. She and her son wrestled at the door when she tried to leave. I introduced Noah to Mrs. Greene, glad I had put shoe-tying ahead of the alphabet.

I could not resist adding: "And he's done his postgraduate work in coat buttoning."

Mrs. Greene grinned. Noah walked to the chair on which she was sitting, put his arm around her and gave her a hug. She looked startled, then delighted. No one noticed me as I left.

The following Sunday, September 15, 1963, a black church in Birmingham, Alabama, was bombed, injuring twenty-three children and killing four little girls. When I picked Ben up at the airport that day after a business trip, we both noticed that no black person met our eyes. I walked Noah to school the next day, fearful this tragedy might affect the feeling of the black children toward anyone white. The trusting smiles that Spike's and Noah's classmates gave me made the tragedy seem somehow even more poignant. Mrs. Greene was, as always. at the front door of the school to welcome her students. That day she had organized them into a game of farmer in the dell. As each child arrived, he joined the circle. Small brown hands held pink hands, healing the alienation that might have begun.

Many years later, a fifth-grade teacher told me she had asked her class to write compositions on "My Favorite Teacher." "Do you know that nearly all the children wrote about Mrs. Greene?" she said. It did not surprise me. From the first hug Noah gave her to the last hug ten years later, a few months before her death when he towered over her, Noah—and thousands of other children who passed through her arms—knew that her "strictness" was as "old-fashioned" as her love.

Sarah was now on her own in her last year of nursery school. Within a few weeks, she had found a substitute for Noah. He was only the first in a long line of little boys who were somehow persuaded to carry, move, lift or fix Sarah's toys or projects. She had also made her choice of a career. She watched Mrs. Jefferson, the woman who cleaned our big house once a week in one efficient swoop. She listened when Mrs. Jefferson and I compared notes on her four children and my three. Perhaps her little computer mind, which had always observed, analyzed and concluded, told her that Mrs. Jefferson's skill and optimistic personality were laudable goals. Sarah announced, "I'm going to be a cleaning woman when I grow up."

I was also learning from Mrs. Jefferson. With one exception, she was to be my most intimate contact with black mothers who worked, not for "creative fulfillment" and not in offices or schools, but who worked because they desperately needed the money and had been taught no other skills.

It is always hard to remember that Mrs. Jefferson is several years younger than I; she seems to have lived much longer. Her history was, and would continue to be, much like the typical low-income families in big cities. She, her construction-laborer husband and four children had come from South Carolina about the same time we moved from Omaha. When her initial quiet caution with me finally gave way to candor, she told me they had moved North to escape segregation and to get a better education for their children than she and Mr. Jefferson had had. During her South Carolina childhood, the schools for Negro children were open for six months; nine months for whites. Attendance was purely voluntary in the crowded classes where the teacher herself sometimes had only an eighth-grade education. At the age of twelve, Mrs. Jefferson noticed that important news could be found in the newspapers—"Negro papers told if there was trouble, like a lynching." She had taught herself to read. Now, in the North, she hoped for better instruction for her children.

I would talk briefly with other women like Mrs. Jefferson at the Home and School Association meetings in our school, their faces and their bodies limp with fatigue. They had worked all day, cleaning other women's houses, gone home to clean theirs and to make dinner. When I heard the often-repeated statement, "The parents who need to be at these meetings never are!" I knew some of the reasons why. Those who did manage to get to meetings often answered my chatter with monosyllables and they had no time to build friendships through afternoon visits. I would get to know some of their children very well, but not their parents.

These were not the kinds of parents who had time to hold offices in the Home and School Association. According to Barbara Hamilton's cynical belief, the HSA was "run by a certain clique of whites. They assign Negro parents to the Hospitality Committee . . . you know, the dishwashing and cleaning up."

Perhaps. But at the first HSA board meeting to which Ben and I were invited, I was impressed with the group. This was no women's club. In fact, most of the offices were held by men. They were, I admitted to Barbara, all white men, but unlike the Omaha group, they were involved in more important issues than organizing programs on golf or lawn care. One man who was referred to as "Doctor" talked of a new math-teaching method he hoped the school might adopt; the president of the group read the news release he was sending to the papers condemning the slow pace of Southern integration. There was a lively debate on his choice of words and on the merits of the New Math method. Ben pleaded later that he had enough meetings at the office and I decided that this dynamic, intellectual group did not need me. I volunteered for the cleanup committee. I told Barbara, "Maybe my best contribution is to integrate that committee!" On the color of the committee, she had been absolutely right.

While I disagreed with Barbara that the HSA officers were working "more for their ego needs than for the good of *all* the children," Barbara and her husband, Leland, were both making other changes in my attitude and my vocabulary. It had taken many weeks after our first meeting for Barbara to persuade Leland to meet Ben and me. He felt, she told me later, that he had met too many patronizing white liberals. When he finally came to our house with Barbara, it was with the eager friendliness of a student serving detention time.

During the conversation, carried mainly by Barbara, Ben and me, I made a comment about the almost fifty-fifty "racial balance" of the lower grades compared to the 10 percent white–90 percent black "racial composition" of the upper grades.

Leland, dark brown eyes watching me closely out of his strong-featured face, said pleasantly, " '*Racial*' is a racist word. Use it if you wish, but it *is* inaccurate."

Leland's patronizing attitude irked me, but as he spoke I became too fascinated to be annoyed. With the ease of a premed student (which he had been before entering the ministry), he sped through the biological reasons why people "with poorly pigmented skin and those with richly pigmented skin" were of the same—the human—*race*.

"The false concept of race," said Leland as he shifted his stocky, heavily muscled frame in our red chair near the fireplace, "was invented by Thomas Jefferson as an intellectual exercise in hypocrisy. By promulgating the theory that Africans were of a different species—a different 'race'—he could convince himself and others that it was all right to own slaves while demanding 'liberty and freedom' for himself."

While Leland's biological facts about "race" were convincing, I could not quite accept Thomas Jefferson as "The Father of Racism." (Five years later, I read Winthrop Jordan's book, *White Over Black*, University of North Carolina Press, 1968. This eminent white historian had carefully documented Leland's accusations about Jefferson.) It was, however, irrefutable that black and white people were physically identical except for pigmentation; more identical physically than men and women.

I protested that "race" was a handy phrase and I would miss it; that I was already having enough trouble revising my vocabulary because I had decided that "Negro" was an *adjective*, not a noun. That evening's paper began an article with the sentence, "The Supreme Court reversed conviction of a Negro for sitting in an all-white section of a Virginia courtroom." The noun divested a person of sex, age, occupation and . . . "well, humanness." Like "race" it seemed a small matter on the surface, but I had come to believe that "Negro *student*" or "Negro *housewife*" or "Negro *man*" indicated *people* rather than a large faceless homogeneous group.

Leland nodded as if I were a bright child. Something in Ben's glance made me remember that since Omaha we had met many black people—especially men—who outpatronized white people in their determination not to be patronized. When the subject of Ben's Southern background came up, I decided that

(51)

if Leland had a prejudice about all Southerners then he was a bigot as warped as any Klansman. Instead, Leland raised his eyebrows, said he was from South Carolina too "so maybe we're related!" When Ben said, "Could be, Cousin," Leland looked at Barbara, hooted and relaxed into the friend he is to this day.

Our friendship changed more than my vocabulary. The following August when Watts exploded, it was Leland and Barbara who could explain the reason behind much of the looting. Barbara who had been raised in Harlem told how her mother walked her past the furniture-store window to show her the living room suite on which she had made payments for years. When her mother died before paying the full amount, no refund was given. Leland told us of the innumerable rackets from which he tried to protect his parishioners; smiling salesmen pressuring people to sign contracts whose language they could hardly read, "insurance policies that pay off only if you're trampled by an elephant at high noon on Market Street."

"In a section like Watts," Leland said, "most kids are pushed out of school unable to read their diplomas let alone a sales contract. They get taken by crooked merchants over and over again. No surprise they looted."

There was much we would learn through Barbara and Leland, much their children and mine would learn together, but it would take time to uncover certain deeply imbedded attitudes of mine less easily changed than my use of the word "race." These would be activated only as my children moved through their school.

From June, 1964, to March, 1965, there was no serenity to reflect on sociological attitudes. Ben was told at the office that his duties were being absorbed by the home office back in Omaha. He was out of a job.

Since Ben's unexplained transfer from Omaha to the Philadelphia branch, we had done some wise and some foolish things. We had saved every penny possible and I had begun doing free-lance advertising writing at home. Foolishly, we had not quite believed that the corporation transferred Ben in order to fire him at a safe distance. Since settling in Philadelphia, Ben had job-hunted but refused to skimp on his job at the office in order to make contacts and arrange interviews. Before his job ended, he had almost accepted an offer from another food company. During an interview with that company's president, the man had said, "Just remember our main competition comes from the Jew-boys. Those damn kikes have been trying to take over for years." Ben decided he would have a chancey future with a company like this. We believed he had lots of time to look around.

By fall, Sarah began kindergarten, Noah entered Mrs. Grant's first grade, Spike was in third grade and Ben was still unemployed. He had had the ironic experience of being told several times that the city and state jobs he applied for were "being given to Negroes only, sorry."

Like poking a sore tooth to see if it hurt, we looked for feelings of bitterness. Ben felt depressed, but resigned. "We whites had the edge all these years," he said. "Evening things up means someone has to lose. Too bad it's me. But if not me, it might have to be Spike's generation."

We had budgeted our savings carefully but they were dwindling. Ben knew how much I dreaded leaving the children to take a full-time advertising job away from home. We could hold out for nine months, but by early March, it looked as if I had to begin making arrangements to leave my children each day as my mother had had to leave me. It was hard to keep smiling when the children came home for lunch, wondering to myself how many more times I would be able to be there to greet them.

Our neatly ironic happy ending would be more appropriate to a work of fiction. All during Ben's job hunt, he had cherished the impractical (to me) hope of finding a job in some field more valuable than business. On March 25, 1965, Ben was interviewed in Washington, D.C., by David Seeley, then director of the Equal Educational Opportunities Program of HEW. To Dave Seeley, the fact that Ben had his own children in an integrated school was more important than experience in government. Ben was hired to work with Southern school districts on their desegregation plans. Unlike many Northern politicians (then and now), he would only be asking of others what he had already accepted for his own children. In spite of the fact that he would be doing a lot of traveling—in Georgia, Florida and Mississippi—Ben had a job and one that he felt was important.

By then, Spike was halfway through third grade. His gentle, sweet second-grade teacher had also worried about his inability to sit still and his lack of concentration. She confessed she was praying for him. Vangie Peters reminded me that Albert Einstein and Winston Churchill had both been slow starters. Ben suggested that Spike be taken out of the "advanced" grouping for third grade. "Maybe it would be better for him to be fast in a slower class than slow in a fast class," he said.

Vangie Peters was aghast. "But Spike reads so well," she said.

True, but his second-grade teacher told me he seldom finished his written work and sat fidgeting, looking around the room, during lessons. When I tried to work with him at home, he was interested and curious about everything but the assignment. I was afraid he would get farther and farther behind. One semester of low pressure could not hurt. Vangie finally agreed, and Spike was assigned to the class of a warm, motherly woman. He adored her. Not enough to change his casual habits, but our pediatrician kept assuring us he would eventually settle down.

We could not blame Spike's study habits on the school. Noah was in Mrs. Grant's first-grade class (Mrs. Schmidt had retired) and was combining an active social life with rapid progress in reading, writing and numbers. Each lunch hour he would bring home friends to wrestle on our lawn or climb trees. After school, he often brought home his neat papers with perfect grades.

The only phone call I had got from Mrs. Grant was the day Noah had brought an old pocketknife of Ben's to school. Mrs. Grant asked that I pick it up. He had been displaying it proudly to his buddies in class, but Mrs. Grant felt it should be transferred safely into my hands.

As I walked home, the pocketknife in my handbag, I remembered the worries of the nursery-school mothers. They had said they heard the children brought knives to school!

The semester ended and America had its first "hot summer" —the explosive incident in Watts. My children had still not met with violence in their school. In fact, Ben and I often listened to their dinner-table talk, pleased at the evidence that they were growing up with a wonderful color blindness. Children were described as "always wears a red coat" or "Billy's brother" or "lives near Amanda's house"—only occasionally and when other descriptions had failed, would they add, "He's brown-skinned." It was easy in those early days to believe that the children in our school at least could grow up seeing each other as people rather than as "them" and "us."

By the time Sarah entered Mrs. Grant's first grade, I had not yet realized that integration was much simpler for my children than it was for me. They had grown up expecting that classrooms and streets and their parents' living room would contain people with brown, pink and tan skins. I had grown up so accustomed to my all-white neighborhood, all-white school and even all-white movies (except for comic characters) that I had never plumbed attitudes I should have known were there.

The year before, I had realized Spike was ahead of me in sensitivity. He brought his friend, Cephas Simpson, home to play. Cephas was now a big, heavy child, slow-moving and quiet. The boys played until dinner time. Cephas politely refused my invitation to dinner and, with something close to alarm, rejected my offer to drive him home. Spike maneuvered me aside.

"I don't think he wants you to see where he lives," he said.

In a while, I said to Cephas, "Gee, I won't have time to drive you home after all, but I'm going to a supermarket near your house. Want a ride that far?" Cephas accepted immediately.

There was so much more I could have learned from the incident—about youngsters like Cephas, about what was really going on in our school. Instead, I was simply proud that Spike had picked up a clue I had missed. By focusing solely on my own children in those years, I was missing many clues.

It may have been that my own subconscious mind decided to send me a signal to end my smugness. It did not alert me to what was going on in the school, but at least I learned to question what was going on inside myself.

I was picking the children up for a dental checkup. The boys were already in the car and I waited, impatiently, for Sarah. Down the school steps she came, arms swingly freely and looking back only occasionally at her friend, Georgie, who was burdened down with the games and dolls she had brought to school for Show-and-Tell that day. Georgie's dark brown face was rigid with concentration as he struggled down the crowded stairs. At the car, Sarah instructed Georgie to put her things in the back of the car. She asked him sweetly, and he looked happy to comply, but I felt impatient.

I said, "Oh, Sarah, who was your . . ." My mouth slammed shut. I had almost uttered that old phrase of my grandmother's, "Who was your nigger *last* year?" Lamely, I stuttered a finish to the sentence, "your . . . uh . . . helper before you met Georgie?"

Sarah looked puzzled. "Leonard, but he moved to Scranton."

I drove to the dentist with extreme caution; my mind was not on driving. Luckily, the checkup was routine. I drove home, still trying to understand how I could have come so close to uttering that nasty little phrase. How could I even have thought it?

At home, I peeled potatoes (some down to walnut size) and made myself admit that the phrase had been there, planted long ago, but still alive. It was probably not a coincidence that I had just finished reading M. Esther Harding's book, *The Way of All Women* (Longmans, 1933). Dr. Harding, a psychoanalyst, wrote of all the complex emotions women experience in growing up, in marrying and in raising children. I had been particularly impressed with her statement that a mother's unconscious attitudes, if unhealthy, can infect her children as surely as physical disease germs. She urged women to try to rid themselves of unhealthy emotions as conscientiously as they kept themselves physically clean to protect their children. I thought I had.

I had often heard other white mothers emphasize color unnecessarily and tried to avoid this myself. Only recently, Abby Goldman had said, in front of her children and mine, "Mark had a fight with a little colored boy today." Noah, who loved using his developing muscles, had "fights" twice a week. I never asked the color of his sparring mate. Half the time it was the freckle-faced Angus Murphy from the next block. Saying "Noah had a fight with a little *Irish* boy today" would, I felt, have sounded equally silly. I had even heard Celia Spears ask, when her child complained of a "dumb old substitute we had today," "Was she Negro or white?" To me, asking the question implied that a "dumb old Negro substitute" was different somehow from a "dumb old white" one. I carefully avoided asking the color of a playmate or a teacher.

Now I wondered whether I had been too self-consciously anxious to avoid the question. As I continued to whittle away at those potatoes, I remembered an afternoon when Spike had brought home a friend for lunch. Noah, always eager to make friends, said to Sidney, a tall, loose-jointed chap with skin the color of rich black soil, "You're Spike's favorite dark-skinned friend." Embarrassed, I had jumped into the conversation. "Noah, don't be silly. There's no difference between light- and dark-skinned people."

Sidney looked down at his arm which was almost touching Spike's as they crowded together at the kitchen counter and said in an undertone, "Is she kidding?" I pretended not to hear.

All right, I told myself, I was not yet truly comfortable with color differences. Until 1961, my world had been entirely white. Perhaps the stupid phrase that pushed its way out of the deepest part of my mind was a reminder that there were more old attitudes tucked away back there that needed to be examined.

As if to prove M. Esther Harding's belief that maternal attitudes are passed readily to children, Noah asked a question the next day that brought out another unconscious attitude of mine.

After his playmates had gone home and I was sewing on buttons, Noah wedged himself into the chair next to me and said, "Mom, how come you never frown at Richard?" I said I did not understand what he meant.

"Well, when the other kids come in the house and don't wipe their feet, you frown. But you never frown at Richard." Richard was the one Negro child in his after-school gang.

To Noah, I said, "Gee, I don't know. Glad you noticed. Richard sure tracks in his share of mud."

That weekend when Ben was home, I told him of the week's events. When I repeated Noah's comment, he said, "He's right, honey. You *do* treat the Negro children a little more protectively."

I opened my mouth to rationalize my behavior, but I was already feeling the now familiar physical sensation of facing an uncomfortable truth. My face felt flushed and I wanted to shake my head in denial. I was also feeling as if I were on a fast elevator, going down. Ben was right. I was emphasizing color to my children just as unnaturally as Abby and Celia—an unnatural protectiveness was no better than unnatural suspicion. Both came from seeing people as "different."

In that moment, I learned something that made the years ahead much easier: Recognition of an unpleasant truth is not fatal. In fact, it made me feel oddly relaxed. I was now able to tell Ben about Sarah and Georgie and the ugly phrase I had come so close to saying out loud.

This was one of the times when Ben's protectiveness toward me was an obstacle. According to him, I was being overly harsh with myself. Perhaps. But close as Ben was to our children, I was with them more. If there were some other unhealthy attitudes I could pass on to them, I wanted to find them.

It was simple to give Richard his equal opportunity to be frowned at. I even hauled the whole troop of second-graders back outside for a lesson in shoe-wiping. By the time Noah was in third grade, I would be in physical combat with a black youth in the middle of the street, feeling protective only of Noah.

Meanwhile, Sarah was attacking her first-grade studies with a single-minded passion we wished Spike might catch. During Parents' Visiting Night, Mrs. Grant said Sarah was a hard worker "and she's learning that making a mistake is *not* the end of the world." Ben told Mrs. Grant, "Funny, I have the same problem with her mother!"

Spike's fourth-grade teacher, Miss Le Duc, had called me in for several conferences. Vangie Peters had told me she was "excellent with boys and a marvelous science teacher. She's just what Spike needs. This will be his best year." Spike did indeed like Miss Le Duc, but before each report-card period, she had asked me to come in and she had apologized for the poor grades she was about to give Spike. She said he had a quick, bright mind. "He gets my attempts at humor when most of the class misses them." She also said he was able to do complicated math problems in his head, but she could only mark him on the work he handed in and on the tests. He did not do his homework and seldom finished a test.

I was spending many anguished afternoons with Spike. He found dozens of excuses to do anything but his homework. If I said he could not leave his room until his homework was done, he read or played there contentedly. I had talked with him, trying to explain how important it was for him to settle down to work. Spike would listen, agree and I could see that his mind was hopping on to some other "interesting" subject. I told him a story about "grasshopper minds and turtle minds." "Grasshopper minds are wonderful," I said. "They get lots of great ideas. But sometimes we have to make our minds act like turtles—slow them down so they can do the not-so-interesting work they *have* to do." Nothing helped Spike sit still and do his homework. Several times I had got angry. Spike and I both ended up in tears. I felt like a monster, shrieking at my child. I felt worse because he did not respond with anger, just with looks of sadness and bewilderment. By now, our former pediatrician had retired from practice. Our new doctor was middle-aged, modern, but just as reassuring. During checkups, Spike examined every object on the doctor's desk and asked dozens of questions. The doctor told me privately, "Let him grow at his own pace. It takes some children longer to settle down."

There seemed to be nothing we could do but wait. Ben and I had discussed private school and rejected the idea for several reasons. Noah and Sarah were doing well at Willis School; if we took Spike out, he might feel he was a failure. If possible, it would be better if Spike outgrew or solved his study problems in the same school as his brother and sister.

There was another reason why private school was, to me, only a last resort. Abby Goldman had, that year, put her children in private school and I did not like what I heard from her. At first she told me firmly, "You're not Jewish. You can afford to be liberal. My kids need the best education I can afford.

They'll have plenty of job discrimination when they grow up." I could not argue. Recently, Abby had reported, casually, that on her car-pool day she heard two of her son's classmates tell him he could not take tennis lessons with them at the Philadelphia Cricket Club. "They don't allow Jews there," one child said. Abby had acted unconcerned. She said, "He has to learn the facts of life someday!" Perhaps, but we did not want Spike exposed to this kind of snobbery if we could avoid it.

Along with our worry about Spike and my own self-criticisms, there were also many amusing and warm episodes sprinkled over those same three years. We invited Miss McGregor, Noah's second-grade teacher, to lunch. She was a young woman, new to the school, and she impressed me as being tense and anxious to impress with her newly acquired training. I listened while she talked of her theories of education, believing that experience would soften her rather rigid expectations. Noah came over to me and began to whisper in my ear. Before he got three words out, I said, recklessly, "Honey, it's not polite to whisper in front of others. Just say what you want out loud."

Noah gave a You-Asked-For-It shrug and said distinctly, "Are you going to tell Miss McGregor you think she gives too much homework?"

I smiled weakly. Miss McGregor flushed.

Spike was having some fascinating experiences as a peacemaker and Cub Scout recruiter. He had joined the same troop as his friends, Sonny Saxon and Neal Brent. One evening, just after dinner, our doorbell rang. It was Neal and his father, Sonny and his father—four brown faces, all scowling.

Neal's father said Neal had been complaining that Sonny harassed him and Spike on the way home from Cub Scout meetings. Sonny's father, an enormous man from whom Sonny had obviously inherited his size, said that Sonny denied this. Sonny had said Spike could explain.

While the two fathers glared at each other across their sons' heads, Spike said, "Oh, sure. I keep telling you, Neal, that Sonny's only playing. He wouldn't hurt us. He's just chasing us in fun." Sonny who had looked so frightening to me the first time I saw him now looked at Spike with moist-eyed relief and gratitude. "See!" he said to his father. "I told you Spike understands me."

Spike was not as perceptive with Neal Brent's mother. She told me it was regrettable that there were two Cub Scout troops in the neighborhood—one, all-white and the other (except for Spike), all-black. Could she ask Spike to recruit some of his "other friends"? Certainly. She must have phrased her request to Spike in the same words. Spike recruited two of his "other friends" for the troop—both black.

Around the same time, Sarah announced that she had been chosen for a dance program that would be "in a big auditorium downtown." For a week, she had locked herself in her room and I could hear the thumps of her practicing. She volunteered me to help sew the costumes. At school, I stitched up the brightly colored fabric into loose sacks. I asked Mrs. Grant what kind of dance the children were doing.

Mrs. Grant grinned mischievously. "I was very annoyed that our school was assigned an African dance while the white schools got to do the pretty ballet and waltz things. I thought Sarah would make a very interesting-looking African."

By the time the 1965-66 school year ended, I believed I had uncovered at least some of my attitudes left over from my childhood. At least I no longer painted an unrelievedly rosy picture of our school to the new residents Vangie Peters asked me to have over for coffee. Our sons, I would explain to the new mothers who wanted to know about the school, happened to be bigger than average for their age; Sarah, while small, was not timid and was used to dodging her big brothers. A small or shy child might not be happy in a bustling boisterous city school. I would also explain that while Sarah and Noah were doing very well in their studies, Spike was having problems. He was, I added, getting special attention from Vangie Peters and his teachers. But I no longer felt pressed to "sell" the school passionately to quell any doubts of my own. I kept myself aware of the protectiveness Noah and Ben had noticed in me, but I was only dimly aware that protectiveness toward small Negro children was easier than it would be when my children and their classmates were older.

When Barbara Hamilton phoned to tell me what she termed "a hilarious" incident between her daughter and Sarah, I did not have time to be realistic. To me, the incident was horrifying and I could not understand why Barbara told it to me in a light, laughing way.

Barbara said she had given the girls an old curtain to play with and had overheard Sarah saying to Paula, "Let's play 'bride.' I'll be the bride. You can't be because you're black."

I hung onto the phone as if it were a life preserver. The floor felt as if it had turned to water beneath my feet.

Barbara continued without giving me a chance to reply. "Then Paula said, 'Don't be silly. My mother was a bride. Anyway, she'll make us take turns.' Then Sarah said, 'I don't have to mind your mother. She's black too!'"

I clutched the telephone tighter, hardly breathing. What attitude of mine could have infected Sarah? Even if I had said that ugly phrase out loud the day Georgie was carrying her things, she would not have understood it. But I had not said it. If Sarah had picked up any unconscious attitude of mine, she must also have picked up the feeling of close friendship between Barbara and me. Was there, perhaps, some attitude toward Mrs. Jefferson who cleaned for us that I had projected to Sarah? That did not make sense either. Mrs. Jefferson had once confided in me that my children were the only ones among the families for whom she worked who were taught to call her "*Mrs.*" (I had cringed inwardly at the lack of dignity implied when other children—and their mothers—called her by her first name.) In addition to these questions, I was also confused by Barbara's tone of voice. Why had the incident amused her?

Barbara was saying, "When Sarah said, 'I don't have to mind your mother because she's black,' Paula said, 'Oh, Sarah Stalvey, sometimes you say the dumbest things.' It was quiet in there for a minute and then your daughter said, 'Okay. Let's play dolls.'" Barbara finished with a laugh. Then she said, more seriously, "I could *never* have handled things that way when I was Paula's age. By the way, who has Sarah been playing with lately?"

I understood one mystery. Barbara was proud of Paula for dealing with Sarah, self-confidently, directly. But I did not feel I could push off Sarah's attitude on some playmate. I was positive that children's bigotries came directly from the home. Sarah's did not come from Ben; he was more natural and relaxed about color than I was.

Barbara, with a confidence I did not share, said, "Come on. I know Sarah didn't get this from you. Who has she been playing with? Abby Goldman's daughter?" Barbara disliked Abby who, she felt, "resents being Jewish." I felt Barbara was being unfair and I did not agree with her theory that some people who resent their own minority status "have strange hang-ups about other minorities."

I had to admit, however, that Sarah had played with Tina Goldman the day before. In defense of Abby, I told Barbara of the unpleasant experience Abby's own daughter had just had.

"Abby said she found Tina had taped adhesive tape across her nose. She thought Tina had hurt herself. Then Tina told her that a child, 'a WASP child' Abby said, at school told her, 'You're a Jew and your nose is going to grow bigger and bigger and bigger!' Tina taped her nose down to keep it from growing."

I told Barbara that, even though she did not like Abby, incidents like this certainly made Abby conscious of the hurts of prejudice. She would not teach Tina anything that blatantly racist.

Barbara said, "No, she didn't, but there's your answer. If that child was anti-Semitic, you can bet she was anti-black too. Along with the junk about Jewish noses, she probably also told her a whole lot of dandy things about black people. And Tina passed her lessons on to Sarah."

Later I learned this was exactly what had happened. Sarah had listened, observed and finally announced, "That Tina says some dumb things."

That day, however, I hung up the telephone with a head full of thoughts. I was thankful that Barbara and I had had time to build a close, trusting relationship. Earlier in our acquaintance, she might have blamed Sarah's remarks on home environment as I had been ready to do. She might have ended our friendship without telling me why. And I might not have confirmed what we suspected in Omaha—that like cold germs, the virus of racism and anti-Semitism can be passed around from child to child.

My own genetic endowment of racism was still far from diagnosed and cured. I had learned it was there. I had learned that admitting it was painful, but not fatal. Many of my unresolved fears involving color would remain dormant for a while as a new phase of school life began for our children. National events took on a different dimension when I viewed them from within our neighborhood. Barbara was there too, to help me understand this new phase, but because they were moving to West Philadelphia to be nearer Leland's church, her reassuring (and cautioning) words would often come through the same telephone I had clutched so tightly that day.

There would also be other days soon when there was no time to talk with Barbara or with Ben. I would be alone with my maturing children, my impulses and the need for quick decisions.

(65)

five

It is now clear that the fall semester of 1966 had in it many clues to the future. During the previous four years, I had been concentrating solely on my own three children, their reactions to school in general, to their particular kind of school and the adjustments I needed to make as a white middle-class mother. The spotlight of attention was focused on my children and myself. The children just outside that spotlight were shadowy figures, only marginally part of my children's lives. In 1966, my view was forced to widen when other youngsters pushed their way into that spotlight and when it flashed briefly over children who would play an important part in my further education.

Part of my ability to see more was due to Ben's having a new job that brought him home every night. Ben was now in charge of enforcing equal job opportunities in the building trades for the Department of Labor and, except for trips to Washington, he would be here with us in Philadelphia. I believed I would no longer have to worry about midweek crises. I could relax, like a passenger instead of the driver, and notice the scenery.

By now, my eye had become so adjusted to color that I did not realize both Spike and Noah had Negro teachers that year until I was asked by a new white mother in the school, "How do your children accept Negro teachers?" The answer was "Variably." Spike's fifth-grade teacher, Miss Jane Banneker, was a gentle, serious woman in her late thirties. Spike enjoyed carrying books for her and staying late to help clean the room. By contrast, Noah's third-grade teacher was an effervescent lady whom Noah usually convinced to drive him home if it rained.

Sarah's teacher for second grade was Mrs. Sczmanski, a white woman with a young child of her own who, Vangie Peters told me, had just returned to teaching after a divorce.

At the first Parents' Visiting Night, Jane Banneker told us she had talked with Spike's former teachers and was going to try not to press him, but to give him as much supportive help as possible. I appreciated her directness and the small frown-line of concern on her broad high forehead.

Noah's teacher grinned at us broadly and reported that he was certainly an affectionate, always-clowning boy. Noah had made a conquest, but it was also reassuring to see that his reading and math levels showed good progress.

We were particularly anxious to meet Sarah's new teacher. For weeks, Sarah had praised Mrs. Sczmanski. "She's so nice and if the class behaves, she buys us all candy bars." Ben said to me, "Either she's rich or she has a deal with a dentist!"

When we entered Mrs. Sczmanski's classroom, she interrupted her conference with another couple to call to us, "I'll bet you're Sarah's parents."

She quickly ended the other conference and led us to chairs at her desk. "Oh, that Sarah! She's so smart and adorable. And I get such a kick out of the way she likes to do things *her* way!"

Ben asked, "Which things?"

"Well, the class is supposed to go into the coatroom by the left door, but Sarah insists on using the right-hand door. She's so cute about it that I just let her do it."

Ben's eyebrows shot up. He said, "Do you think it's good

(67)

for her to think she can break rules?" Mrs. Sczmanski said she had never thought of it that way. She regretfully agreed.

It never occurred to me that our children were getting other less blatant special privileges. If Vangie Peters always had time to invite me into the teachers' room for coffee and a chat, I thought it was because we had become friends. She took great interest in every detail of Spike's study problems and together we explored every possible way to help him. I assumed that all parents got nearly the same attention.

Neither Barbara nor Ben shared my liking for Vangie. Barbara's son Jimmy was an unusually advanced child and Barbara contended that Vangie always seemed surprised "that such a brown little boy had a high IQ." Ben felt Vangie manipulated people. I insisted that in many instances she had to.

Vangie had told me the story of her first years at Willis School. For years, she said, Willis School had had "a martinet woman principal who simply kept Negro students out—one way or another. When she finally retired, our school had a very weak black principal who, well, he just did nothing, Lois. The man you bought your house from—he was president of the Board of Education—personally asked me if I would accept the challenge."

Vangie smoothed her black hair away from the whiteness of her temples. "You have no idea what I went through that first year! The neighborhood had just begun to integrate, Lois. My white parents were running like frightened chickens! With a few other sensible white parents, I organized a group to visit the homes and sell the values of integration. I talked to realtors about our wonderful school. I got publicity for us, Lois."

We were in the teachers' lunchroom; Vangie lit another cigarette and pressed her other hand, small and blue-veined to her temple. "But, Lois, you can't *imagine* the hypocrisy I had to deal with! In the most crucial time, when I was *desperately* trying to hold my parents, the *president* of the Home and School Association moved to the suburbs without a word of warning. *All* the time he had been telling others to stay, he was *actually* in the process of selling his house!" She closed her eyes, put her hand to her forehead and shook her head, remembering the shock apparently.

"Five, *five* other white families moved out right behind him," she said. Then she shook her head once more and looked at me smilingly. "But other families stayed and now we're getting families like yours, Lois, and I feel I've won."

I protested that our children had got much more than we had been able to give the school. Our suburban school would never have given them the same broadening experiences; some having nothing to do with color. Sarah had been fascinated to learn that her new friend, Amanda, the daughter of an Australian exchange professor, went to the beach at Christmastime. The children had been to a Chanukah party at a friend's synagogue; Spike decided that year to make a Chanukah decoration in class. ("I did Christmas stuff since I was a child!") Sarah had a new "boyfriend" whom she described as "so polite and handsome and he wears a shirt and tie every day." When her brothers tried to figure out which child he was, they finally asked, "Black or white?" Sarah said she didn't know. He was, it developed, a child from a Hindu family. Sarah went to lunch at his house and came home wide-eyed over the beautiful saris worn by his mother and grandmother.

Our children's experiences were also contradicting color-income stereotypes. One of Sarah's friends, the daughter of a black realtor, talked of the swimming pool her family was having built at their splendid new house; one of Noah's classmates, a WASP child whose bruises Vangie had once shown me—bruises inflicted by his parents—happily wore one of Noah's outgrown coats to school after Vangie had telephoned me to gasp that the child had been sent through the snow in a sweater.

That day, talking in the teachers' room with Vangie, I also told her about driving Noah to the suburban home of one of his summer day-camp friends. As we drove through block after block of similar houses where children played in driveways or on the sidewalks, Noah said, "There's something funny about this neighborhood." I had glanced around. "What, honey?" Noah said, "Everybody's white!"

The neighborhood in which Noah was growing up was much more like the international world his generation would have to live in. I felt we had Vangie to thank for the opportunity.

Even that summer's "Black Power" cry had not disturbed the smooth surface of the school. While conservative black "leaders" made apologetic denouncements of Stokely Carmichael, and black moderates "explained" him to nervous whites, Noah adopted the phrase along with his friends. To Spike and Noah, "Black Power" was what their teachers had and their teachers used that power wisely.

The first months of school moved along predictably. By now, our children's characteristics had become humorously evident. After Sarah's complaint that Mrs. Sczmanski made her go through "that other door," Ben said to me laughingly, "It seems that if Spike's teacher calls you, it's about his work. If Noah's teacher calls, it's to complain about his mischief. If Sarah's teacher calls, it's because Sarah is complaining about the teacher."

I had just been through some of Noah's mischief that should have told me more than it did at the time. The school nurse, Mrs. Helgstrom, had called to say, "Could you come to get Noah? A colored boy kicked him in the stomach. He's all right, but he is upset."

When I rushed into the nurse's office, Noah's face was tear-stained. There was something else in his expression that I could not quite identify, but my mind was on getting him home. As we passed Vangie Peters' office, she rushed out into the corridor. "Don't worry. I've notified the boy's parents. He'll be punished."

At bedtime, Noah wanted to talk to me "privately." "It

wasn't exactly the way I said it was, Mom. Sonny Saxon and me were trying to grab Harold's lunch. That's how I got kicked."

Ben and I told Noah how proud we were of him for telling the truth. Ben thought I should call Harold's mother and explain before he was punished. Harold's father answered the phone, listened to my story and said stiffly, "Yes, I know. Thank you. Good-bye."

When I called Vangie the next morning, she too seemed unconcerned that Harold had been unfairly blamed. I decided that perhaps I had made too much of the incident.

In late November, Spike broke his sad little pattern of failure by winning the prize at the School Science Fair. Vangie called to tell me and I asked her to pretend she had not; I wanted Spike to feel he was breaking the wonderful news. And it was truly wonderful news. Spike had worked on the project almost secretly, asking only that Ben bring home cardboard and formaldehyde. Spike had caught and dissected a grasshopper, labeled small medicine bottles and drawn (crudely, but accurately) a large picture of the grasshopper with strings to each embalmed part. Spike shot up the driveway to "surprise" me with his news. The triumph did not spur him on to better work in his day-to-day subjects, but it did give us hope that he might be gradually overcoming his study handicaps.

The school year moved along with no other unusual incidents. In January, 1967, the Board of Education ratified a new contract with the Philadelphia teachers' union and averted a threatened strike. The main issue in the new contract was whether a teacher could be transferred against his will "in order to further integration." The union objected to "forced transfers" and the Board backed down.

I agreed with the union. If a white teacher did not want to teach in a predominantly black school, I believed he should not be forced to do this, more for the good of the children than for the teacher.

The fluttery, harassed-looking first-grade teacher, Mrs. Greenberg, was a typical example. None of my children had ever had her for a teacher, but she had often spoken to me about "lower-class children—not what I'm used to—so different from the way the school used to be." One day in the hallway, I had noticed a tiny little Negro boy, tears rolling down his cheeks as he stood next to the water fountain trying to reach up for a drink. As I lifted him, Mrs. Greenberg came out of her room. "Why do you bother with *him*? He's such a bad child and comes from a terrible family," she said.

I gave her the nastiest look I could manage and she fluttered away. I talked to the little boy until I could make him smile. Later, I reported the incident to Vangie Peters. "Oh, you're so right, Lois," she said, "But I can't get rid of her. The union would crucify me!" It was hard for me to believe that the union would defend a woman like this. Like the Bar Association or the AMA, they would certainly feel that she reflected badly on all their members—if they knew about her. Vangie said, "You wouldn't believe the methods the union uses to defend members. Anyway, Greenberg is retiring soon."

That day, Vangie had said she had something "marvelously exciting" to show me. She shuffled through a pile of papers on her desk and produced a yellow-covered sheaf of mimeographed pages.

"Look," she said. "This is a ten-year report of the distribution of Negro pupils in the Philadelphia schools. Our school is the *only* school that had a decrease! We went from seventy percent Negro to sixty-nine percent Negro!"

I tried to return her broad smile of triumph, but the statistics were, to me, unimportant and deceptive. It was nice if other white parents had discovered the benefits of our heterogeneous school, but not all the new white students were what would be considered by some as desirable classmates. In fact, Sarah had complained about "Annabelle. She says she's going to beat me up! And she's *big!*" By then, we had developed a system of inviting belligerent children home for lunch. I had told my children, "Sometimes people act mean because they want attention—they want to be friends and don't know how to do it." Annabelle, a pale, blond child with unhealthy-looking stoutness, did indeed want attention. She chattered on, talking about her family's moves from place to place "so Daddy can find a job now that he ain't drinking" and about her two sisters who "got babies but they couldn't get the guys to marry them." This first grader's worldly toughness was heartbreaking. She became, for Sarah, a living example of a coarseness that Sarah recoiled and learned from. By contrast, some of the new black families were making valuable contributions to the school. Another new classmate of Sarah's, Vanessa, was the daughter of an unusually creative mother who invited the entire class to her house for candle-making projects and other musical or artistic afternoons.

I also wondered how the children of black and white marriages were counted—as Negro or white? There were a number of families like this in our neighborhood, probably one of the few neighborhoods where children of mixed marriages could grow up normally. I wondered wryly whether they were counted in fractions.

Vangie was so eager for me to look at the list that I scanned it at her insistence. For whatever it meant, Willis School was indeed the only school in our district—or any other district, I learned later—where the percentage of Negro students had decreased even slightly.

I noticed Germantown High School's listing. During seven years, the percentage of Negro students had risen from 32 percent to 69 percent. Some of the white parents of older children were already worrying about whether their sons and daughters would qualify for the academically selective Girls High or Central High School for Boys. "If not," one mother said to me, "it means private school. I could hardly send him to Germantown High!" When I asked why not, the woman had looked at me incredulously. "Well, the quality of the school and the gang fights and all," she said.

I reserved judgment. When I drove past the big brick building—as I had when Spike had gone to Germantown Settlement House day camp his first summer in Philadelphia and now when school was in session and the students gathered around the building—it had seemed peaceful and not too different from my own high school. True, I noticed that black and white students seemed to segregate themselves into groups, but surely the friendships our children made in elementary school would continue if any of them went to Germantown High. According to Vangie's list, the color ratio was the same as Willis School. I was not conscious of the other differences.

Vangie insisted I take a copy of the report home "for your marvelous husband." The next year, the *Bulletin* newspaper's yearly Almanac began to list the color percentages in each public school for the first time.

The first disruption to the serenity of the semester came near the end of March, 1967. At lunchtime, I saw Sarah marching up the driveway, small mouth set. In the kitchen, she said, "I hate that Jelly Stowe! And Mrs. Sczmanski won't be our teacher anymore." She burst into tears.

When I finally got the complete information from her it was that Jelly Stowe, a child Spike's age, had come into Sarah's classroom, "yelled at Mrs. Sczmanski and then slapped her."

"Mrs. Sczmanski started to cry . . . and she said she won't teach at a school like this anymore . . . and Mrs. Peters told us we'd get another teacher tomorrow." Then Sarah's tears increased and she said, "But I want Mrs. Sczmanski and I hate that Jelly Stowe and I hate his brother!"

Jelly's brother, Cyril, was in Sarah's class. "He's bad too," Sarah said. Her little body was trembling from the shock of seeing her teacher slapped. Sorry as I was for Mrs. Sczmanski, I wished it had been possible for her to have considered the little children instead of bursting into tears. However, if someone slapped me, I might react the same way.

I walked to school with Sarah that afternoon. She was afraid of Jelly Stowe and I wanted to talk with Vangie Peters. Why would a fifth-grader slap a second-grade teacher, or any teacher, for that matter?

Vangie said, "Oh, Lois, I'm so sorry Sarah troubled you with this. I thought I had calmed the children. Solomon Stowe was expelled from our school months ago. Very emotionally disturbed child. Impossible to handle. But believe me, he will *not* get into the school again. Don't worry."

She said, yes, Mrs. Sczmanski had indeed resigned. "She hasn't taught for years, you know, and the poor thing is still shaky from her divorce. Dr. Kornreich—the District Superintendent—has a *marvelous* teacher he's sending us tomorrow."

The new teacher, when I met her a few weeks later, looked utterly harried. She was middle-aged, black and out of breath when I introduced myself one afternoon. "This is," she sighed, "the most undisciplined class I've ever seen!" I told her about Mrs. Sczmanski's candy-bar rewards for good behavior. "It figures!" she said as she walked wearily away.

After the Jelly Stowe incident, I added a demurrer to my statement that "mean people are often just unhappy people." If Jelly Stowe was emotionally disturbed, as Vangie Peters said, he was no one to fool with. I told my children, "Some people are very, very full of angry feelings. It's best to stay away from them if you can." Spike replied that Jelly was not "*that* bad"; Noah looked fascinated and Sarah nodded with wide-eyed solemnity.

During the first four days of April, 1967, the Philadelphia newspapers carried stories of school incidents that were as confusing to me as the Jelly episode. On April 1, nearly every room of Roosevelt Junior High, a school near us, was vandalized. Three days later, four of its pupils, aged twelve to fifteen, were arrested for the vandalism. I wondered why students would want to destroy their own school.

On April 3, newspapers reported "racial violence" at South Philadelphia High. At the school (which was 51 percent white), black students demonstrated in protest against a twenty-seven-year-old white male teacher who allegedly made an anti-Negro remark in his class. Cecil Moore, the charismatic president of Philadelphia's NAACP, demanded the teacher be fired. Instead, the teacher apologized for the remark and was allowed to stay.

The school that Barbara Hamilton's children now attended in West Philadelphia made the news on April 4. A twenty-three-year-old white woman teacher used the rhyme, "Eenie, Meenie, Minie, Mo, Catch a Nigger by the Toe," with her predominantly black class. This time, the teacher was transferred.

Barbara was angry. "She was a better teacher than some of the others who are truly vicious and don't get caught. For her, it was only a slip of the tongue." I could sympathize with that. The slip may have made the teacher think carefully about her attitudes as my near-slip had done.

Barbara told me about the "light-skinned, middle-class Negro teacher" who told Paula's class when the vandalism at Roosevelt Junior High occurred, "It's *your* kind of people who cause all the crime in this city. *You* make it harder for *decent* Negroes." This teacher kept her two white students in class during recess, telling them they might get hurt on the playground. The teacher's encouragement, Barbara said, was given to children according to how light they were. Barbara had protested the remark and the general treatment of the children to the principal. The teacher said Paula was lying.

"Perhaps I should have kept my mouth shut," Barbara told me. "Lord knows what that teacher can do to Paula now. But I couldn't let it pass."

All these incidents were hard for me to absorb. I knew of the snobbery some light-skinned Negro people felt toward those with darker pigmentation, but it was horrible to think a teacher would carry this snobbery into the classroom, horrible too that Barbara now worried because she had complained. But surely bad teachers were the exception. Each teacher my children had had—with the exception of Mrs. Schmidt who pinched Spike's chin in first grade—had ranged from good to excellent. The anti-Negro remarks and attitudes reported by Barbara and by the press were certainly wrong. Vandalizing a school was wrong too.

Earlier in the year, the new president of the school board, ex-Mayor Richardson Dilworth, had said that white teachers were hostile to Negro students. He recanted his remark the next day. Yet I had seen that hostility clearly when the fluttery Mrs. Greenberg berated the child I was lifting up to the drinking fountain. Her classes had literally changed color before her eyes and, for some reason, she hated them for it. She still approached me in the hallways to talk about "lower-class children—impossible to teach."

On the other hand, handling a class was something I felt I could not do myself and, in 1967, believed I would never try. When I reflected that no one who disliked her students should be in a classroom, it was with the same detachment that I might have criticized a trapeze artist—I was not planning to try it myself.

Before solving the problems of the school system, I reminded myself, we still had Spike's erratic progress to wrestle with. Jane Banneker looked woebegone when she showed me the result of Spike's Iowa Achievement Tests. Earlier in the semester, she had asked if I wanted her to request a psychological examination by the Board of Education psychologist. Ben and I welcomed any insight that might help. The psychologist had praised Spike's "excellent mind," reported that he was friendly and outgoing, but confessed that he had no idea how Spike could be slowed down and encouraged to concentrate. Ben and I decided we appreciated his simple candor. The psychologist speculated that maturity would eventually help Spike focus his energies. Still Jane had hoped for more progress. So had we. I reminded Jane that Spike's winning of the Science Award showed that he could work carefully when he wanted to. Soon, I hoped, he would learn to work when he *had* to.

Noah and Sarah seemed to be finishing up the semester with excellent progress. Noah's teacher told us, smiling fondly, "He certainly livens up the classroom!" but his math and reading levels were rising well too. Sarah complained that her new teacher "doesn't give us candy for being good like Mrs. Sczmanski did," but Sarah, as usual, was working hard with single-minded devotion. Just when I began to worry if she was too single-minded about her studies, I saw her one day, bending over a tiny, weeping kindergarten child whose big brother was late in picking him up. Sarah did not know I was standing behind her as she affectionately reassured the child and offered to go find his brother for him. It was good to know that she had compassion along with her spirit of competition.

On a beautiful sunny day in May, a month before the end of the semester, Sarah's frightened little voice on the telephone shattered the serenity of that day and, in the end, some of my assumptions about our school.

I was rushing to finish a batch of gingerbread men for the children to eat when they came home at 3:30. The phone rang. Sarah said breathlessly, "Mommie, come quick. Jelly Stowe is beating up Noah at the trolley stop!"

I switched off the oven, jumped in the car and shot down the driveway, surprised at the force of anger in me. Be he ten feet tall, I was going to stop Jelly Stowe from hurting my son!

I do not remember driving the two blocks to the trolley stop.

I remember only running to a cluster of children in the middle of the street and seeing blood coming from the nose of a tall, blond eighth-grade girl, a girl who was much bigger than I was.

Someone yelled, "Here's Noah's mother!"

Suddenly, a small gingerbread-colored face was looking up at me. "I ain't gonna let Noah call me no name," the small wiry fellow said. He started toward the curb where Noah, tear-stained, but fists cocked, was standing.

I followed this unfamiliar youngster. "Are you Jelly?" I asked. Some child shouted, "Yes, he is, Mrs. Stalvey." Jelly turned around to glare at me defiantly. I grabbed his wrists. "You are not going to touch Noah," I said.

Every bit of my anger went into the grip I had on Jelly's wrists, but I steeled myself for a blow. Jelly was much smaller than I expected, but if he had the daring to slap a teacher and the reach to bloody the nose of a girl much taller than I, then I was an easy target. I hung on desperately.

Out of the corner of my eye, I saw Sarah. She was crying and saying, "He'll hurt my Mommie!" Two very brown-skinned girls had their arms around her; one wiped Sarah's eyes with a handkerchief, the other was patting her to soothe her. I could do nothing but hang on to the struggling Jelly.

A child yelled, "Come on, Mrs. Stalvey, you can beat him!" and I suddenly felt like an idiot. What was I doing, at the age of forty-one, fighting in the middle of a street?

And then I became aware that Jelly's arms were trembling. Good Lord, this child was terrified! And as I looked down at him, I realized that he was, after all, only a child—the same age as Spike.

I said, "Did Noah really call you a name?" and, with some trepidation, I released his wrists. Jelly took two steps away from me, then one step back. "He called me a black bitch!"

Noah was now inside our car. I saw his face and the two

brown faces of his friends. I said to Jelly, "That doesn't sound like Noah. Let's ask him." I walked toward the car with Jelly beside me.

"If he apologizes, it's okay," Jelly said. He was panting and his eyes were darting around the crowd. He was exactly the color of the gingerbread men I had left cooling on racks.

I opened the car door, sat down and turned to Noah and his friends in the back seat. Jelly leaned over my shoulder.

"Noah, did you call Jelly a 'black bitch'?"

"No. I just called him a 'bitch,' " Noah said.

Jelly reached over my shoulder and put out his hand. "Okay," he said, "I accept your apology." Noah looked startled, took Jelly's hand. Jelly was out of the car, onto his bicycle and gone.

I sat there limp. Noah was obviously unhurt. He said, "Well, David dared me to." I summoned just enough strength to explain, furiously, about dares and consequences and "this is the last time I pull your irons out of the fire, young man!" The audience began to disperse.

The two girls who had been wiping Sarah's eyes had delivered her to the car, been thanked and had gone on their way. Now they came running back.

"Jelly just got into another fight on Wayne Avenue," one said.

I drove slowly, carefully around the block, too drained to trust my driving. Then suddenly Jelly worried me. He had gone from one fight directly into another. Vangie Peters had said he was emotionally disturbed, but he was also frightened and in no condition to be running around by himself. I said to the children, "Let's go find Jelly and see if he wants to come home with us."

Noah said, "Mom, you gotta be crazy! He's the baddest kid in school!"

I said, "He didn't call *you* a name, young man!" It seemed doubtful that Jelly would come home with us, but the ginger-

bread man story kept running through my mind: "I ran away
from the little old lady and the little old man and I can run
away from you, I can, I can." In the end, as I recalled it, the
gingerbread man had been eaten by a fox.

We found Jelly furiously pumping his bike up a street
nearby. I honked. He looked frightened. I smiled broadly and
waved him over to the car.

"Hey, Jelly, I haven't had a street fight in thirty years! Come
on home and let's have some milk to celebrate!"

Jelly said, "Okay." He suddenly reminded me of Spike, the
same constant movement of his hands, the quick impulsive
nod. "I'll follow your car, okay?"

Spike was waiting when we got home. In our kitchen, we
ate gingerbread men and listened to Jelly lie. He said his
father was director of the United States Mint; he was an only
child; he was getting a motorcycle for Christmas. Noah
looked at me to see if I believed this. I pretended I did. Spike,
I noticed, followed my lead. "That's cool," Spike said.

Jelly laughed. "I was only kiddin'." Then, looking down at
the gingerbread man he was crumbling on his plate, he said he
wasn't getting a motorcycle; there were really ten kids in his
family and that his father *worked* at the mint. "But I really can
get coins for Spike." He jumped up, taking his plate and glass
to the sink. "Do I have to go home now?"

No, he could come with us to the supermarket if he wanted.
I had watched for signs of the "emotional disturbance" Vangie
Peters mentioned. To me, Jelly's lies were childish boasting,
but his ability to admit them and tell the truth was impressively
mature. In our street encounter, he was all chin; now, he was
all eyes. The change in mood was fast, but explainable. And
he wanted to stay with us. He collided with Spike, helping take
dishes to the sink. Spike had homework to do, so Jelly herded
Noah and Sarah to the car.

At the market, Jelly said, "I'll watch the little kids." At the
checkout counter, he told Sarah, "Now, you be lookin' out

for that movin' belt"; to Noah, "She said no candy." As we stood in the line, I felt Jelly's small wiry body move close to mine. I thought I felt a strong, insistent appeal for affection. I reached over in a gesture that could have ended in a tug at Sarah's collar. Jelly leaned into my arm. I hugged him. "Thanks for helping, Jelly." The "baddest kid in school" cuddled.

Driving home from the supermarket, I said casually to Jelly, "Why did you hit Mrs. Sczmanski?"

Jelly's wiggling little body stiffened. He muttered, "She was hittin' my brother so much. Tryin' to make her stop."

Over my shoulder to Sarah, I said, "You never told me *that!*"

To my dismay, I learned, for the first time, that my children *expected* teachers to slap, hit, kick children. My children, except for Mrs. Schmidt's pinching Spike, had never been touched, but Sarah confirmed the fact that Mrs. Sczmanski "used to hit Cyril when she got mad at him. She slapped other kids too."

Noah added reports of what Miss McGregor, his second-grade teacher, had done. I believed he was exaggerating to top Sarah, but his story of Almira Stampp's humiliation was beyond even Noah's imagination. Almira was a blank-eyed little girl I had noticed who, Noah said, "didn't talk even when she was supposed to." Miss McGregor made her stand in the waste-basket all one afternoon "because she wouldn't say, 'Yes, ma'am.'" When Almira asked to go to the bathroom, Miss McGregor said No. Almira had wet her pants and Miss Mc-Gregor called the class's attention to "the pig in the pig pen!" Noah added, "Miss McGregor was always hitting Josh Pitt too. Then he'd laugh and she'd hit him again."

I pulled the car to the curb, turned around and said to my children, "There is a law that says no teacher may hit a child without his parents' permission."

Noah misunderstood my vehemence. "Would *you* give permission?" I said, "Noah, you know I wouldn't!" Though I was not above losing my temper occasionally and spanking in anger, neither Ben nor I used physical violence as a punishment. It was too contagious. "I'm-bigger-therefore-do-what-I-say-or-I'll-hurt-you" was a bad lesson to teach a child. When I did strike one of my children, I was sorry and said so: "You pushed me too far, but I was wrong to hurt you."

To Jelly, I said, "But instead of hitting Mrs. Sczmanski, why didn't you let your mother handle it?"

Jelly said his mother "took off from work and went to see Mrs. Peters when Cyril had that bad mark on his face. Mrs. Sczmanski said Cyril got hit by some kid, not her." Jelly's face went back to its chin-up rigidity. "And that teacher just kept on hittin' him."

Mrs. Sczmanski was gone now, but Miss McGregor was not. I planned to talk with Vangie Peters.

In our driveway, Jelly took charge of unloading, hefted the biggest bags himself, assigned the lighter ones to Noah and put Sarah in charge of the doors. It seemed impossible that this happily smiling youngster was struggling in the street with me two hours ago. He announced he had to go, but he would bring some coins for Spike soon.

The next day, I stood on the sidewalk outside the school telling Vangie Peters of my experience with Jelly. Her blue-black hair glinted in the June sunlight and her bright yellow linen suit looked fresh and pretty and a bit incongruous as we talked near an overflowing trashbasket.

"Oh, you're so right, Lois. All that child needs is a little attention, but his home environment is incredible."

But, I said, he did not seem "emotionally disturbed" to me. Vangie said, well, of course not, but she had to give "a bureaucratic word to it to get him out of the school. After all, he did hit a teacher."

Vangie's eyes were darting around, watching the children. I felt guilty taking her time from nine hundred responsibilities, but I had to tell her what Sarah and Noah had said about teachers hitting children.

"I'm so glad you came to me with this, Lois. I'll talk to Miss McGregor. She's an excellent teacher—the parents adore her, but she is new. Don't worry. I'll work with her."

I left the corner, feeling inept and dissatisfied. With thirty children in each class, perhaps no teacher could give a child like Jelly the understanding he needed. But he had needed so little to respond lovingly. My children needed so much less from their teachers. In fact, Ben and I had used "bad" teachers to prepare our children for adult life. ("Yes, the teacher was being cross and unfair. Someday you will have bosses who are hard to work for. We all have to learn to work with difficult people.") Yet no teacher should use physical violence on a child. Children could not hit back; they would discharge their anger at another child, mine perhaps, or on school property. How much of Jelly's reputation as the "baddest kid in school" was caused by teachers like Mrs. Schmidt or Mrs. Sczmanski? This same anger may have been what caused the vandalism at the local junior high? And, if so, what on earth could I do about it?

When I told Ben about the afternoon, he had been concerned mostly with me. "You did fine, honey, but you can't solve all problems for all children."

Barbara Hamilton, when I called her after leaving Vangie Peters, said almost the same thing, but added, "You might be surprised how much you did for that child, even if you never see him again. He knows most mothers would have called the police." (I said I probably would have too, if I had had time to think of it.)

Barbara said, "But you didn't. You saw him as a scared kid and you gave him maybe the only hug anyone's had time to give him in a long time. Anyway, didn't you ever have just one short experience with someone that you never forgot? I did."

Perhaps because I wanted to believe Barbara, I remembered

a few incidents of my own: my elementary school principal who somehow made me feel special, even without a father; a high school English teacher who said, "You write really well"; a boy in high school who said, on a day I felt sad, "You have the prettiest smile in school"—all brief moments that I never forgot.

I still try to believe Barbara because I never saw Jelly Stowe again. He affected the lives of my children only one more time and that time, over a year later. When Jelly came to our house a few days after our street fight, I was not home. He brought Spike some coins as he had promised. Jelly stopped by once more during that summer. Ben was home and told Jelly how sorry I would be to have missed him again.

When school resumed in September, 1967, I did not forget Jelly, even though we became deeply involved in solving Spike's study problems. Whether or not Jelly was helped by our brief encounter, it had had a far-reaching effect on me. Jelly was the first child to bring me into contact with a side of big city schools I might have missed; solving Spike's problems would free me to take an even closer look.

six

By the summer of 1967, Ben and I had been through five years of worry, optimism and self-criticism about Spike's school performance. In view of Noah and Sarah's excellent progress, we could not blame Spike's under-achieving on the school. Except for Mrs. Schmidt in first grade, each teacher—and Vangie Peters—had devoted a remarkable amount of attention to Spike. Could we blame ourselves? Ben and I had both tried (often reinforcing each other's patience) to give Spike help without pressure, to show our concern without making him feel we were disappointed in him. Our pediatrician assured us Spike would organize his energies as he matured. Vangie Peters told me of all the famous men who had early school problems. (Albert Einstein and Winston Churchill were her favorite examples of underachievers. She also pointed out that Woodrow Wilson never did learn to spell.) Spike's Science Award had made us optimistic; the low scores on his Iowa Test at the end of the 1967 semester worried me, but what worried me much more was Spike's comment when he handed me his report card: "I'm just stupid, I guess."

I said, "You're *not*. You'll tame that grasshopper mind one of these days and then you'll see." He looked as if he did not believe me.

Over the years I had compared notes with my friends. Celia Spears, the minister's wife, had no problems with her high-achieving son. Barbara Hamilton's Jimmy was finally skipped a grade when the teachers could not keep up with his talents and ambition. Only with Mrs. Jefferson, when she came to clean each week, could I compare problems. There were, we decided, many similarities between Spike and her son, Ernie. I had met Ernie several times when Mr. Jefferson came with his family to pick his wife up after work. Ernie was four years older than Spike, but his quick constant movements, his spirited friendliness reminded me of my pell-mell son. Many times, Mrs. Jefferson and I had sat on the edge of half-made beds, comparing our sons' problems and reassuring each other that they were lively boys who were simply not quiet and plodding.

At the end of the school year, when Jane Banneker showed me Spike's low Iowa Test scores, she asked if I would be willing to have Spike tested at the Reading Clinic of a local university where she had been taking a course. "Spike reads way beyond his level, but they test other factors too and perhaps they can find out how we can help him concentrate," she said.

I discussed it with Ben and we agreed. There was, I thought, some risk to Spike's self-image in too many special tests, but we felt we could not risk missing some important clue to his problem.

Earlier in the year I had asked our pediatrician if a psychiatric evaluation might uncover the cause of Spike's study problems. He discouraged us. "If a child makes friends and if he gets into a *normal* amount of mischief—not too much or too little—it's unlikely he needs psychotherapy," our doctor said. I mentioned this to Vangie. "You're so right, Lois. Spike certainly does not need psychotherapy," she said.

We had also tried tutoring. A retired teacher in our neighborhood spent many afternoons with Spike and finally said, "Look, I hate to take your money. Spike is delightful, but I have found no way to get him to work unless I literally stand over him. Even then," she said, laughing, "he gets me off into interesting discussions that have nothing to do with the work at hand."

Perhaps, Ben decided, the Reading Clinic was the combination of scientific practicality we needed. The appointment was made for the end of June. On August 11, 1967, we received the four-page report.

Now that Spike is achieving even more than we dreamed for him, I can look back at that report with bitter amusement. It is not amusing, however, to imagine how this smoke screen of jargon might affect parents less experienced and self-confident.

Ben read the report first and passed it to me without comment. I read it three times, the second and third times to be absolutely sure of what I was seeing in it.

The first page was devoted to Spike's virtues: "An evaluation of intellectual functioning which utilized the Wechsler Intelligence Scale for Children placed Spike in the superior range . . . superior ability to form concepts . . . to make social judgments . . . superior ability in the sequential thinking skills."

I said to Ben, "Okay. That means 'Here's a smart kid who can think straight.' Right?"

The second page listed the tests given Spike for "Evaluation of the Personal Adjustment area" and concluded: "The results show that there may be some basic physiological factor responsible for Spike's hyperactivity." (A vital clue had been found and was quickly dismissed in the next sentence.) "His problems, however, do not seem typically organic." (Why not? The clinician never said.)

I read the rest of the report out loud to Ben and said, "They take two and a half pages to say that Spike can't sit still and that he works impulsively and too rapidly if someone forces him. Right?" Ben looked as bleak as I felt.

The recommendations at the end of the report suggested the Clinic's own Directed Reading Activity program and a psychiatric evaluation.

"All right," I said. "The report says, 'Here's a smart kid who can't sit still. We don't know why. So try our Reading program and a psychiatrist.' " I was ready to weep with anger and frustration. At least the Board of Education psychologist had said he did not know what caused Spike's disorganized energies; this report hid its failure to find an answer behind obscure, meaningless jargon.

I had told Ben about Spike's comment, "Guess I'm just stupid." Spike, I feared, had stopped trying and was accepting himself as "dumb."

Ben said, "Maybe we could try their Directed Reading Activity thing—but honestly, I don't have much confidence in any group that writes such pretentious, meaningless reports."

"Not only that," I said, "but reading is the one thing Spike does eagerly and well. It doesn't seem right to make his one source of pride into a 'directed' *chore*."

Ben and I discussed private school again. Unfortunately, I had just talked with a woman who had taken her daughter out of the public school the year before because of study problems. The woman had greeted me wearily, announced she had gone back to teaching. "Debbie," she said, "sees a psychiatrist twice a week and a tutor three times a week. It's so expensive." Apparently the private school had wrought no easy solution.

Ben said, "Then I think we ought to talk to the pediatrician again. With Spike's beginning to doubt himself, maybe the doctor will feel differently about a psychiatrist now."

This time, our pediatrician agreed that a consultation might be valuable. He recommended a child psychiatrist in whom he had confidence, a Dr. Bartell.

During our first whole-family interview at Dr. Bartell's office, his appearance dismayed me, but I chided myself for my reaction. He was a tall, thin, slouching man with gray skin and narrow yellowish eyes that never met ours. He stared at the desk top as he talked with Ben, Spike and me.

On the way home, Spike said, "He looks like a vulture, you know?"

Ben said, "Now, son, you know you can't judge people by how they look on the outside."

We had explained to Spike that Dr. Bartell had studied a great deal about children and families and might be able to help us help Spike to catch up faster with his school work. Spike seemed resigned to more tests.

During the last weeks of August, 1967, Dr. Bartell interviewed Spike, Ben and me. At my private interview, I again gave the information that had always seemed unusual to me. "Spike was very much more active inside me during pregnancy than either Noah or Sarah," I said to the top of Dr. Bartell's head. Dr. Bartell did not comment. Instead, he asked, "Did he walk and talk on schedule?" I said proudly that he never walked; he ran. And had talked early and clearly.

"Experiences during weaning from the bottle?" Dr. Bartell asked, eyes down, pencil poised over a form. I explained he had never had a bottle. He had weaned himself from breast-feeding because he finally refused to lie still. "Too much to see. He wanted to sit up and look around. He was able to handle a cup at seven months." I had the feeling I was giving Dr. Bartell more information than he needed, but any small clue might help.

Dr. Bartell wanted to see each parent twice and it was just before Ben's last interview that new information came out at our dinner table.

Noah told us about his new fourth-grade teacher, a tiny blonde in her first year of teaching. "She got mad and slammed the door . . . and all the glass broke!" Noah said laughing.

Spike said, "That's nothing! Mrs. Schmidt broke three rulers on Gus Clifford's head!"

Ben's eyes enlarged to twice their usual size. "Did she ever hit you on the head?" he asked.

Spike said, "No. Just the black kids. Me, she just pinched . . . and other things."

What "other things"?

Under Ben's quiet, patient persuasion, Spike finally told us that Mrs. Schmidt had held up his messy papers to the class and said that this was how "stupid" people wrote and that "Spike Stalvey is too stupid to sit still."

Spike looked up at Ben, his eyes searching for a denial of what the teacher had said. While Ben reassured Spike that he was far from "stupid," I clutched my dinner knife, wishing Mrs. Schmidt were within reach. I also wished Spike looked more convinced than he did by Ben's reassuring words.

Ben told Dr. Bartell of Spike's first-grade experiences. Ben reported, after the session, that Dr. Bartell requested we enroll Spike in a tutoring service in Chestnut Hill. I arranged this immediately and took Spike, twice a week, to the tutors, a patrician trio of women. Spike went willingly, but I was still hearing the same old comments from his sixth-grade teachers. He was now in a cycling pattern with a different teacher for math, English, science and social studies. Each one said, in effect, "Nice fellow, but doesn't finish his work." The tutors made no comments at all.

For the next three months, Spike continued his sessions with Dr. Bartell. In December, we were to receive his final recommendations.

I wish I could remember which woman's magazine contributed so much to my son's future. I have only a page of scribbled notes I took as I read the small paragraph in a medical news column. The magazine reported that Dexedrine, a drug used primarily for dieting and to prevent sleepiness, was also being used successfully to treat *hyperkinesis*. Hyperkinesis, the writer explained, was a "dysfunction in children, usually boys, that causes excess physical activity, distractability and learning problems." Neurologists had found that the drug had a "paradoxical effect" on hyperkinetic children, calming them and helping them to concentrate.

In three days, we were to have our final conference with

Dr. Bartell. I took the magazine clipping along and gave it to him before we settled ourselves in his office. He read it, scribbled a prescription and pushed it across the desk to me.

Spike was asked to wait in the reception room while Dr. Bartell read aloud to Ben and me from a typed report. As Dr. Bartell read on and on, I waited, as patiently as possible, for him to get through the descriptions ("difficulty in concentrating, short attention span") that we knew so well.

Finally, Dr. Bartell cleared his throat and said, "Summary and Recommendations . . . Spike seems to need remedial help directed primarily toward improving his work habits and secondarily . . . albeit necessarily . . . toward removing his skill deficiencies." He put down the paper.

I looked at Ben. He was looking at me. I said, "But, Dr. Bartell, I don't understand. *How* can we remove his skill deficiencies? The tutoring hasn't helped. *What* exactly can we *do* to improve his work habits?"

Dr. Bartell looked down at his desk in silence. Then he said, "Get the boy in here. I'll show you how deficient he is in skills."

It was not an answer, but I went to the door and brought Spike into the room, settling him in the chair near mine. For once, Spike sat absolutely still, looking at the doctor.

Dr. Bartell began to talk, fixing his eyes on Spike instead of Ben or me. "This child doesn't even know his multiplication tables! Listen to this! Spike, how much is seven times seven?"

Spike sat rigid in his chair and whispered, "Forty-five?"

Dr. Bartell's voice rose. "You know it's not! How much *is* seven times seven?" He stood up, glowering down at Spike who shrunk down in his seat. Spike was swallowing and unable to speak. Dr. Bartell began to shout, "Seven times seven! How much is it? You see, he won't try!"

It was hard to believe I was seeing and hearing correctly. Dr. Bartell was standing, pointing a long bony finger at Spike. The doctor's face was contorted in anger and his voice was almost a shriek. I told myself that this must be some surprise technique. Dr. Bartell was acting in the way I acted when I lost my patience. If he was trying to show *me* how terrible it looked, he needn't. I knew. And this technique was not successful with Spike. I had reached over in an irresistible impulse and put my hand on Spike's arm when Dr. Bartell began to shout. Spike's arm was trembling. I put my arm around his shoulders. What was the doctor trying to accomplish? Was it possible he had simply *lost* his temper?

Suddenly, Dr. Bartell sat down and said, "All right. I'll see him next week at the same time."

Ben said, evenly and slowly, "Oh . . . no . . . you . . . won't." In a quiet, furious voice, Ben told the doctor that he had never witnessed such unprofessional behavior and under no circumstances whatsoever would he consider allowing his son to be alone with such an obviously uncontrolled personality. Dr. Bartell never looked up from his desk. If there had been any reason for his attack on Spike, he made no attempt to explain. But as Ben spoke, I felt Spike's body stop trembling. He sat up straight and looked at Ben with a broad beautiful smile.

Ben and I walked out of Dr. Bartell's office with Spike between us. I remembered the Dexedrine prescription and slipped back in to get it. Dr. Bartell turned his head away and gazed at the wall until I left.

The next day, I got a telephone call from the tutoring service. One of their former students had returned unexpectedly from boarding school. They could no longer give Spike his usual hour . . . or any other hour.

Our pediatrician agreed that Dexedrine was worth trying. I asked him to arrange for an encephalogram (brain pattern test). The test showed evidence of hyperkinesis. I made an appointment with a neurologist and he confirmed the diagnosis. "In a way," the neurologist said, "it's almost too bad that Spike has such a happy disposition. I usually see the trouble-making children sooner." Yes, definitely get him on Dexedrine. It would help him concentrate until he outgrew the disability . . . "probably in his late teens."

One week after Spike began taking the spansules each morning, his sixth-grade English teacher phoned me. "*What* has caused the wonderful change in Spike?" she asked. "He's suddenly calm and working away like a beaver."

Until she called, we wondered if it was wishful thinking. Spike was the same intellectually curious, active eleven-year-old, but instead of running his motor with the throttle full out, he appeared to be able to idle normally.

On Parents' Visiting Night in January, 1968, all of Spike's teachers in the sixth-grade cycle made similar comments. Ben and I told each one of them of the long, sad search, of the sheer luck of reading the small paragraph in a woman's magazine. We hoped they might be aware of the symptoms and get help for any other child like Spike.

When Mrs. Jefferson came to clean on the first Friday after Spike's remarkable change, I told her the good news. When I told her of the symptoms and diagnosis, she said, "Lord, that sounds just like Ernie!" But, by now, a pill was unlikely to change Ernie's life; at the age of fifteen, he was serving a sentence in a boys' reformatory for burglary and assault.

In the six years that Mrs. Jefferson had cleaned for us, I had watched Ernie's misfortunes as helplessly as I had watched Spike's. From the beginning, teachers had complained to Mrs. Jefferson that Ernie did not listen and walked around the room instead of sitting still. By second grade, he was put into a "slow" class. He complained, "Don't do nothin'. Teacher just yells all the time." He also complained that the teacher ripped up his drawings "if I don't be drawin' what the class s'pose to draw. I can draw better than *pumpkins!*"

When Ernie was the same age—eleven—as Spike was when his problem was diagnosed, Ernie and a group of friends were playing, tossing stones back and forth. A child's eye was hit and badly damaged. When the police arrived, they said it was Ernie's stone that had hurt the child. Ernie was taken to the police station. Mrs. Jefferson searched for him frantically before the police finally called her at ten o'clock that night. She was not allowed to see her child until the next morning at Youth Study Center. Even then, she was not allowed to talk to him or touch him until Visiting Day three days later. He was kept at Youth Study Center, a notoriously understaffed, overcrowded place for juvenile offenders, for three weeks until "some hearings downtown." Mrs. Jefferson got a lawyer and Ernie was released to his parents after the hearing.

Mrs. Jefferson had often said, "Ernie got different after that." There were marks on his body and he told his parents he had been beaten at Youth Study Center by a guard. "He acted like he blamed us about what happened to him in that place," Mrs. Jefferson said. He began to fail in his school work. "He said the teacher hit him all the time." The Jefferson family decided they had to move to a neighborhood with better schools. At the new school, at age twelve, Ernie was put into a Retarded Educable class. Whites quickly fled the new neighborhood and the school became as overcrowded as the school they had left. By now, Ernie was thirteen. Mrs. Jefferson had to force him to attend school each morning. He usually was a truant by noon.

Mrs. Jefferson did not yet know that Ernie had never been taught to read. Her personality reminded me very much of my own mother; timid with teachers, gullible about "expert" advice, not a fighter and blaming herself for whatever went wrong. Ernie's teacher reported only his misbehaviors and truancy. Mrs. Jefferson did not guess that a nonreading sixth-grader was likely to flee from days of defeat in a classroom.

By the age of fifteen, Ernie and his family had moved again, chasing after a "good" school. Whites again fled the neighborhood and the same pattern was repeated. (I had suggested to

Mrs. Jefferson that she move to our neighborhood. Realtors showed her no houses the family could afford.) Ernie was beaten up by white students in his new school.

One Monday in winter, Ernie did not return from school. She finally called the police. On Wednesday, she received a call. Ernie had been arrested for burglary and assault.

Later, he told his mother he had not run away, had got on the wrong bus, could not read the street or bus signs and could not get home. He had broken a window to get into a gas station to get warm and to sleep. When the police woke him up, he tried to get away and was charged with assault as well as burglary.

Mrs. Jefferson had said to me, "My other kids read okay, but I just found out Ernie can't. He opened four cans of soup last week and when I scolded him, he say, 'Mama, I don't know what's inside 'til I opens them!' He wasn't lyin' to those police! An' if he was burglaring that place, he wouldn't go to *sleep!*"

In view of Ernie's record, the lawyer advised them that they should accept a "light" sentence at the Youth Development Center in Cornwall Heights where Ernie could be "helped."

When Ernie ran away from the Development Center to come home, I had talked on the telephone with his probation officer, unable to believe what Mrs. Jefferson told me he had said. The man repeated the words to me: "He's just a bad apple. No good. His mother just ought to forget about him." The man then proceeded to tell me of his own sterling character and virtuous life: "I'm colored myself, ma'am. I pulled myself up by my bootstraps. It's trash like Ernie Jefferson that makes it bad for folks like me. They ought to throw away the key on that little b . . . baby." Mrs. Jefferson was sitting next to me as I talked, rubbing her hands nervously. When the man's words made me react with open mouth and wide eyes, she stood up. For her, and because he could make things even worse for Ernie, I did not tell this man that I thought he belonged *anywhere* but working with troubled black children.

Now, as I gave Mrs. Jefferson the happy news about Spike, I could not help making some comparisons. If I had been born black in South Carolina, convinced I was irredeemably inferior, afraid of "experts," forced to work so that I could chase "good" schools from neighborhood to neighborhood, would my Spike be where her Ernie was now?

I could tell Mrs. Jefferson about incompetent "experts," about "hyperkinesis," encephalograms and Dexedrine. She did not have the leisure I had to read magazines or the self-confidence to reject the jargon that cloaked ignorance. And Spike was eleven years old—Ernie had had four extra years to believe he was "stupid." Spike had Vangie Peters, giving him maximum attention, worrying "why aren't *we* reaching *him*?"— Ernie had simply been labeled "retarded," belatedly or indifferently, when he reached the sixth grade. And Spike could not be casually written off as the child of a laborer and a domestic "impossible to teach with his home background."

While these thoughts raced through my mind, Mrs. Jefferson was shaking her head, slowly, thoughtfully, and then she said, "Maybe some pills like that might of helped Ernie. That doctor at the Development Center, though, he said Ernie's IQ is only sixty-nine and he's got para . . . para . . ." I asked, "Paranoid?" "Yes, paranoid tendencies."

Mrs. Jefferson looked alarmed when I exploded. She winced at the profanities she never heard me use. "HOW in HELL," I said, "can they give a valid IQ test to a troubled kid who's never been taught to read! What's been done to Ernie by the cops and by teachers is enough to make a DAMN paranoid out of ANYONE!"

Mrs. Jefferson put her rough, callused hands on my arms to calm me. "Hush now," she said, "I been praying for Spike and he's okay now. God will help Ernie too."

So far, He has not.

seven

WHILE SIXTH GRADE WAS TO BE A PERIOD OF ACHIEVEMENT
for Spike, after so many lost years, it was the opposite for
Willis School. By now, I have lived through our school's
Sixth-Grade Panic with each of my children. It has always
followed the same sad and predictable scenario. The Sixth-
Grade Panic, I believe, not only sets the stage for predominantly black junior and senior highs in big cities, but I also
suspect it answers the question asked at the beginning of the
1970's: "What happened to the liberals when school integration came North?"

Until February of 1968, it seemed that the semester would
be uneventful. Noah was more or less settled in fourth grade
with his stocky blond teacher who slammed doors but who
told us Noah was working well. Sarah now had the same effervescent teacher Noah had charmed the year before. (Serious,
diligent Sarah was a contrast and a surprise to the teacher.
On Parents' Visiting Night, she said Sarah worked hard, be-
haved well . . . "And how is my Noah?" she asked fondly.
Ben said to me, "Brace yourself for Sarah's complaints about
her." But Sarah and the teacher managed a peaceful coexis-
tence.)

In Spike's sixth-grade cycle, three of his four teachers appeared to be excellent. His English teacher was a middle-aged white woman, relaxed, direct and well-liked by all the students. For the first time, Spike had two male teachers; one was Mr. Thomas, a richly pigmented black man who, Spike said, made science easy to understand and who had "a cool sense of humor."

Math was taught by the other new male teacher, Carter M. Kellogg, a red-faced, red-haired young man with a gravelly voice who told us he was "a dropout from the Peace Corps." He had glanced around, dropped his voice to a muted grate and said to Ben and me, "I decided it would be more meaningful to work with underdeveloped *Americans* rather than with foreign countries." Carter M. Kellogg was enthusiastic about the New Math. (I listened politely, not having mastered the Old Math yet myself.) He told us he was not using "those silly old conventional approaches on unconventional kids like Spike." He felt he was getting through now that the pills helped Spike to concentrate.

The only teacher I felt dubious about was Miss Grenelli, a gum-chewing, miniskirted young lady fresh out of teachers' college. She slouched behind her desk, doodling and chomping gum while talking with parents. Spike said that in her social studies class, she gave the students "busy work" while she addressed wedding invitations. Ben said, "Well, maybe she won't be here long." Even so, three good teachers out of four was not bad.

That February, I had had a chance to see the large sixth-grade group all together when the English teacher asked me to speak to the students about advertising-writing. I was impressed with the behavior of the youngsters and with their bright, perceptive questions. The only disruptions came from Miss Grenelli's Advisory Group and then, largely from her harsh, frequent stage whispers to her students. In the corridor after my speech, I saw Miss Grenelli trying to shake an enormous youngster whom I recognized as Spike's old friend,

Cephas Simpson. Since Cephas and Miss Grenelli were the same size, it seemed unnecessary to interfere. Cephas soon shook her hands from his shoulders and walked away.

In what has since revealed itself as a predictable pattern, the special meeting of the sixth-grade parents was held in late March. Celia Spears, the minister's wife and one of my closest friends, told me that several white parents had demanded a special meeting to discuss "some of the terrible things happening at Willis School." I asked Spike. He looked puzzled. Nothing "bad" was happening that he knew about.

Celia and I came to the afternoon meeting together. Vangie Peters opened the meeting by saying, "I thought we might all get together to share the marvelous progress of our wonderful school." Celia whispered, "My God!"

By then, Vangie's misleading statement about the purpose of the meeting was not as disillusioning as it once might have been to me. Reluctantly, but gradually, I had come to realize that Ben and Barbara Hamilton were right about Vangie's special treatment of white parents. I still believed it was necessary in some cases. As yet, I could see no real harm in Vangie's flattery and dissembling.

It had hurt, though, when I had put Vangie's honesty to a personal test. When Spike's hyperkinesis was diagnosed, Vangie had praised me lavishly for my "common sense" in rejecting the peculiar Dr. Bartell. I reported to Ben that Vangie had said, "Spike does not need a psychiatrist!"

Ben said, "Honey, don't you know that she would agree with you if you said you were having leeches applied to Spike or taking him to a Bantu witch doctor?"

I wanted to prove Ben wrong. The next time I saw Vangie, I said I had decided that Spike might benefit from psychotherapy. "Oh, you're so right, Lois," she said. "It would be marvelous for him!" I felt lonely, as if I had been speaking to a mirror all this time.

That afternoon, Vangie, in a bright red silk suit, stood as

tall as her short stature allowed and smilingly explained that we parents would follow the same cycle as our children to each room to talk with each teacher.

Celia whispered, "Very smart. Divide the mob."

In Mr. Thomas' science room, I was astonished to hear Beverly Statz, the pretty, fluffy mother of a pretty, fluffy little daughter, berate Mr. Thomas for "poor science equipment and an unchallenging program. At the private school my friend's daughter goes to, they're a year ahead of you," she said. Her stern tone was bewilderingly different from her usual pleasant attitude. Mr. Thomas looked as bewildered as I felt. "Why, Mrs. Statz, I had no idea your daughter was that *interested* in science. I can certainly give her extra work." Beverly Statz's face became pink. She said, "But you don't have any lab equipment for her to work with." Mr. Thomas said he had ordered some new things and hoped they would come through soon. At the door, I thanked him for giving Spike an enjoyable experience in science. He was still shaking his head, "The Statz child never seemed interested in science. I never dreamed she felt held back."

As we walked across the hall to the English class, Celia said quietly, "Tim Statz has just joined a big new law firm. Even if Thomas put in electronic microscopes, the Statzes will be in private school next year."

I wondered why parents like the Statzes did not simply leave if they wanted to instead of finding a rather thin excuse.

In the English room, a dignified-looking father, who had apparently taken the day off, said to the English teacher, "I wish you could use more advanced reading material. My daughter reads Salinger and Tolstoi at home."

The English teacher, smiling brightly, said, "Why, that's great! Maybe it will help Fredericka with her spelling. That's what we're working on now. Could you work with her a bit at home?" The dignified man adjusted his suitcoat. Celia whispered to me, "Now *that* one is worried his daughter isn't going to qualify for Girls' High! And he's sure not going to send her to Germantown High." Girls' High, Philadelphia's academically selective high school (Central, for boys), required high Iowa Test scores and report-card grades for admission; Germantown High was rapidly becoming all-black.

In Miss Grenelli's room, the parents took over while Miss Grenelli lounged at her desk, doodled and chewed her gum. Some of the "terrible" things began to be aired but in such vague terms that it was hard for me either to dismiss them or become concerned.

A woman with horn-rimmed glasses and red-brown hair pulled so tightly into a bun that her eyes looked strained said, "Even if it makes some people uncomfortable, I do think it advisable to air grievances. I am concerned, yes, concerned at the harassment of our children by the older students. My son is afraid to go onto the playground . . . petrified."

A thin-faced, brown-skinned woman sitting in the back of the room said, "Why?"

The woman with the bun hairdo sputtered, "Well, he's afraid." During the dialogue with the thin-faced woman, it developed that, no, her son had not been hurt or threatened; no, he was not unusually small for his age. The thin-faced black woman, who I noticed suddenly was one of three black people in the group, finally said, "Perhaps *you're* afraid?" The woman with the skin-tight hair blinked behind her horn-rims and stared at the other mother, then turned her head away.

Another white woman, Sally McGeorge, entered the discussion by saying that her daughter wanted to go to private school. "I feel I must listen to her." Again, the thin-faced Negro woman (who I recognized now as Mrs. Harris, mother of Linda who Spike said was the "smartest in the class") asked, "Why?"

I understood the question, although Sally McGeorge said, "Why, I *must* listen to my child!" I remembered nagging my own mother to let me go to a Catholic school in Milwaukee because I liked the uniforms. Under the questioning by Linda's mother, Sally McGeorge could never state specifically *why* her daughter wanted to go to private school.

In the hallway, Celia said that several of the complaining parents had already left her husband's church for the more "fashionable" Chestnut Hill congregation.

In Carter M. Kellogg's math room, the same vague comments continued. Vangie Peters, I noticed, was somewhere else. Of the three black mothers, two exchanged puzzled glances; Linda's mother had a tight-lipped, weary attitude, as if she had gone through meetings like this before. She had and I would too.

Madelyn Drinker, mother of Spike's friend Tony, began the discussion. She had the appearance of always being late for something and, as she spoke, she often glanced at her wristwatch. "I am afraid that 'other children' are holding my son back," she said. Good Heavens! I hoped she was not referring to Spike. His pills were helping him do so much better than before, but he still had six years to make up for.

Linda's mother gave a huge sigh and said, "Do you mean 'other children' or black children?" Carter Kellogg cut in to say that he would be happy to give extra credit work to any child who felt held back.

To me, this was similar to the attitudes of the mothers in Trinity Nursery School. But these women were not outside the school; they were *inside*. And they were all active in liberal activities. Even frivolous Beverly Statz had worked collecting clothing to send to black Mississippians, who had lost jobs through voting demonstrations; Sally McGeorge's husband had been in the demonstration at Selma, Alabama. It was true that many white parents in our neighborhood were now working for the candidacy of Eugene McCarthy instead of for integration, but it was hard for me to suspect, as Linda's mother apparently did, that they were fleeing from more integration than they had expected.

As Linda's mother worked (fruitlessly, it developed) to get Madelyn Drinker to be specific about her discontent with the curriculum, I searched my own memory for any experiences my children had reported. Spike, of course, had not complained about being held back or about any excess roughness on the playground; Noah, who would enjoy the roughness, never complained that he had got more than he gave out.

Even tiny Sarah had had only one period of being unhappy there and, with Barbara Hamilton's help, I had learned from it. The first week of school, Sarah had come home weeping. "Nobody likes me because I'm white!" she said. It did no good to remind myself that black mothers all over the country were going through the same experience; this was my daughter and her pain hurt me. I reminded Sarah that Paula Hamilton liked her and I named the other little girls who came home with her to play. Inside me, however, the old question was reactivated: Had we been wise in choosing this kind of school for our children, even with all the benefits we knew it had? Questioning Sarah more closely revealed that "nobody" was one little girl who, after Sarah lost the class election for president, told her, "I didn't vote for you because I don't vote for *whites.*" I had lost class elections too, I recalled, and it had hurt. I had been called Four-Eyes because of my glasses. And I remembered with shame I had called one classmate Lizzie Longfeet and another, Fatso.

When Sarah was calm enough to go to sleep, I sat staring out of the window and trying to come to terms with my emotions. Children are cruel, I knew. Was being called "white" any worse than being called "fat" or "Four-Eyes" or "Skinny"? With the same bad luck that would continue for several years, Ben was in Washington. I phoned Barbara to air and explore my feelings. I told Barbara of the incident and of my own memories. I said, finally, "It's not easy to find something to tease Sarah about!" Sarah had developed with average height, a well-formed little body, neither thin or chubby, and thick, yellow shining hair. Barbara had listened and then said quietly, "I'm so glad you can see it that way." She told me then about being teased in her all-black school in Harlem because of her dark complexion, her lisp and her then-sparse hair.

Other than that—and the fights Noah confessed to inciting —my children had had no complaints. However, some children were more retiring or timid than my two big-for-their-age sons and my small, but determined daughter. If this were the case, why did their parents not simply take their children out of our school instead of discussing the problem in vague terms at meetings?

On the way home, Celia thought she knew why. "Up until sixth grade, it's a nice social experiment that these liberals can brag about to their suburban friends. But if their child is not doing A-plus work, they want out. These parents are thinking in terms of Harvard and Princeton and Radcliffe now. They'd rather believe there's something wrong with the school than with their own not-absolutely-brilliant kids."

Celia's remarks were, to me, both proved and disproved in the next few months as more and more white parents prepared to leave the school. On the train from Center City, Ben sat with a neighbor, a lawyer who had just received a lucrative political appointment. Ben came home bristling. The lawyer had said, "It's just terrible what's happening at Willis School. We're putting our children in private school next year." Ben asked what terrible things were happening at Willis School?

Ben said to me angrily, "You know, that s.o.b. would never get specific! He just kept saying he didn't want to talk about it."

The lawyer, I told Ben, had a child in Spike's class and one in Noah's class. Neither was doing well from what I had observed during classroom visits or from what our children casually mentioned.

Some white parents seemed to be genuinely if belatedly concerned about a religious education for their children. Several white Catholic families and Jewish families were taking their children after the sixth grade into religious schools in the area.

Yet I had to admit that racism, in some cases, was a factor. A new friend, Ginny Arthur, whose daughter Amy was in Noah's class, told me of her next-door neighbor. The neighbor began to complain about the smallness of their house, their inability to find a larger house in the area. Ginny, daughter of a professor of philosophy at a black university, told me she had listened to her neighbor with reservations during the frequent, elaborate explanations. "Then her son told my daughter, 'We're moving to the suburbs where there aren't no colored,'" Ginny said bitterly.

Yet there were other white families—admittedly only a handful—who were apparently pleased with what their children were learning; Celia, of course, but others too. Was it my imagination that the white families who quietly kept their children in our school through the seventh and eighth grades were unusually close-knit and free from family tensions? Some of the departing families evidenced inner turmoil that a change of school would be unlikely to cure. Most of the half-dozen white children who had graduated the previous June seemed markedly independent and secure. Was this because the family practice was to face problems rather than run from them—in school as well as in other areas of life? If so, what were the other white children learning when their parents constructed false reasons for running away?

As if to compound my confusion about neighborhood attitudes, I got a phone call from Madelyn Drinker a few days later. "What do you think of the school *now*?" she asked. I did not understand. "Well, I *saw* Spike shaken down for money yesterday at school . . . by that terrible Jelly Stowe, in fact." I had to confess I knew nothing about it.

When Spike came home, I asked him. He looked clearly astonished. Jelly had not tried to get money from him, he said.

I wondered if Spike could possibly be lying to protect me from disappointment with Jelly or because he didn't want me involved in his problems. But he continued to protest that, though he had seen Jelly at school, nothing had happened. I was willing to drop the subject. Spike kept it going, shaking his head, wondering out loud why Mrs. Drinker got "that weird idea."

Finally, his face cleared and he laughed. "You know what she must have heard, Mom. Jelly was at school with a friend. When they saw me, Jelly said, 'Here's a kid who's got lots of coins.' Jelly was talking about my *coin collection*, Mom, and about how he gave me those coins that time."

Madelyn Drinker had apparently heard the comment about "coins," put her own fearful interpretation on it and assumed Spike had then been "shaken down" for money.

When I called Madelyn Drinker to set the record straight, I had the unpleasant feeling that she believed Spike . . . and I . . . were covering up.

She said, "Well, I just don't think integration works as well as you like to think it does. They *are* different from us. Don't forget, I teach them every day. A psychiatrist friend told me that they're used to being hit at home and that hitting them is the only way to communicate with them. And they *do* harass our children. Tony has had several unpleasant incidents . . . and I'll bet Spike has too, if he's truthful with you."

There was no way to be positive that Spike always told me everything, but the coin incident was certainly beyond his powers of invention. I did not argue this with Tony's mother, but I protested her psychiatrist-friend's theory. She said, "You don't know what it's like in a classroom!" No, I did not.

Later, when Spike came home for a snack I told him that Tony's mother said Tony had had some unpleasant incidents with black students and that she seemed to doubt our explanation of Jelly Stowe and the coins.

(107)

Spike listened. It was hard to tell whether he was politely listening to adult "foolishness" or if his mind was on something else. He said he was going to Tony's to play chess. He'd be back by six.

At six o'clock, Spike came in the kitchen, grinning. "It's okay, Mom," he said, "I had a good talk with Tony. He just didn't notice that he never told his Mom if he had a fight with Ricky or Adam or Eric." (These were all white boys.) "But if a black kid even teases him, he tells her. And then she gets nervous. But it's okay. Tony sees what I mean."

On April 4, 1968, Dr. Martin Luther King was murdered. The next day at school, several black classmates of our children proclaimed loudly that they would never speak to white people again. In a week, they had forgotten their vow. So, it seemed, would the many whites who rededicated themselves to equal rights during the emotional outpouring over Dr. King's murder.

A few days after Dr. King's death, Ginny Arthur told me that Celia Spears had registered her children in private school. I simply did not believe Ginny. A friend of a friend, Ginny said, had seen Celia at the school. I protested that Celia could have been there for other reasons. Celia had been so critical of those who left public school, surely she would not change her attitude so quickly. Close friends as we were, she would certainly have told me of any problems her children were having or any discontent she was beginning to feel. I told Ginny that it was just a rumor, spread because Celia was the minister's wife.

When I telephoned Celia to laugh with her over the silly rumor, she was silent at the other end of the line. Then she said, "Oh, Lois, we discussed it with everyone and decided that private school was best for the children. I really don't want to talk about it any more."

That evening, I got an additional shock when Spike said,

(108)

"Oh, yeah, I knew Archer Spears was going to private school. Tony knew, but he wasn't supposed to tell me."

Ben, as usual, provided the sounding board for my confusion and hurt. I said, "Every parent has a right to do what he thinks is best for his children, but it hurts that she tried to keep it a secret. And a lot of other parents are acting peculiarly. They're leaving . . . and that's okay . . . but they make up funny excuses for doing it . . . excuses that make the school look bad."

Ben said, "Honey, they'd rather make the school look bad than look bad to themselves. Weren't a lot of those families involved in civil rights things?"

Yes, and that's what was so contradictory about it.

Ben said, "Look, honey, it's easy to get involved in fashionable causes and demonstrate for integration in the South. Maybe they're having to face their feelings about integration in their own neighborhood. And they can't admit what they feel."

I could not agree with Ben. I even wondered if his South Carolina childhood was, for once, coloring his view of northern liberals.

"But, Ben, these parents have stayed in public school for six years. Why do they want to leave now? Celia Spears said that some of them were scared that their children were not going to make Girls' High or Central, but her son couldn't have missed qualifying."

Ben said that was a hard question to answer. "But can't you just write it off as a disappointment?" he said.

I wished I could, but the sixth-grade exodus appeared to go deeper than my disappointment. In trying to justify leaving our school, these parents spread unpleasant and untrue rumors. Other white families could become afraid to enroll their children. It did not matter to me how many white classmates my children had, but the Kerner Report had predicted two Ameri-

(109)

cas—one, white and one, black—and any false fears that kept white children out of our school helped push people farther apart.

In the next few months before school was to close, I learned only that more white families were not returning for seventh grade. Celia, instead of explaining her reasons for leaving, managed to avoid me. In June, Vangie Peters added a few more pieces to the emerging pattern.

I was again going with a class for an outing and as I waited outside Noah's classroom for the children, Vangie clicked down the empty corridor toward me.

"Isn't it terrible," she said, "about the Spears family putting their children in private school? A minister . . . a neighborhood leader! I understand there's plenty of criticism about it at the church."

I said simply that I did not understand why Celia had decided to leave.

Vangie's smooth white forehead wrinkled in surprise. "But I thought you knew why! Calvin Spears' grandfather died and left him some money. They couldn't afford private schools until now!"

It hurt to realize that Vangie was probably right. This explained Celia's leaving, but not the others. By now, I knew Vangie Peters told me what she felt I wanted to hear, but I asked her a direct question. "Why are so many other white families leaving after the sixth grade?"

Vangie moved closer to me and lowered her voice. "Ah, Lois, there are several reasons." She began to tick them expertly off on her fingers. "Don't forget, this neighborhood has some fabulous bargains in big, well-built houses—much more spacious and comfortable than these families could possibly afford in the suburbs. The husband isn't making much money, so in the early school years, they can live in their big house and play liberal by sending their kids to an integrated school. By the time the kids are in sixth grade, the husband is making more money. Maybe the wife is on some prestigious committees by now. They've met a few upper-class people and the upper class send their kids to private school. So the former liberal can now afford to pay to have his child among conservatives. That's one type."

Ironically, the next "type" Vangie described had first been described to me by Celia. Vangie said, "By sixth grade, some parents find out that their superior little darlings are not likely to qualify for Girls' High or Central. That's when they begin to wish they'd moved out to the suburbs where the intellectual lines aren't so plainly drawn. They're not about to send their children to Germantown High School. They never wanted *that much* integration! Many flee the city entirely. The others flee to private schools." I did not interrupt Vangie. Her crisp, if biting, analysis was too fascinating, especially from someone who usually spoke with careful idealistic optimism. But I had heard that our own (white) superintendent of schools, Mark Shedd, sent his daughter to Germantown High. Could it be as bad as everyone seemed to believe? As I listened, I felt hopelessly naïve and disillusioned, but I also felt a new respect for Vangie's insight and sudden, refreshing candor.

She smiled, perhaps sensing my absorption in her words, and continued. "But *most* important, my dear, is that the seventh grade is when boys and girls really begin to notice each other. They begin to pair off. Those white parents are not going to run the risk of any interracial dating!" Vangie put her small head back and looked up at me, raising one eyebrow. "In most schools, the seventh grade is when school dances begin. Haven't you ever noticed that we never have dances in our school?" she finished triumphantly.

No, I had not. I blurted out, "You mean our children don't have dances just because a few more white parents might leave?" I must have shown my distress. Dancing had been my favorite recreation in my teens.

Vangie stepped back a pace. "Oh, you're so right, Lois.

Our children do need dances and I'm planning some for next year." She glanced at her watch. Oops, she was late, she said, and hurried off.

In the few minutes while I waited in the corridor until Noah's class was ready to leave, I thought over Vangie's words. They were disillusioning, but they had an air of expertise about them. Had Vangie watched the same exodus each year, knowing what caused it, but not how to stop it? Her words, much as I hated to admit it, explained the evasive and unfounded complaints of the departing white parents.

For a moment I wondered if I would have chosen a big city public school knowing all the complexities involved. Probably not. I would have been afraid. The safe conveyor belt of suburban education would have seemed preferable to this constant self-searching.

I remember that moment vividly now. That day, as I stood in the corridor examining my attitudes with Vangie's words in mind, I had been through the easiest years of our children's —and my—education. The real complexities were ahead.

Yet that day our decision to keep Spike in Willis School for the seventh and eighth grades seemed sound. Spike was slowly catching up in the same school where he had experienced failure. As for his dancing with or dating a young lady who was black, it was foolish to be sure how I would feel. I had had plenty of surprises—good and bad—in the last six years. However, no parent could make his child's world totally white forever and some of the mixed marriages I had observed were clearly the product of rebellion. Wasn't it better for a teen-ager to see people of other colors as *people* instead of as a means to rebel?

And what about Spike's qualifying for Central High? During the last six years when he was falling farther and farther behind, we had given little thought to high school. It was possible, but not likely, that Spike might catch up enough in the next two years to qualify for Central. If not? I reminded myself again that Mark Shedd, the superintendent of schools, sent his children to the junior high where Spike would spend ninth grade and to Germantown High. Mark Shedd knew better than anyone what went on in those schools and if he sent his own children there, we could. Perhaps Germantown High's reputation stemmed from the same self-justifying scare talk that was taking white children out of our seventh grade.

Noah's class was ready to leave for their trip now. I walked out of the school in the midst of the children. In the time I had waited in the corridor, I had stirred up and examined our decision to remain in this school. These thoughts would serve us for the next two years but there would be a time during those two years when I wished I had joined the sixth-grade exodus—but for reasons unlike any I had examined that day.

eight

MANY CHANGES IN AMERICA BEGAN IN THE SUMMER OF 1968. Robert Kennedy, one of the last idols of our young people, was killed in June. That summer, Lyndon Johnson, who had pushed through historic civil rights legislation, appointed the first black men to the Cabinet and to the Supreme Court and who had personally identified himself with black Americans in his ringing "We Shall Overcome" speech, was now a villain. Riots had moved from big city black ghettos to white colleges. The war John Kennedy began was now the issue; Eugene McCarthy, who said little or nothing about the unwon battle of civil rights, was the new hero. In Chicago in August, young people who were ages eleven or twelve during the days of the Freedom Riders were treated by Chicago police in much the same way as their elders had been treated in Selma, Alabama. Liberals in our neighborhood urged us to join them in "punishing" the Democratic party by staying away from the polls. Much of this was as hard for me to understand as were the vague reasons so many sixth-grade parents had given for leaving our school.

The week school opened in September, 1968, I had another disillusioning experience. Sarah had forgotten her notebook. I had brought it to school and found myself walking behind

Vangie Peters and a young white woman. Vangie's words drifted back to me. "And you'll notice," she said, "that our school is rebalancing itself racially. Note how many white children we have in the primary grades." Vangie's candor, I realized sadly, was transient. She and her guest reached the office and went in without looking back.

On my way home, I tried to take an unemotional look at Vangie Peters. All right, she was misleading the young woman (probably a parent); she had misled me by agreeing with whatever I said, by giving me the answers she believed I wanted. She was trying, through means I would not have used, to keep white parents in the school. I would probably have tried, had I been Vangie, to be candid about the sixth-grade exodus and to use frankness instead of flattery, but perhaps Vangie had tried this in the past and it had failed. Perhaps she felt forced to try other tactics.

There were, I had come to believe, good reasons to keep white parents in our school. If we were to have integration it was easier for whites to do the integrating. Time and money and anguish had been spent trying to integrate black pupils into white schools. Getting eight students into Little Rock's Central High School, getting James Meredith into the University of Mississippi had required national guardsmen. Bringing white students into our school required nothing but Vangie Peters' persuasion.

In addition to the advantages of our children's growing up among all kinds of Americans, I had learned that school integration gave black children a vital lesson too. Recently, Mrs. Jefferson had paused while dusting, looked at me carefully for a moment and then said that her daughter, Ernie's younger sister, had told her, "Mom, I always thought white people were smarter than us, but there's some white kids in my class who aren't as smart as me!" Mrs. Jefferson was worried that her daughter was becoming "big-headed"; I was delighted her daughter had learned the truth.

I decided, as I walked home from school that day, that even though I wished Vangie Peters would use more honest methods, she was doing a service by wooing white parents to the school. It did not, as I saw it then, harm either black or white students. By the end of the semester, I learned I was wrong.

On November 5, the liberals in our neighborhood did indeed "punish" the Democratic party by writing in Eugene McCarthy or Dick Gregory or by staying away from the polls. Richard Nixon was elected and promised to bring us together.

On November 18, I read that the New York teachers' ten-week strike had been settled. It seemed tragic that over a million children in the New York public schools had lost so much time (Philadelphia children would eventually lose more). The New York strike was not over salary, but over the ousting of ten white teachers who were considered incompetent by the new decentralized Oceanhill-Brownsville school board in this mostly black area. The teachers' union had won the strike; the ten white teachers would stay where they were. Perhaps this was what Vangie Peters meant when she said the union would not allow her to get rid of some of the teachers at our school who hit or humiliated children.

I had been surprised, however, to learn that Vangie had helped Miss McGregor (the teacher who had made Almira Stampp stand in the wastebasket) get funding for an Open-Classroom experiment for the new semester. When Vangie asked me if I wanted Sarah in "Miss McGregor's fantastic new kind of class," I said no. Even if another teacher had been in charge of it, the open-classroom concept was too untried for me. It might have been successful in England where children from a more formal culture needed a relaxed learning situation, but it seemed to Ben and me that our uninhibited children needed a structured school situation. But I wondered why Vangie would help a teacher she "couldn't get rid of" to conduct this prestigious experiment.

This semester was to remove my naïveté in many areas. It

started, however, with only a few hints of what was ahead. Sarah was to be in the fourth-grade class of Miss Le Duc, the shy teacher who had stimulated Spike's interest in science. Before Christmas vacation, Sarah brought home the news that Miss Le Duc was leaving to go back to college for a while. She was replaced by Mr. Schwartzkopf who, Sarah said, came from Germany and yelled. I did not take this seriously. By now, we had learned that beneath Sarah's determination was a sensitivity to criticism and even a low-voiced reprimand from me brought a "You don't have to yell, Mom!"

As I did with all our children's teachers, I invited Mr. Schwartzkopf for lunch. He was short, blond and moved with the precision of a Bavarian clock figure. He announced, between enormous forkfuls of food, that he was a German national, here originally to get a Ph.D. in his field, but was marrying an American girl and would be a citizen. I asked if he found American children different from German children. He shrugged and asked me to pass the salad. After school, Sarah said to me, "He talked with his mouth full of food!" I told her that while table manners were important, that did not mean he could not be a good teacher.

Spike, who was now almost thirteen and in the seventh-grade cycle, had decided that having teachers home for lunch was "baby-ish," although he liked all but one of his new teachers. Carter M. Kellogg had been moved from sixth-grade math to seventh-grade art and had always taken a special interest in Spike. Spike also liked his math and science teachers. The new tall blond man who taught social studies was, according to Spike, "learning how to handle the class," but Spike disliked Miss Arnold, the English teacher. "Weird" was the only specific description I could get from Spike. After a few months, he asked if I would talk with her. "She's always making fun of my handwriting," Spike said. Since Spike seldom complained about teachers, I knew Miss Arnold must really be upsetting him and made an immediate appointment through the principal's office. Miss Arnold, a tall, bony woman in her sixties with a thin mouth and a yellowish complexion, quickly assessed my clothes, snubbed out her cigarette and patted her chemically blond hair. "I didn't realize Spike came from such a fine background," she said. I explained that Spike was on medication for hyperactivity and that his bad handwriting was part of his symptoms and his inheritance.

"Oh, certainly," she said, "with his background, he should have no problem." I did not know what his "background" had to do with it, but Spike reported dryly the next day that she had stopped making fun of his handwriting. "Now she sorta flutters around me," he said. "Maybe I shoulda settled for the old way!" Spike, however, shortly developed a philosophic attitude toward Miss Arnold. He had survived Miss Grenelli the year before. "At least Arnold is trying to teach something," he said.

Noah was in Miss Banneker's fifth-grade class that year and by late April, 1969, the only unusual event in his semester was ironically humorous. Noah announced one day that he and Lester Northrup, a classmate, were being tutored in math by "some kids from Chestnut Hill Academy," an exclusive private school. Jane Banneker was coming to lunch the next day and I asked her whether any other child needed tutoring more than Noah. I had the time, I said, if not the talent, to drill him in math at home if this would free the tutors to work with another child.

Jane explained that Noah and Lester Northrup were the best candidates. "These students from Chestnut Hill are only tenth graders themselves, so they can't handle any severe study problems." Then her soft mouth twitched with suppressed laughter and she said, "I had to assign someone. It seems that we are Chestnut Hill Academy's *poverty project!*"

Before the Chestnut Hill Academy tutors led me into an unexpected area of education, Sarah's fourth-grade class took my attention. Sarah had settled down to a quiet dislike of Mr. Schwartzkopf in spite of my attempts to explain away her complaints. She admitted she would rather be in his class than in Miss McGregor's "open classroom." When she was sent there with notes or to borrow things, she said, "They're always making vegetable soup in class and running around." Always? "Well, Mommie, every time I'm in there," Sarah said. But Mr. Schwartzkopf was "mean."

I discounted Sarah's appraisal of the open classroom and her reports that Mr. Schwartzkopf was "always yelling at Donald and Warren and Ralph." Sarah had developed a tender but possibly overprotective, maternal relationship with several of her classmates, especially Ralph. She had told me one day that "Ralph curses all the time and I told him it sounded ugly and he said he'd try to stop." Her face had turned soft and wistful when she added, "He says he doesn't have a mother. So I'm going to help him talk better." I knew if Mr. Schwartzkopf "yelled" at Ralph, Sarah would see it in a fierce protective way.

In the middle of May, Sarah told me at lunchtime that "Mr. Schwartzkopf broke the window with Donald Johnson's head." I did not believe her and decided that this was an opportunity to confront Sarah with her exaggerations.

I said, "All right, honey, if he did, then let's go look at the hole in the window." Sarah must learn to tell the truth even about people she disliked. Noah and Spike were at a lunchtime meeting of the safety cadets and Sarah was finished with her lunch. We could go right now, I told her. Her unabashed willingness to leave immediately was, I believed, a deplorable bluff.

I followed Sarah across the playground to the portable classrooms and there was the hole. It was just the size of a child's head. Someone was in the process of repairing the window; tools and a jar of putty rested on the window sill.

As we walked into the building toward Vangie Peters' office,

I said to Sarah, "Honey, I apologize. I thought you were making it up."

Vangie was alone in her office with its window that overlooked the area we had just left. She said, "He's leaving." I had not said a word. I was glad I did not have to.

Still feeling speechless with shock, I turned to leave and walked into Mr. Schwartzkopf as he entered the office.

The smile on his face changed into open-mouthed surprise as Vangie Peters said, "I just told Mrs. Stalvey you are leaving our school."

The mechanical apparatus that ran Mr. Schwartzkopf's precise, patterned manner seemed to break down. His mouth opened and closed; his arms moved purposelessly. He said, "I . . . but . . . he . . . I was only shaking the Johnson boy."

"So hard that his head broke the window?" I said. I turned away from him and asked Vangie, "Where *is* Donald Johnson?"

Before she could answer, Mr. Schwartzkopf said, "I gave him *my* comb to get the glass out of his hair."

Vangie Peters now beamed benevolently, took my hand and Mr. Schwartzkopf's and began to lead us back into her inner office. "Why don't you two just take my office and talk this over. I'll take Sarah to get some chocolate milk." Sarah grabbed my other hand tightly, shaking her head.

I said, "Vangie, I have nothing to talk over with Mr. Schwartzkopf. If he's leaving the school, that's all I care about. Where is Donald Johnson?"

Vangie said he had probably gone home for lunch. I walked out of the office with Sarah. Mr. Schwartzkopf followed us down the corridor. "But that child is bad," he said. Then, "Surely a woman of your intelligence . . ." I ignored him all the way to the street. He turned and went back into the school.

As I was getting into the car, I saw Donald Johnson, leaning against the iron fence around the school yard. Sarah had gone off with her friends and I walked over to Donald.

Donald looked at me fearfully. I asked, "Are you all right?" He relaxed. "Sure." His big fluffy Afro had, luckily, protected him from any physical damage, but his brown eyes looked down at the ground and his mouth was clenched tight and thin. I said, "Did you tell your mother what happened?"

Donald's head snapped back and he looked up at me now with alarm in his eyes. "Please don't tell my Ma. Please!" I squatted down and looked into his pleading face, assuring him that I would not tell his mother. But I added, "Teachers are not supposed to hurt children. I think your mother would *want* to know what Mr. Schwartzkopf did . . . because it wasn't right, Donald."

He looked away. "Okay," he mumbled, "I'll tell her." I knew he would not. Spike had been afraid to tell us about his teacher's pinches and cruelty. I wondered if I should call Donald's mother. As if he read my thoughts, Donald gave me another pleading look. Recently on a trolley, I had heard a well-dressed man who was sitting behind me boast to his companion that "old ways of discipline were best. When I was a kid, my dad said that if a teacher had to hit me in school, he'd give me another wallop when I got home." I had never met Donald's mother. What if she had the same philosophy? I decided that, with Mr. Schwartzkopf leaving, I would keep my promise to Donald.

Vangie Peters, I learned, had taken over Mr. Schwartzkopf's class that afternoon and the next day, Miss Le Duc returned.

I expected the last month of school to proceed peacefully. Vangie Peters had telephoned shortly after the window-breaking incident to tell me that Spike's Iowa Test Scores had risen from a national percentile rating of eighty in the sixth grade to an eighty-eight on his seventh-grade test. "You were so right, Lois, in the way you handled his problems," she said.

Sarah, it appeared, had worked as determinedly under Mr. Schwartzkopf as under other teachers she liked. Her national rating was ninety, but she was now much more excited about her friend Ralph's improvement than about the *A*'s she brought home on her own papers. "He doesn't say 'ain't' and he doesn't curse, not never!" she said. "Not *ever*," I corrected. "That's right," Sarah said.

I knew Noah was doing well except in math, but he was still working with the tutors from Chestnut Hill Academy and, I assumed, getting the kind of drill in multiplication tables that he needed.

Just after Noah's eleventh birthday on May 24, we learned he was getting something other than multiplication tables in his bi-weekly tutoring sessions. At the dinner table, Noah said to Spike, during an unexpected lull in the family chatter, "Bet you don't know what a rubber is!"

When Noah heard his words ringing out in the stillness, his round pink face turned red. He looked nervously at me, then at his father.

Ben said, calmly, "And who told you about rubbers, son?"

Noah said, "Well . . . uh . . . Bill, the guy from Chestnut Hill Academy, was telling me and Lester . . . well, Bill showed us one."

Ben, straight-faced and mild, said, "Well. Thought you were supposed to be learning math." I felt I knew how Ben was handling the situation. We had always answered our children's questions about sex as openly and simply as possible, careful, however, to avoid overexplaining or adding more than they wanted to know. Birth control information had, to put it mildly, seemed premature for Noah. If he had any questions about it, however, Ben would naturally prefer that we talk about it rather than have Noah get the information from a tenth grader.

Noah saw Ben's calm attitude as permission to share his fascinating new information, information he was sure his big brother did not have. He said proudly, "Bill says he always has a rubber in the trunk of his car and he keeps one in his wallet. And he showed it to me and Lester."

"Lester and *me*," I corrected. "Yeah, Lester and me. And he said he goes with this girl, Jane, and . . .." Noah looked around, not sure now whether he wanted to go into details. "He told us what it's for," Noah finished. Spike was looking at him with scientific interest. When Noah stopped, Spike turned to Ben, waiting to see what would happen next. Sarah looked disinterested.

Ben said, "Son, let me tell you a *real* fact of life your friend Bill probably skipped. First of all, a rubber . . . it's also called a condom . . . is something a man puts over his penis during intercourse to keep sperms from going into a woman's uterus and making her pregnant. Okay? But I'll tell you something else. Kids Bill's age like to pretend they've got experience that they don't really have. That's okay sometimes, and lots of teen-agers talk like that. But it's very, very wrong of Bill to drag a girl's name into the talk."

I added what was on my mind. "Noah, some times older boys talk big about things they don't know anything about. Daddy and I want you to have the right facts, so if you hear something that sounds strange, will you be sure to check with us?"

Spike had a question immediately, "Why would he keep that rubber in the *trunk*?"

We had a comfortable family discussion of sex questions and I felt the incident had provided us with a necessary reminder that our children were facing new questions. It was good to let them know we were at ease in helping them find the answers, through asking us or through some books we had made available to them.

When I talked with Ginny Arthur the next day, I told her about Noah's hilariously abashed look when his question smashed into the silence of the dinner table. Ginny shared my amusement, but she felt I ought to report the incident to Vangie Peters.

"It worked out fine for Noah," she said, "but I wonder

about Lester. You know, we black people still have an uptight attitude about sex. There's still that old myth about us being oversexed and some black families don't know how to handle the talk with their children."

I did not know Lester's mother, but I agreed that perhaps I had better tell Vangie and Jane Banneker that the tutors had switched from math to sex education.

When I phoned Vangie, she gasped. "How *dare* those tutors show condoms to Noah!" I assured her that we had simply used the episode to update our discussions with our children, but that I thought she should know what had happened. Vangie said she would certainly do something about it immediately.

When I talked with Jane Banneker, she said, "Of all children, Lester doesn't need this kind of nonsense. I'll take both boys out of the tutoring project today."

I felt the episode was ended. On Saturday night, Ben and I went to what was supposed to be a carefree, relaxing party to welcome some new neighbors. Ginny and her husband were there as well as a white couple who had British accents, a black computer specialist and his wife who was a nurse and, adding to the interesting mix, a Nordic-looking man, Derek Jones, with a pretty blond wife who had been raised in Mississippi and who now had the almost-incredible name of Mary Jones. Far from being the quiet fragile southern belle of my stereotypes, Mary Jones was gregarious and uninhibited.

In the middle of the evening, I listened to her tale of registering her oldest child in our school. In a rich southern accent, Mary Jones told how she had telephoned Vangie Peters to ask if Tinky could attend kindergarten for the last month of the semester.

For a Southerner, Mary did a fair imitation of Vangie's crisp "Out of the question. Good-bye."

"But ah was just so desperate with Tinky beggin' me to go to that school. Ah decided to see if ah couldn't get fahtha talkin' to the lady in person," Mary said. She had gone to school; Vangie Peters registered Tinky immediately and said to Mary, "Now let me show you our *marvelous* school!"

Mary grinned at Ginny Arthur. "Ginny, d'you get the feelin' Miz Peters thought 'Mary Jones' was black?"

While Ginny laughed ruefully, I felt stunned. By now, I knew that white children got special attention. It had never occurred to me that Vangie would keep a child out of our school if she thought he was black.

I had no time to deal with this thought. Ginny, who was sitting next to me, said quietly, "Lois, didn't you tell me that the tutors from Chestnut Hill Academy brought those condoms to school?"

Yes, of course. Why?

Ginny told me that Lester Northrup had been accused of stealing her daughter's money on Banking Day and that Vangie Peters had said to Ginny, "I don't know what to do with that boy. Why, just yesterday he brought condoms to school and shocked the Chestnut Hill Academy tutors so badly that they canceled the program."

Totally confused, I sputtered, "But she knows better! How . . . Why would she say that?"

Ginny shook her head sadly. "I suppose it was because there was no real proof that Lester took Amy's money. This was probably Vangie's way of *proving* Lester was 'bad' and settling the problem."

On Monday morning, I cleaned my clothes closet vehemently, trying to work off my anger before deciding what to do about Vangie's destructive lie. Until then, I believed that her dissembling to keep white children in the school did no harm to the black children. I was obviously wrong.

The closet-cleaning went well; it was a good day to throw out old useless things and to examine beliefs that might be old and useless too. Vangie would not have admitted Mary Jones' daughter if she had been black; Vangie had casually ignored the truth in order to create evidence that Lester

(125)

Northrup stole Amy Arthur's money. Lester, as I knew him from occasional lunchtime visits, was a big, slow-moving child, quiet and cheerful. He would not be cheerful much longer if he had been accused as unfairly of stealing as he was of bringing condoms to school. It was Ginny's opinion that Vangie wanted to build up reasons to expel Lester and as many other black students as possible. "By expelling black kids and wooing whites, she can keep her precious school integrated," Ginny had said. Vangie's appraisal of Jelly Stowe had shifted from "emotionally disturbed" to "just needs attention" when I got to know Jelly, yet he had been permanently expelled. Had my children gone through all these years of special attention and privilege while their black classmates were treated quite differently?

A phone call, just before noon, interrupted my thoughts. By evening, when I found the pile of clothing and bags of discards outside my closet, it seemed impossible I had begun the task only a few hours before. The questions I had been asking myself that morning were thoroughly answered.

The telephone call was from Mrs. Helgstrom, the school nurse. Noah, she said, had been "beaten up" by Lester Northrup. He was not hurt, but he was upset. Could I come to school?

By then, I had learned that Mrs. Helgstrom's assessment of damage to my children was likely to be overstated and so, without real alarm, I drove the three blocks to school. As I walked into her office, I saw her standing in front of Noah, tissue in hand, wiping each of his tears as they fell. Even I felt that much service was excessive.

I was more experienced with Noah's fights than was Mrs. Helgstrom. Noah knew it. When I asked blandly what happened, he glanced at her and then at me. "Well . . ." he began, blushing.

If Noah realizes his present goal to be a politician, he will have to be an honest one. His face and his voice are incapable of obscuring the truth. In a few minutes, I learned that while Miss Banneker was out of the room, Noah and Lester had fought over the last available geography book. Noah lost and threatened to tell Mrs. Peters. Lester intended to stop him. He got a wrestling hold on Noah and held him until Miss Banneker returned and sent both boys to the office. Noah confessed to me that his tears were from injured pride. "Mrs. Peters sent me to the nurse," Noah said.

I asked Mrs. Helgstrom, "Where's Lester?"

"Oh, he was much too out of control to stay around school. I sent him home."

"Is his mother at home?"

Mrs. Helgstrom did not know. She was, I reflected, too busy wiping Noah's tears to make the phone call.

I said to Noah, "Lester has had a rotten time lately and it was wrong of you to threaten to tattle to Mrs. Peters." Noah nodded. I said, "Let's try to find Lester so we can have a glass of juice together and clear this up." I was also anxious to know if Lester's mother was home or if he was roaming the neighborhood with no place to go at lunchtime.

No one was in the principal's office but Jerry Washington, the school's nonteaching assistant. His head with its huge Afro was bent over two cartons while he tried to untangle his Black Power medallion from their strings.

"Mr. Washington," I said, "could you please give me Lester Northrup's phone number?"

"Sure. What's he done now?"

"Nothing. He and Noah got into a fight and I want to call his mother to be sure he got home all right."

Jerry Washington now had his Black Power medallion untangled and he looked at me in alarm. "Oh, no, you don't want to call *her*! My God, she's a black militant! She'll curse you out. You can't talk to that one!"

"Now, look," I said. "If this school treated Noah the way they've been treating Lester, I'd curse people out too."

Jerry Washington went to the files, wrote the number on a piece of paper and handed it to me. "Don't say I didn't warn you," he added.

At home, I sat in front of the phone for a while before dialing. I was not anxious to be cursed at. Jerry Washington was a thirtyish, streetwise, tough-acting fellow. If she scared him . . .

But risking a conversation with an irrational woman was better than worrying whether a child Noah's age was wandering around with no place to go after a bad experience. While I dialed the phone, I organized my words so that I could get the main points in before she could interrupt me.

A woman's voice answered after two rings. Yes, she said, this was Mary Northrup.

I began rapidly, "Our sons had a fight. They were both at fault. But I wanted to be sure Lester got home all right and to ask whether he can come over for a glass of juice so the kids can make up." Then I held my breath.

There was what seemed a long pause. Then Mary Northrup said, "My, that's nice of you to call. I sure appreciate it. Lester's here."

After a short, pleasant conversation, I invited Mary Northrup to have coffee with me while our sons had their juice. "Sure. Be there in maybe ten minutes."

When she came up our walk with Lester, I understood why she scared Jerry Washington. Mary Northrup was nearly six feet tall, broad-shouldered and muscular, but there was also a regality in the way she walked. Her head was held high and her eyes flashed quickly around her. Her skin was blue-black; no white blood had ever diluted the African blood in her veins.

We sat on the terrace while Noah and Lester wrestled on the lawn. Her proud manner overcame her tight, washed-out cotton dress and worn shoes. At first, we discussed generalities, then her large clear eyes looked soft as she told me about Lester's interest in drawing and how he had had one of his drawings chosen for a city-wide exhibition displayed at a local department store.

"We didn't know his drawing got picked, though, 'til a friend told us she seen it there. I took Lester down next day, but the show was over and the drawings was taken down." Mary Northrup's face had gone from a look of pride to a look of disappointment.

Lester must have been, I realized, the child Jane Banneker talked about when she told me, bitterly, that the art teacher for the district had not bothered to tell her that Lester's drawing had been chosen. "She said she didn't have time to inform the students. But it would have meant so much to this particular child," Jane had said. "Yet when Michael Colby won a dictionary for sending a question to a quiz show, Vangie Peters took him around to every classroom." Michael Colby was the son of a white lawyer.

Lester, apparently, not only was cheated of honors he had earned, but tagged with blame for what he did not do. I began to tell Mary Northrup about the episode of the condoms and Vangie's changing the story around. Mary Northrup's face now took on the kind of expression that must have frightened Jerry Washington.

I said, "Perhaps what we ought to do is to go up to school together right now and get it straightened out. I know what really happened because I'm the person who told Vangie."

As Mary and I marched down the school corridor together, I saw Jerry Washington up ahead. I linked my arm with Mary's. He looked at us, widened his eyes and headed immediately in the other direction. Vangie was in her office, waved us in and I told her that Ginny Arthur said she had blamed the condom incident on Lester.

"But, Lois, Mrs. Schwartz, the counselor, told me Lester brought the condoms to school!"

"Mrs. Schwartz has nothing to do with this, Vangie. Don't you remember, I reported the incident to *you*."

Vangie Peters was speechless for the first time in the seven years I had known her. Her face was blank and as rigid as her lacquered black hair. Mary and I had both remained standing and I returned Vangie's silent stare, looking down at her. Inside me, three emotions—anger, embarrassment for her and curiosity about what she would say—fought for dominance.

She shook her head quickly as if to clear it and said, plaintively, "But, Lois, we've been such close friends. I've always had such a deep respect for you."

My anger swept away everything else; Vangie was again using flattery to cover the dirty face of the truth. I knew I was about to say something cruel, but I could not suppress it. "And I had respect for you, Vangie, until I learned that you lie."

Vangie looked up at me silently. She had never glanced in Mary Northrup's direction or acknowledged her presence. At last Vangie said, "Well, if I was wrong about the condoms, then I owe Mrs. Arthur an apology."

"Mrs. *Arthur!*" I gasped. "No, you owe Lester and Mrs. *Northrup* an apology!"

Vangie was silent. Mary Northrup said, "Lois, forget it. Her apology don't mean nothing to me. But, Mrs. Peters, I know my son and you ain't going to destroy that boy. I'm gonna watch you like you was a snake. Cuz that's just what you are." Mary's voice had risen and she leaned on Vangie's desk, her two enormous fists pressed tight to its surface. Vangie looked past her at me.

I found my voice was coming out as loud as Mary's. I said, "And I'm going to be watching you too. You're not doing any favor to my children by making them *vehicles* of injustice. I will *not* have you teaching my kids they've got special privileges just because they're white." I too had moved toward Vangie's desk and was leaning forward in the same position as Mary Northrup. I said, "Don't you understand, Vangie? If you protect my kids unfairly, the black child is going to get them after school anyway. And, worse, my kids are going to start believing that justice doesn't apply to them."

Vangie finally spoke. "Does this mean you're leaving our school?"

Vangie's question loosed another wave of outrage. "Leave?" I said, "I'd be afraid to leave this school! If I hadn't been here, you could have got away with blaming Lester for that condom thing. If I took my children out of this school, I'd have to worry about what other dirty tricks you're playing. I'm staying right here, Vangie. I'm gonna watch right along with Mary."

Mary said, "Okay, you told her. Let's get out of here." I followed Mary out of the door and down the corridor. Mary may have read my mind or my face. I had had a strong desire to grab Vangie Peters by the throat. In the end, Vangie had cared nothing for what she had done to Lester; she was concerned only that she might lose three white faces from her school.

On the sidewalk, I found that Mary Northrup had walked to our house. I drove her home. Outside her neat row house, she tried to calm me. "You made your point okay. Let it sit awhile." She laughed. "Lord, I thought that Peters was gonna choke. She ain't used to being talked at like you was doing."

Then Mary became serious. "Let me try to tell you something about this integration stuff. Black folks don't like to make it look like we want whites in the school so we can learn from *them*. Sounds like we think our little kids can't learn unless there's a white kid sitting next to 'em. What we gotta have is—now, you hear me all out because it sounds funny—we gotta have like white *hostages*. I mean, if there's white kids in the school, it ain't gonna get as bad as if it's all black."

Mary saw the birth of a new insight on my face. She laughed. "You gettin' it okay! An' that's how it *is*. They ain't gonna let the school get all run down and with bad teachers long as there's some white folks there sayin' 'Uh-uh, you ain't gonna do my kids that way.'" Mary patted my shoulder with her large hand. "See, I been in there yellin' at Peters for years. She never looked scared like she looked when you got yellin'. Ain't no thing like Black Power, honey. That fool Jerry Washington, he wear his power sign and play his games, but there ain't nothing but White Power, honey. Only White Power gonna keep that school straight."

She peered at me soberly and said, "You gonna hang in there?"

Yes, I was. But it was not with a sense of do-gooder sympathy that I realized we had to stay. To me, it was only common sense. What Mary said was true. All those schools that Mrs. Jefferson had moved near had deteriorated when the whites ran away. If my children were "hostages" for the quality of the school, that was all right with me. If their being there helped make things better for Lester, if it helped make things better for a child like Ernie Jefferson, it was worth it. Spike, Sarah and Noah would meet children like Lester and Ernie when they were adults. If their presence in a school helped Lester and others get a better education than Ernie Jefferson had gotten, my children would then meet Lester as a proud, self-sufficient productive citizen. As of now, they would meet Ernie as an angry, illiterate man.

There was also, I know, a superstitious sense of gratitude that made me feel a responsibility toward our school. Spike was thirteen years old; Noah, eleven and Sarah would be ten in October; their personalities were formed well enough for us to be proud of what they had become. They were far from perfect—they quarreled with each other, put off chores, scattered their belongings far, wide and deep—but they were healthy, loving, open young people whose future would never be limited by the prejudices of teachers or employers. If staying in the school helped, as Mary Northrup believed, it was a debt we owed for our children's good fortune.

Mary Northrup gave me a friendly whack on my shoulder, climbed out of the car and said, "It sure's good meetin' you."

I said something polite because it was impossible to articulate how much meeting Mary had meant to me. She may have felt impotent at our school for all her regal, imposing appearance, but she had given me a blunt description of what integration was all about and what "hanging in there" was going to mean.

nine

IN SPITE OF THE NEW VIEWPOINTS MARY NORTHRUP HAD given me, I had no plan to become any more closely involved *physically* with our school than before. I intended to watch closely and to speak out, but only as a parent. For years now, I had heard neighborhood women who were also teachers say, "You don't know what it's like in a classroom." I did not. I did not expect to find out.

During the last week of school, I thought I had found another way to use the insight Mary Northrup had opened up in me. Sarah had come home, tears at the edge of her eyes, to say that "the reading teacher slapped Ralph and I could see the marks on his face all afternoon!"

Once, I would only have hoped that Ralph would tell his father and that the father would lodge a complaint. Now, I realized, I could protest teacher violence because it disturbed my child.

Complaining to Vangie Peters was now more futile than ever. The day after the confrontation in her office, I had sincerely regretted my emotional outburst. Open enmity between Vangie and me was no solution to school problems. I had written her a note, apologizing for losing my temper. I had had no reply. I decided instead to telephone the teacher. When I told her that I objected to having my daughter witness a teacher slapping a child, the woman cleared her throat several times and then said, "It . . . uh . . . was an accident." This seemed unlikely, but I thought perhaps these "accidents" might happen less often if she knew other parents heard of them.

The semester closed and, for our family, it was to be a quiet summer. For America, July and August of 1969 brought wonder, disillusion and horror. On July 16, Apollo 11 began its flight to the moon and Spike never left the television set, surprising me by explaining details he had gathered from his reading. Before the craft landed, four days later, Edward Kennedy's private indiscretions were in the headlines. America had fulfilled his brother's 1962 promise of "a man on the moon by 1970"; Chappaquiddick, sadly and ironically, competed for public attention. On August 9, a group of frighteningly amoral young people murdered movie actress Sharon Tate and her friends. Their wealth and fame had not protected them from the depraved whim of Charles Manson, leader of this pathetic "family" of white middle-class runaways.

On August 28, national publicity was given to another event that was to have wide and continuing influence on America's attitudes. The Sunday *New York Times Magazine* published an article *about* an article: Arthur R. Jensen's article in the *Harvard Educational Review* in which he concluded that no amount of compensatory education could overcome the inherited intellectual inferiorities in the Negro students he tested.

As I understood *The New York Times* article when I read it on our terrace that bright Sunday morning, Professor Jensen had found that Negro students tested out poorly in abstract reasoning and problem-solving. But as I read the information as carefully and open-mindedly as I could, it astonished me to find that he had tested only American Negro children. If, as he seemed to believe, this inability to do abstract reasoning was in the genes instead of the environment, it only made sense to test children—black and white—in a black-dominated culture such as Kenya or Ethiopia or Liberia. It would, I was convinced, take a generation of equal education before a fair test could be made here. Surely Arthur Jensen must know that the 1954 Supreme Court decision was as infrequently implemented as the Golden Rule. And even in integrated schools, children like Lester Northrup, Jelly Stowe and Mrs. Jefferson's son Ernie were not treated with the care, concern or empathy that my children were given. Comparing their achievements was ridiculous.

It would once have been hard for me to challenge, even in my own mind, the opinions of renowned authorities, but during the summer a black friend had brought two educational experts to our house. Our friend, Fred Hayden, was an adviser to a nationally known educational research company and told me that he had been trying to convince his superiors that there were differences in the black educational experience that white-oriented research ignored. Fred felt that the two directors of the project might listen more believingly to my observations at our school than they had to him.

Fred's own educational history was, I had once thought, unusual. Later, Ben and I learned it was not uncommon among black men and women now in their thirties and forties. Fred had dropped out of a ghetto high school after two unsuccessful, frustrating years and enlisted in the armed forces. There he found he *could* learn and that learning was rewarding. After his discharge, he finished high school and then, for six years, worked nights and attended a Philadelphia college during the day. He now had his master's degree and was working on his Ph.D. I reluctantly accepted his belief that his present employers would be more impressed by the opinions of a white high school graduate than by Fred.

In our living room, Dr. X and Dr. Y enthusiastically explained their newest project in the kind of sociological jargon they were apparently most comfortable using. They proudly showed me charts and reports and brochures, impressively printed with funds from a generous foundation grant. I thought

(136)

I understood what the project was about, but I finally had to ask, "Are you saying that you are picking a group of children, studying them for five years and working with their mothers in order to find out if the health of a child has anything to do with his ability to learn?"

Well, yes. The older of the two Ph.D.s, a thin man with bright blue eyes who was in his late fifties, sat back in our red chair and said, "What do you think of our exciting project?"

Fred gave me a nod that I read as a signal to say what I thought. I said, meekly, "I'm afraid I think it's silly to study whether a sick child can learn as well as a healthy child. Isn't it obvious a healthy child will learn faster?" To fill in the silence that followed, I offered my experiences at our school where conscious and unconscious racism, physical abuse and psychological humiliations were, to me, a factor in a child's ability to learn. "I wish the money could be spent instead studying teachers," I said.

The two Ph.D.s listened politely. It was difficult to study teachers, the older man said mildly, but they had certainly enjoyed meeting me. At the door, the younger man said that my experiences and viewpoint were certainly valuable and would I come to speak to his researchers at the main office? I said politely that I would, but reflected that any renowned research group so isolated from schools that they need my opinions was in trouble. I never heard from them.

That Sunday afternoon in August, reading about Arthur Jensen's theory, I could only feel depressed that expensive, prestigious "studies" were being made far away from the realities of the classroom. On the other hand, I was no expert either. I had seen certain things that concerned me in our school, but I too had never spent time in charge of a classroom.

In the fall of 1969, when I volunteered to take an eighth-grade class for one period each week, it was not through any conscious desire to prove or disprove what I believed. It was through an impulse as casual and innocent as my offer in Omaha to help the black doctor find a house in our neighborhood.

I had come to the first Home and School Association meeting of the year, hoping to bring up the problem of teachers who hit children. The meeting, however, had erupted into an angry argument between our school's black parents and a group of white parents who had got permission to open an Open-Classroom school in an underused building across town. Vangie Peters insisted she knew nothing of the new school until someone leaked the story to Philadelphia's black-owned newspaper. The black parents were angry that the group had got special bus transportation ("when we can't even get buses for field trips!"). By the end of the meeting, tempers were too hot for me to introduce a new, albeit important, topic.

As the auditorium was emptying, Mrs. Hallette Spain, the seventh–eighth-grade teacher who was also serving as Vangie's "liaison to the black community," asked to make a last-minute announcement. Mrs. Spain, a tall woman with military posture and a face as long and thin as an ebony piano key, said, "We are in desperate need of parents who can take a class during the union-required rest period for the seventh- and eighth-grade teachers. We've had no trouble getting volunteers for the lower grades, but no one will volunteer for the junior high cycle."

I looked around. No hands were raised. Since I had spent most of the last seven years avoiding committees, working instead as cake baker, dishwasher and chaperone for school trips, I felt I should be contributing more. This was something I could do without going to meetings. With no additional thought, I raised my hand.

Next day, Spike said, "Good grief, Mom, did you *have* to?"
I said, "Well, if you see me in the halls, you can pretend

you don't know me, okay? Mrs. Spain promised I wouldn't have your class."

Spike rolled his eyes, shook his head and walked out of the kitchen, his tall, slim frame slumping under the burden of raising a parent properly.

Mrs. Spain had indeed promised I would not have any classes that Spike was in. When she phoned to arrange the matter, she told me that "Mrs. Peters feels you should have Carter Kellogg's advisory group."

All right. I asked Mrs. Spain what she wanted me to do with the class. My quick, impulsive move was now beginning to seem a little formidable, but challenging.

Mrs. Spain had a high nasal voice and precise diction. "Oh, you can do anything you want," she said. "It doesn't matter. Just be there at one-thirty on Friday."

The Thursday night before my first class I sat up late, aware suddenly that my preparation for teaching consisted solely of seeing two movies: *Up the Down Staircase* with Sandy Dennis and *To Sir With Love* with Sidney Poitier. It would have been reassuring that night had I known that real teachers have not much more preparation for controlling a class. Since then, every teachers' college graduate I have asked has told me that maintaining order in the classroom is not formally taught. A professor from Illinois State University said recently on television that all the research done on student discipline could be carried home by a first grader. Whether I knew it or not, I was going to begin "teaching" under conditions similar to those of a new teacher. And, like many new teachers, I would be teaching in a predominantly black school.

Do new teachers sit up late the night before their first class? Do they dream of what they will say and imagine the satisfaction of reaching each pupil, bringing out all those sparks of individuality hitherto ignored? I had decided to teach creative writing, the only subject I knew and a subject that might encourage most children to express their feelings. Oh, there would be behavior problems, of course, but I rehearsed the calm and persuasive words with which I would explain to a restless pupil why he must cooperate. In those movies, Sandy Dennis and Sidney Poitier had finally reached even the most troubled Harlem and English slum children. By midnight, I knew exactly what I would say under every possible condition.

I arrived early at Mr. Carter M. Kellogg's classroom. His red face had changed subtly from the first time we had met him as Spike's sixth-grade math teacher in his first year of teaching. This red-haired man, who had described himself as a "Peace Corps dropout," had now developed two deep frown lines between his bristling red eyebrows and a tight set to his small mouth. His gravelly voice was more harsh than I remembered. "Have fun," he growled, raising one eyebrow and gathering some papers from his desk. He left the room quickly.

The students filed in, one by one and in small groups. Many of these children must have begun school with Spike. I searched for the familiar faces of those I had chaperoned through zoos and museums. Several students said, "Hi, Mrs. Stalvey," and I recognized youngsters who were now triple the size I remembered. One young fellow had a moustache. I smiled at everyone; some smiled back, some regarded me suspiciously.

The room was filled. I stood in front of the teacher's desk and began, "Class, I will be with you each week at this time. There are a lot . . ." A small youth sprinted behind me, pursued by a tall, heavy young man.

"Make Cephas stop hittin' on me," the smaller student said. The heavy youth had gone back to a desk. Good heavens, he was Cephas Simpson, the child who had not wanted me to drive him home when he and Spike were in second grade!

Again, I began, "There are a . . ." A yelp came from the corner of the room. A buxom young lady leaped up and shrieked, "Gus, you stop that," at a chubby laughing young man.

I continued, "We are going to try creative writing. Now, by creative writing, I don't . . ."

Two boys walked up to the front of the room where I was standing. "Can we go to the library? Mr. Kellogg always lets us go to the library."

Go.

When they went out the door, something about the room looked different. Then I realized they had been the only two white pupils there.

"Now, class, there are . . ." From the corner of my eye, I saw a beige-skinned fellow whose face was turning a dark red. Cephas Simpson had his large hand around the youngster's neck. I kept talking, walked over and, finger by finger, Cephas allowed me to remove his enormous hand from his classmate's throat.

". . . I don't mean the kind of writing that . . ." I said. And then, for no apparent reason, the classroom erupted into chaos as if a string of beads had been broken. Erasers, bodies, spitballs flew in every direction.

I roared, "CLASS . . . I NEED YOUR ATTENTION . . . PLEASE."

There was a moment of quiet and I recalled how I deplored screaming teachers.

"I thought we might . . ." I finished quietly.

"Poncho, God damn you . . . give me back my m.f. pen." A tall slim fellow whom I recognized as Donald Welles from Spike's Cub Scout troop leaped up and hit another lad I now knew was Bradley Webster ("Poncho"?) on his broad back. Poncho was on his feet, 150 pounds of muscle and rage. The other students backed away from them, leaving a wide circle where Poncho and Donald stood, fists cocked, faces tight with rage.

In the two seconds I had in which to think it over, the best plan seemed to be to walk between the two young men. After all, no one hits women . . . with glasses. It worked. Poncho allowed me to lead him back to his seat; Donald looked relieved.

Someone plucked at my sleeve and a feminine voice said, "I don't want to do creative writing. I want to do my homework and Lydia won't give me my book."

Going on with my remarks to the class was obviously ridiculous. I followed the young lady to where Lydia sat, glaring, holding a book and sucking her thumb. She slammed the book down on the table. She was an enormously fat child, bulging from unpressed, too-tight clothes. Her hair looked like a pile of discarded sweepings. I said, "Thank you, Lydia," smiled and patted her arm. Lydia looked at the spot I had touched on her dark-brown skin, removed her thumb from her mouth, and brushed off her arm contemptuously.

The rest of the period was a blur. I felt like a one-woman baseball team, trying to field an endless number of hits by the opposing team. One group of sophisticated youngsters sat together at a table in the corner laughing, I suspected, at my desperate sprints from fight to shout to knocked-over chair.

There was a sudden silence. I looked around in panic, certain that someone had got seriously hurt. It was only Mr. Kellogg. The bell had apparently rung. He dismissed the class. He said to me, "Well, did you enjoy the zoo?" I smiled weakly and walked out of the room.

Outside in my car, I sat, trying to control my emotions and to recall some other time when I felt as defeated. I could not. All I could think of was my own patronizing feeling when people who knew I wrote advertising said, "Oh, I've always intended to be a writer. I just never get around to it!" As if writing were only a matter of "getting around to it"; as if teaching were only a matter of being in a room with students! I told myself that the second week would go better; I did not ask myself *how* I could make it go better.

The second week was worse. The students knew—and I knew they knew—that I felt as if I were trying to balance forty ball bearings on a pane of glass. When I moved to one end of the room, disorder erupted at the other. I could only hope no one would get hurt and wait, watching the clock crawl until Carter Kellogg's red beaming face was poked through the door.

After the first week, Spike had asked how "everything" had gone. I told him, "Well, the first time is the hardest." But now, after the second week, I again sat outside the school in my car, aware that there had been more regression than progress in my ability to handle a class.

I stared up at the dark red brick building, too drained to start the engine. All right, I decided, bleakly, my ego was very badly bruised. I had volunteered for something I could not do well. There were lots of other things I could not do: sing, work with numbers, play tennis. But I had dreamed that I would be different from the teachers who slapped and shrieked and humiliated students. I was going to relate to them through understanding and respect for them as individuals. Well, I had not been able to keep them quiet long enough to give them respect, individually or in a group. Whatever it took to be a teacher, I did not have it. And I did not have the strength to take my ego inside that school the next week for another battering. I would tell Mrs. Spain that I could not continue. She would have to understand.

And then I thought of telling Spike that I was quitting.

The problem with parenthood, I realized, is that—like pregnancy—it cannot be abandoned in the middle of the process. Once I could have given up my volunteer teaching and forgotten it. Now I would have to explain to Spike that when I could not do something well, I gave up. Spike, who was struggling to catch up for all his lost years, dared not see me as an example. His sense of defeat and humiliation may well have been as painful as mine. Yet he had to keep trying. So did I. I remembered the day I was being wheeled into the delivery room to give birth to Spike. At the door, I voiced a panicky thought to Ben, "Are you sure we ought to go through with this?" Then—and now—I had no choice.

Spike was the first home that day. He strode into the kitchen and leaned against the refrigerator. "How did it go today?" he asked.

"*Not* well."

"Wow, I don't know why they gave you Mr. Kellogg's class. Mrs. Peters calls them the worst class we've ever had in school!"

How interesting!

After Sarah and Noah had come home and Noah was playing basketball in the driveway with friends while Sarah worked on her homework, Spike returned to the kitchen, sat backward in a chair and twined his long legs around the rungs. "Not going so good, huh, Mom?" he said, seriously.

Why not let Spike know that grownups have failures too; that we too hope to accomplish something, try to do it well and, for no reason we can understand, fail? I told Spike everything that had happened and finished with: "Well, maybe next week it will go better. Any suggestions?"

Spike picked up the A-1 Sauce bottle, began to scratch the label off with his long thumb and said, in an avuncular tone, "Sure. Look, in the first place, they gave you what's *supposed* to be the worst class in the school."

I interrupted. "What do you mean 'supposed to be'?"

"Well, everybody keeps telling them how bad they are. Most of the teachers won't take 'em on trips. The smart class gets to go all kinds of places and my class gets to go most places, but those kids just get yelled at. And they're not that bad. Anyway, they were testing you." Spike grinned. "It's fun."

Yes, I remembered, it was . . . when I was a child. We gave substitutes a terrible time. It was a challenge to upset a powerful grownup, especially if she was boring or cross or pretentious. But, I told Spike, I had tried to be friendly.

"Well, you can't be *too* nice either. If we know we can get away with everything, we do. But, Mom, you've got a problem. Those kids know you can't give 'em a bad mark or anything." Then his long, lean face with its strong developing jaw brightened. "Hey, why don't you tell 'em you'll write down the names of the kids who get out of line and give the list to Kellogg?"

That, I told Spike, was the best idea yet.

Spike, who by now had half the label off the A-1 Sauce bottle, said, "But, Mom, don't yell at those kids, okay? And don't say anything . . . you know, mean. Some of those kids get treated mean all the time."

Spike had not wanted me to volunteer for the job, but now he did not want me to feel hurt or to hurt others. "Don't worry, Mom," he said, standing and looking down at me. "You can do it."

I said laughing, "Okay, coach, I'll go back in there and win this one!" My now-anonymous A-1 Sauce bottle was worth the opportunity to learn that my son was growing up more than I knew.

I had a week in which to figure out how to be friendly, but firm and how to keep forty students out of each other's books, faces and reach. During the weekend in October that Spiro Agnew made his "effete snobs" speech, I had decided that teaching creative writing to my eighth graders was not feasible. Once a week might be enough for a student who was interested in creative writing, but, according to Spike, "writing compositions and stuff" was not exactly popular with most of the students.

The next day, Saturday, Spike said, "Y'know, some of those kids might just want to do their homework in your class. Can you think of something *interesting* to talk to the other kids about?"

I tried to remember my own blasé eighth-grade state of mind. The only thing I could think of that would have been interesting to all my classmates in those days was sex.

On Sunday, October 19, after Sarah's tenth birthday party, Spike said, "Hey, Mom, why don't you have a discussion group in your class on Black History?"

The idea had occurred to me, but in a class of forty students—thirty-eight of them black—what would the reaction be to a white person's teaching Black History?

Black History was, however, a subject I had been studying with growing excitement. Barbara Hamilton's husband, Leland, had stirred my curiosity with his statement that Thomas Jefferson was "the father of racism." I found this documented in Winthrop Jordan's book, *White Over Black* (University of North Carolina Press, 1968) and I wondered what else my school history books had ignored. Barbara and Leland had lent me their copies of Lerone Bennett's *Before The Mayflower*, Basil Davidson's *The African Past*, and Arna Bontemps' *Story of the Negro*. I began a thrilling, if disturbing, study of what white history books had neglected.

It was fascinating to speculate on why I had been taught about the French Revolution but not about the Haitian Revolution with its colorful heroes, Toussaint L'Ouverture and Henri Christophe. Was it because this successful slave revolution in 1818 was not what slave-holding America wanted to publicize —then or ever?

My school books had described Africa solely in terms of which European country had conquered, occupied and exploited its riches. Africans themselves were depicted as savages without a history. Yet white historian Basil Davidson translated ancient African documents that told of sophisticated African cultures that flourished while England was still uncivilized.

In his book, *The African Slave Trade*, Davidson also told the true tragic story of how slave trading began. To me, the most vivid, typical and poignant documentation came through the correspondence between King Nzinga Mbemba of Mani-Congo and his "royal brother," the King of Portugal. A "missionary" expedition from Portugal had been welcomed in 1490. King Mbemba loaded the Portuguese ships with gold, ivory and copper in return for the promise that Portuguese experts in medicine, shipbuilding and other needed specialties would be sent to train his people. In spite of King Mbemba's eloquent pleas, the experts never came. When, in desperation, King Mbemba sent his most brilliant young men to Portugal to learn the European techniques his people needed, they were seized and made into slaves.

Meanwhile, word spread throughout Europe of African riches. The trading of cloth, utensils and medicine for Africa's gold and ivory proved too slow for greedy Europeans. Hostility was created deliberately among African kings in order to start wars and open up a new and endless market—for guns. Eventually an impoverished, but beleaguered African king offered to trade prisoners of war to the Europeans as slaves in return for guns. The slaves were soon known as "black gold" when their demand as servants grew in Europe (and later in the Americas where vast newly occupied land required endless supplies of enslaved labor).

The King of Mani-Congo was the first to predict the devastation, decimation and ruin of his continent. He pleaded for help from the King of Portugal in the name of the Christianity to which he had converted. For forty years he wrote to Lisbon. He was ignored. History—and commercial greed—took the course he feared.

While Europeans eventually occupied the African gold- and diamond-producing areas, America bought its kidnapped people. The complex emotions with which "the land of the free" justified slavery produced historical deceptions that still exist today: famous men of African ancestry were carefully "whitewashed," their Negro blood ignored. These men of literary, musical or scientific genius would have contradicted Thomas Jefferson's—and Arthur Jensen's—theory, expressed in Jefferson's *Notes On Virginia,* that "blacks . . . are inferior to the whites in the endowments of both mind and body." Thus men with enough African blood to panic a neighborhood in America—Pushkin, Dumas, Haydn and others I was yet to discover —were presented as "white." After reading of John James

Audubon, the renowned artist-naturalist, in Bontemps' *Story of the Negro* (Knopf, 1955), I had checked the *Encyclopaedia Britannica* and found that his Haitian mother was completely ignored. It seemed strangely evasive to read only that he "was raised by a French stepmother." *World Book* acknowledged his mother and printed a portrait of a dark-skinned, Negroid-featured man. Yet in our school library, I found a copy of Margaret and John Kiernan's *John James Audubon* (Random House, 1954), a book written for children, where Audubon was shown as a yellow-haired child! (I wondered if his Negro blood explained the mysterious fact that his books on American birds were not published in America until *after* their enormous European success.)

I had found myself studying these clues to honest history with an energy that would have confounded Mr. Hercher, the high school history teacher who had once flunked me in his course. This was no boring study of flawless heroes; this was a dramatic story of conflicts and human weaknesses and struggles between ethics and greed. It still went on. Arthur Jensen was being rebutted by white and black scholars with almost the identical arguments presented to Thomas Jefferson. And, from what I saw in the history books Spike brought home from school, American children were still being taught the European-only version of "world" history I had flunked in the forties.

Late that Sunday night in October, when the children were in bed, I thought about the Black History I knew, but wondered if I could "teach" it any more successfully than creative writing. I had not gotten "my" class to keep quiet long enough for me to finish three sentences.

Then Ben, who knew what I had been going through, said casually, "Maybe you could use some advertising techniques on the kids?"

Ben's idea made sense. I had to get the attention of the class and hold their interest—exactly as a television commercial had to do. A white woman announcing she was going to teach Black History was, at least, attention-compelling and if I organized the information into brief, dramatic "headlines," perhaps I could hold the interest of the students. I sat up late, organizing the material in my mind.

On Monday, October 20, 1969, the newspapers headlined a black student demonstration at West Philadelphia High School. The students protested the "inadequate" job of teaching Black History done by a white teacher. "No white can teach Black History" was their attitude; they demanded a black teacher.

What dandy timing! And there was simply no other subject I knew well enough or that had the same potential to interest the students.

Several times during the week, Ben said, "I wish I could do it for you, honey." So did I. He said, "It's really *not* a matter of life or death, darling." No, it was only a matter of feeling humiliatingly inept.

Friday came too fast. When I entered Mr. Kellogg's room, he growled cheerily, "Didn't expect you back!" This time, the students did not even bother to look at me; they simply continued with whatever talking, strolling, throwing things that they had been doing.

Feeling like Daniel making an announcement to the den of lions, I boomed as loud as my voice could manage: I AM WRITING DOWN THE NAMES OF ALL UNCOOPERATIVE PEOPLE. I waved a notebook. There was a silence. I knew it was decidedly temporary. But I also decided to use it to tell the youngsters exactly how I felt.

I said, "Look, the last two weeks I have found out that I'm probably the world's worst teacher." Several students looked interested, if not amazed. I continued, "It's no fun feeling that you can't do something well, so I'm going to try a new idea and maybe it'll work out better." The class was still quiet. I said, "Let's try this. If you want to do your homework quietly, go to *that* end of the room." Some of the youngsters began to move. I said, "Just a minute. Those who do *not* want to study, go to the other end of the room because . . ." I took a breath and plunged . . . "I'm going to teach some Black History."

Before anyone had time to react, I said, "I'll bet I know more Black History than you do and if you don't believe it, I'll see you over there right now."

One laugh would have squashed me. I heard none. The class moved about while I walked to the end of the room near the doorway. (The two white students again asked if they could go to the library and went.) In my corner, I saw round, chubby Gus Clifford, Donald Welles and, with an openly jeering look on his face, Poncho Webster. Cephas Simpson, the class strangler, slouched at the edge of the group, along with six or seven other youngsters, all boys.

I sat among them, took a breath and plunged. "If you've been reading about that demonstration at West Philadelphia High . . . well, you might be wondering why there's such a problem about teaching Black History. I'm afraid it's because the history books written by whites don't tell the whole truth. For example, the history books I read in eighth grade made it sound as if Africans were a bunch of savages who were dumb enough to get captured and then happily stood around singing 'Old Black Joe' until Abe Lincoln did the kind deed of freeing them."

No one in the group moved. They did not look at me either.

I said, "But that's not the way it really was. Almost a thousand years before Columbus discovered America, there were universities in the African city of Songhay. Askia, the ruler of Songhay, had done such a good job running the city that strangers could leave their possessions in the street overnight and know they would be safe. The first Europeans went to Africa to learn about the good things the Africans were doing."

(150)

Now I had ten pairs of dark brown eyes looking at me. With a sickening flash of insight, I understood why I had grabbed their interest. All through school, I had been taught that my Anglo-Saxon ancestors had civilized the world and, single-handed, built our great country. What kind of pride could these children feel if they were led to believe they were the descendents of docile primitives, fit only for bondage and labor, freed finally through the benevolence of high-minded whites? No wonder they looked hungry for contradictory evidence!

Poncho shifted his heavily muscled shoulders and said, "How come those slaves let themselves get grabbed?"

I said, "Well, what happened was this—The Europeans who came to learn also learned that there were a lot of diamonds and gold and ivory and things. They started trading with the African kings. But the Europeans started running out of things the Africans needed before the Africans ran out of gold. Then some European got the idea that if they made the African kings mad at each other, they could do a terrific business in trading guns and gunpowder. And that worked fine. Then some king—in about 1445—who was losing his wars and was fresh out of gold traded some of his prisoners of war to the Portuguese. Up until then, in African wars, the armies captured their enemies instead of killing them and made them into slaves until their relatives bought them back—ransomed them—or maybe traded them for the prisoners of the other side. Shipping prisoners of war out of the country, selling them to someone else was a whole new thing. And it worked out well. It started to be kind of a fad in Europe for people to have a black servant just because he looked different. Then about fifty years later, Columbus discovered this great big piece of real estate called America and in a while slaves became more valuable than gold. In Europe, where there wasn't too much empty land, people had peasants to do the work, but in America, there was more land than they had people to work it. The native Americans—what Columbus thought were 'Indians'—were not about to stay captured and be slaves. They knew the territory too well and got away. But Africans couldn't. Then too, the white servants—people who were in jails in Europe and could be bought by the American settlers —they escaped and it was pretty hard to find them because they looked like everybody else. Africans didn't."

I was oversimplifying the information for these youngsters, but, as I heard myself speaking, I was surprised it came out as near the facts as it did. Next week, I could tell them about the terrible decision made in America that the *children* of slaves were the property of their owners. In South America, African slaves were allowed to earn their freedom, their children were born free and were allowed to marry whom they pleased. The blurred color lines in South America had saved them the centuries of tension we were still suffering.

To my surprise and unexpected pleasure, Gus Clifford raised his hand, exactly as if I were a real teacher.

"Okay, I getcha. But din't none of them cats try to get away?" he said.

Tall, slim Donald Welles had been sitting absolutely still, his long legs under the table, his arms folded across his chest. He turned his head quickly toward Gus. "Don't be stupid, man. Like puttin' you in some country you don't know . . . like Chicago. You don' know the place; you ain't gonna get outa there. See?"

I said, "That's exactly right, Donald. But a lot of men did try to escape and I'll bring you a book about that next week." I had read Leland's copy of the *Narrative of Solomon Northrup* and Leland brought me a copy of a brand-new paperback edition (*Puttin' On Ole Massa*, Harper Torchbooks, 1969) which included the autobiographies of three former slaves whose escapes made James Bond books seem dull.

The bell rang. No one moved. Poncho raised his bulgingly

muscled arm. "Hey, listen," he said, "how come you talk like this . . . and you *white*."

Donald was on his feet, glaring down at Poncho. "You shut your mother mouth. You don' talk like that to her." Poncho looked ready to spring. It was painful to realize that Donald considered my being called "white" an insult.

I said, "Sure, I'm white. Been white for *years!*" I got a laugh for my joke. I continued, "And, Poncho, that's a good question. You see, white people have been kind of covering up some things for a long time. What I'm telling you is the truth. I happen to think that it's better to tell the truth about the bad things whites did than to get all mixed up about history."

Bulky, heavy Gus Clifford turned his head toward Poncho who looked elaboratedly unalarmed at Donald standing over him. Gus said, "Poncho, she don't want white folks' heads to get messed up. You lie to yourself, you get your head messed up."

I beamed. I had actually taught and my students had listened and they understood. I said, "You're absolutely right, Gus. I'll see you all next week."

I got up and bumped smack into Carter M. Kellogg who had apparently been standing behind me.

He growled, "They gotta put their chairs under the table."

Right. "Chairs under the table, kids," I said. The chairs I helped move were light as feathers. The defeat and hopelessness of the last two weeks was upside down now. It was exhilarating to feel I had given some new information to a group of youngsters and watched their minds work on it. The typically feminine parallel was serving a meal that someone ate with appetite. The humiliation of the last two weeks was worth the feeling I had when I walked out of the room. This must be, I believed, why people became teachers.

ten

FOR THE NEXT EIGHT MONTHS OF MY VOLUNTEER TEACHING, I felt like a spectator who had accidentally wandered out onto the baseball field and got involved in the game. Whether by luck or a knack I never knew I had, most of what I tried worked out astonishingly well. Like any amateur, however, I was to learn gradually that the game was more complex than I thought.

Carter M. Kellogg had, during the first two months, feigned surprise that I came back each week. "You must like punishment," he growled as he left for his rest period. It was no longer punishment for me. I found myself looking forward to Friday afternoons.

The students began to emerge as individuals, some as quickly as photographs in developing liquid, some as reluctantly as buds during a cold spring. Fat, raggedy Lydia Adams never spoke and seldom took her thumb out of her mouth, but Donald Welles, whose physical characteristics reminded me very much of Spike, was obviously the class leader, not by virtue of his size, but through his quick-talking, persuasive wit. He had appointed himself my adviser and protector.

Poncho had found himself in the point of a triangle between me and his stunning girl friend, Althea. She sent him angry looks and sent notes via the short lad I had saved from being strangled. Poncho refused to return to the homework corner where she sat, turning his broad back to her and listening expressionlessly to the Black History discussion. Poncho had a talent for math. Each time I stumbled over the number of years between one event and another, Poncho mumbled out a quick answer. The first few times, I checked the figures after class, using pencil, paper and my fingers. Poncho's instant answers were absolutely accurate.

Although Donald Welles had adopted the paternal protective role with me, Cephas Simpson was the person I intended to hide behind in the unlikely (now) event violence erupted. He looked like an enormous light brown lion, quiet, but coiled to spring. I had looked over his shoulder one day and been surprised by the delicacy of his doodling. This enormous, lumbering fellow had written his name over and over in beautiful, small well-formed script. I had said, "Gee, I wish Spike could write like that! Are you good at drawing too?" After that, Cephas had given me several traced pictures, each meticulously copied in fine, graceful lines.

Gus (Augustus Lamont Clifford) was slow moving, chubby and trilingual. In the hallway, I had heard him spitting expletives at Donald in what I decided was Italian. I learned he had "picked up" Italian and German *and* Polish from neighborhood merchants. Gus said, grinning, "If I curse Donald out in Italian, ain't nobody gonna expel me. Nobody can't tell what I'm sayin'." Gus said he liked learning languages. I offered him my three words of Swahili: *kitabu* (book); *umoja* (together); *uruhu* (freedom) and my one Swahili phrase: *Kama Mama, Kama Binti* ("like mother, like daughter"). I offered to write them down. Gus said, "It's okay. I learn 'em better in my ears."

By the middle of November, the Black History discussion group had expanded to about twenty youngsters: some with vivid personalities like Gus, Poncho and Donald; and some quiet and unobtrusive. Gus and Donald asked most of the questions. Gus, who seemed old for his years, had replaced a brooding skepticism with serious interest. He questioned me closely about Benjamin Banneker, the brilliant black astronomer who also constructed the first American-made wooden clock and who memorized the plans for Washington, D.C., thus preserving them when the French designer left in a huff, taking all the papers with him. Poncho was most fascinated by Garrett Morgan, the black man who invented the gas mask and the electric stoplight, while Donald Welles pulled answers from me about Henry Bibb's frequent escapes from his owner in Kentucky—and his frequent recaptures when he returned to get his wife and child.

While getting to know the youngsters, I was having the same experience of getting to know the teachers in the eighth-grade cycle, partly through what "my" students reported and partly from what I saw and heard in the corridors. The math and science teachers were most liked by the students and least heard shouting in the hallways. The high nasal voice of Miss Arnold, the English teacher who assessed Spike's "background" by my clothes, echoed through the halls angrily, often instructing some child to "go straight to the office." The new history teacher, a bland-faced young man with straight, colorless hair, was, according to Spike, "learning how to handle his class." Perhaps. But I often saw him chatting in the hallway with another new young white male teacher while their classrooms exploded with noise.

It was interesting that the respect and affection the students showed for the math and science teachers had nothing to do with sex or color. The math teacher was a middle-aged white woman; the science teacher a fiftyish black man. Their personalities were strikingly dissimilar: the math teacher was vivacious; the science teacher quiet and serious. Each, however, appeared to enjoy his work and his students.

Carter Kellogg was disliked intensely by the students and it was easy to see why. Several times he had said loudly to me when I came into the room, "Don't forget to watch your purse." Donald and Gus retaliated by asking me, in front of Carter Kellogg, "Why can't you be our real teacher?" Gus added, "Yeah, you're better than *some*." They both looked directly at Carter Kellogg, whose red face got redder.

I laughed quickly and said, "You just like me because I can't flunk you! Anyway, real teachers have college degrees. I only made it out of high school."

The animosity between Miss Arnold and her students was also sadly apparent. Students entering the math or science classrooms looked relaxed and wore smiles; those going into Miss Arnold's room dragged their feet as they passed her tall, lanky figure with its frowning face. Miss Arnold, like the fluttery first-grade teacher, had been at our school for many years and had watched her classes turn black. She had not, for some reason, obtained a transfer and reminded me often that she was "not used to teaching *this* kind of student."

One afternoon, Miss Arnold again stopped me in the hall-way to say she was trying very hard to improve Spike's hand-writing. "He's one of the few *worth* helping, you know. I take him home in my heart every night. The others . . . well, you know, whatever we do for them, the home undoes."

I forced myself to smile up at her and suggested that then it might be better if she took some other child "home in her heart." I did have time to help Spike at home, I said, "so wouldn't it be better to help some child whose parents aren't able to?"

Miss Arnold's lined, yellowish face turned slightly orange. She said, gaily, "Ah, you're such an idealist, Mrs. Stalvey! But you must have heard of Arthur Jensen's discoveries. After all, one can't make silk purses out of sow's ears." She began to close her classroom door.

My smile was more a baring of my teeth and I said, "Or lead a horse to water!"

Carter Kellogg was waiting impatiently at his classroom

door. "They're all yours," he growled and walked quickly away. It was more difficult to understand his antagonism toward the students (and, though I may have been imagining it, toward me lately) than Miss Arnold's. He was young and his Peace Corps work marked him as somewhat of an idealist. He had been eager and enthusiastic when we first met. Now he stomped off to the teachers' room, glaring at students as he passed.

I went into the classroom where the students reminded me immediately that I had promised we would discuss the possibility of an afternoon dance for the seventh and eighth grades. It seemed to me that there was something valuable I could teach about organizing projects and these active, healthy youngsters could use an outlet for their energy. In my own teens, the city of Milwaukee had opened a number of high schools for dancing on Friday and Saturday nights. I could still remember the exhilarating exhaustion and relaxation after these weekends. Sports programs required equipment, coaches, rules and scorekeeping; dancing required only a phonograph and a floor. If the youngsters were closely involved in the planning, I felt we might avoid potential problems.

Donald Welles had already formulated a plan. "Mrs. Peters don't want no dancing," he said, "so she's gonna say that the gym teacher won't let us use the gym. But the gym teacher's okay. What we gotta do is you talk to the gym teacher first, Mrs. Stalvey. Don't tell Mrs. Peters. Then when she say the gym teacher don't let us, you say she already say okay. Got it?"

I thought so. Donald understood Vangie Peters better than I did. He and Gus also explained that the dance should be only for Willis School kids. "We have it too wide open, we gonna get gangs here and trouble." Some of the girls wanted a nighttime dance. Poncho shook his head. "Daytime," he said positively. I agreed. It was easier to get permission to keep the school open an hour longer than to open it up again at night. Poncho said, "More fights at night."

It was an unpleasant shock to find these children had to plan against violence. Gangs, however, were a fact of life, just as they had been generations ago when the children of European immigrants ran in gangs throughout their low-income neighborhoods. A white neighbor who taught a course in urban problems at a local university told me that each immigrant group had gone through the same experiences. "Young people reject their parents' values. They see that the parents are unsuccessful in the American culture. The children formed their own groups for recreation and protection and as a way to develop their own 'success.' There were Irish gangs, Italian gangs, Polish gangs—and 'native' American gangs one rung up—all of whom fought each other. The white children eventually grew up and blended into American society." For black children, the blending had not been as easy.

That day, the students appointed me as emissary to the gym teacher and Vangie Peters. It was also decided that I should be in charge of the phonograph. "Or everybody's gonna be pushin' the songs they want next," Gus explained. The youngsters also chose their adult chaperones, people they liked: a minister, the popular manager of the luncheonette across from school and several other parents.

My visit to the gym teacher and to Vangie Peters went exactly as Donald predicted. Our dance was scheduled for the Wednesday before Thanksgiving. Carter Kellogg said, "Those gorillas will kill each other." Even the popular science teacher raised a dark eyebrow.

On the day of the dance, I sat with the phonograph and two piles of records, fast and slow, while over two hundred students, the seventh and eighth grades, milled around the gym. At first, only the mature, sophisticated youngsters like Poncho and Donald and their friends from their block danced. Soon, other youngsters slipped out onto the gym floor like pieces of dark iron drawn by the magnet of the music. I watched Spike through the crowd as he followed several girls around, apparently trying to work up courage to ask for a dance. He caught my eye, glared at me and I tried to keep from watching him. The next time I sneaked a look, he was gyrating opposite a slender, brown young lady. Even Spike's left-footed friend, Tony, had joined in the dancing.

From the corner of my eye, I caught a glimpse of someone who should not be there: Noah. Sixth graders were not invited. I put on a new record, walked over to escort him out the door. On my way, I met three tall lads who were entering the gym. They were not from our school. I said, including them in my remark to Noah, "Only seventh- and eighth-grade kids and only from our school." Noah said, "Aw, Mom!" One of the tall fellows said, "He your kid?" Yes. He said to his companions, "Okay. Fair's fair. Let's go." They left.

Donald met me on the way back to the phonograph. "What did those guys say?" I told him. "Wow. That's Dogtown gang's top men."

The dance was over sooner than I expected. I had enjoyed the music and watching the children dance. The cleanup crew got to work quickly while I checked the school grounds and the luncheonette across the street to see if the excitement of the dance had created any problems. The waitress at the luncheonette told me, "My only complaint is that nobody invited me." The students, she said, had been unusually orderly.

Even though Vangie Peters told me the union would not allow her to ask the teachers to chaperone the dance, all the teachers had come to observe. The next week, Carter Kellogg said, "None of the white kids came." But they had. The math teacher told me, "I think the children have been calmer since the dance." Miss Arnold said, "They were dancing too close

(160)

during the slow tunes. But they do have a natural sense of rhythm, don't they!"

The youngsters were anxious to plan another dance. In the end we had one each month. After the first dance, Spike, who now was willing to acknowledge our acquaintance in the hallway, told me, "That was cool, Mom. Your class is always called 'the worst class.' Now they're known as the class that planned the dance."

That bonus had not occurred to me, but I was becoming aware of several advantages to me and to my children from my "teaching" position. Spike was at an age when he did not want too much maternal interest or advice. Students in my class now pulled me aside to ask my opinion on hairdos, life and romance. I was able to use up all the excess maternity.

Noah and Sarah enjoyed the idea of My-Mother-the-Teacher. Noah said that Miss Grenelli "was gonna hit Georgie. Then you came around the corner and she put her hand down." (Miss Grenelli, who had addressed wedding invitations when she was Spike's social studies teacher, had apparently wasted her time. The wedding, I learned, was called off that year.) Sarah thought it was "cool" that I was teacher to "kids bigger than you are!"

By spring, our discussion group had got to contemporary Black History and I had told the students about black men who had made outstanding contributions to America: Jan Matzeliger who invented the shoe-lasting machine, Frederick Jones who developed the first refrigeration system for railroad cars and trucks, Elijah McCoy who perfected the self-oiling machine and gave a new phrase to the American language when industrialists insisted on "the *real* McCoy" machine, not an imitation.

After this subject was discussed, Poncho said, "Can I talk to you?" He led me to a corner and glared away other students. He whispered, "What d'you call those guys who made that stuff?" I told him, engineers, but I wondered why it was such a secret question. The next week, when we got off on the subject of careers, Poncho announced casually to the group, "Engineering is my bag." Proud Poncho had not wanted to reveal his ignorance by asking a question.

The following week, I brought in a clipping from the black-owned *Philadelphia Tribune* to give to Poncho. It gave biographies of McCoy, Matzeliger and Garrett Morgan. Poncho thanked me, but after class, I noticed he had forgotten to take it with him. His next class was with Miss Arnold and I decided to take the clipping to him there.

The class was in session when I tiptoed into the room. Miss Arnold graciously gave me permission to give the clipping to Poncho and then turned to where he was sitting and shrieked, "Don't you even know enough to rise when Mrs. Stalvey enters the room?" I was appalled by her unfairness; Poncho did not know I had come to see him. He rose, looking at the floor. I rushed to him, handed him the clipping and slunk out, feeling helpless.

I had stood by just as helplessly the week before when Carter Kellogg berated another student. As I came into his room, he was growling to one of the smaller boys in the class, "Don't open your dumb mouth! You don't have the brains to say anything I want to hear." The boy seemed to shrink as Carter Kellogg sneered. As Kellogg left the room, Gus Clifford looked as if he wanted to hit him. I grabbed Gus and asked, "What happened?" Gus said, "Albert was only trying to borrow a pencil." I said to Albert, now sitting head down and deflated, "People don't mean the things they say when they get angry." Albert said, "*He* means it."

I had also learned that unfeeling attitudes were not limited to white teachers and that they did not begin in the upper grades. A few weeks before I had been walking through the main part of the building on my way to my class when a thin, light-skinned Negro teacher called to me.

"Mrs. Stalvey, I'd like your opinion," the woman said. "This boy brought me some flowers and I think he stole them." A little boy, one of her second-grade students, looked up at me with tears just beginning to roll down his dark-brown cheeks.

I had crouched down to the child. "You are wonderful to bring flowers to your teacher. If I were your teacher, I would be so pleased." (And if I were your teacher, I said to myself, I would know that seven-year-olds may not yet know that flowers can be owned by anyone.)

The teacher's whining voice continued, "Maybe he's not lying. It's so hard to tell with children of this type."

I said to the little boy, "If you gave me flowers, I'd know you liked me and I'd be so happy."

The teacher said, "Well, all right, Robert. Thank you."

I had told Jane Banneker about the incident. She shook her head and sighed. "Unfortunately, Lois, our group has its bigots too. Some light-complexioned Negroes are more hostile to darker-skinned children than whites are. The 'almost-whites' hate being identified with the 'purely black.'"

But white or black, I was beginning to realize, teachers had tremendous, unsupervised power over their pupils. Some of the wounds I had seen left no visible scars and could be inflicted in the privacy of a classroom. Yet if a student retaliated, he would be the one punished.

I did not know what to do about what I was seeing. If I spoke to Vangie Peters, I would be told how "right" I was and nothing would happen. Carter Kellogg and Miss Arnold were not likely to welcome my amateur views on child psychology. Carter Kellogg was already treating me with a distinct coldness while Miss Arnold blithely ignored my hints that "children like Poncho respond so well to friendliness."

All I could think to do was to steer my class discussion group to the subject of what do we do with angry feelings. There were, I told the group, harmless ways of working off angry feelings. "You, Cephas, can draw a picture of what you wished would happen to the person you're mad at. You can punch a pillow instead of the person. Honestly," I told dubious-looking faces, "it works. Try it. You can also write a letter—but don't mail it—telling the person how angry you are."

These mild middle-class ways of dealing with anger seemed puny indeed the following week when Gus Clifford shot out of Miss Arnold's classroom and nearly knocked me down. He walked to the wall and punched it. I said, "What's the matter?" "I'm gonna kill that woman," Gus said, pounding a fist into his hand. I got him into the empty teachers' room. He breathed as if he had been running. I repeated several times, "What happened?" Finally, he heard me.

"She started picking on Lydia. She said, 'I can see why five foster homes sent you back! Your grandma *had* to take you.' She ain't got no right doin' us that way."

Gus confessed he had called Miss Arnold a "bitch" and left the room—"before I killed her." I felt empty and aching. So that was why Lydia sat, thumb in mouth and hostile. It was too painful even to imagine how she must feel.

I was the lightning rod for Gus's anger. As he raved, I sat, nodding and sharing it. A psychologist can probably explain why, but when his anger had drained into me, Gus suddenly appeared calm. He said, "Well, she's old. Nobody gonna change her. No kids, no husband. She got nothin'. Maybe she worse off than Lydia."

I opened my mouth to argue with Gus, then closed it. If he, at fourteen, had the incredible maturity and resilience to try to understand Miss Arnold, I should not argue. It was terribly upside down when a child had to give understanding to a teacher, but if Gus could do it, he had won.

The bell rang. Gus stood up. He looked exhausted, but calm. He said, "Gotta go now. Thanks." He went into the hall to join the group of youngsters around Lydia.

On May 4, 1970, four students were killed by national

guardsmen at Kent State in Ohio; on May 14, more students were killed at Jackson State College in Mississippi. My eighth-grade class showed a remarkable lack of interest in both events. Perhaps these events were less real to them than the thirty youngsters killed in eight months in Philadelphia in gang wars.

By the end of May, I had exhausted my lecture material on Black History and had become a bit disappointed that none of the students had been motivated to do any further study on their own. I had brought books to school and offered them to the youngsters. Some of the students leafed through them, but they were always left lying on the desk at the end of the period. Yet during the discussions, the children were full of questions and comments, seemingly eager for information. Perhaps, I decided, I had made it too easy by giving them the information instead of encouraging them to look it up for themselves. I announced that I had told them all I knew about Black History and hoped they would go on through their own reading.

I asked for suggestions for new topics of discussion. Donald Welles said "Shut your mouth" to Gus Clifford when Gus grinningly suggested we discuss sex. I said there was nothing wrong in discussing sex, and we had a session in which it developed that these children were far less informed than my own children. They also showed great relief when I told them I had been extremely curious about sex when I was a teen-ager. Again, I brought in books on sex written for teen-agers. Again, no one took the books home.

Luckily, I had no illusions about being a real teacher. I wished I had been taught how to get the children to build on what we discussed. This apparently was what was taught in teachers' colleges and I envied Carter Kellogg this knowledge. My popularity with the students which seemed to irritate him was only because I did not need to demand that they study.

It took a confusing incident with Carter Kellogg and then

Jane Banneker's interpretation before I could understand the strange change in him since our first meeting years before and his present antagonism toward his class and toward me.

He had telephoned me at home shortly after I had left his classroom. His growly voice cracked with anger. "Those monkeys . . . those . . . those . . . You cannot have them in my classroom anymore. You'll have to take them to the auditorium. They wrecked my room. They threw India ink over everything."

"While I was with them?" I asked. Could the students have done this without my noticing? If so, it was my responsibility. I added, "Did the ink get on the carpeting?" The side of the room where the homework group sat was carpeted and ink there would be disastrous.

"Yes, while you were with them and yes, it got on the carpeting."

I said I would be right there and hung up the phone. At least I could help him clean up.

When I walked into the room, Carter Kellogg said, "It's all cleaned up." I asked if he had got it out of the carpeting. He said yes. "But there's some I missed," he said, pointing to a Formica tabletop.

But that smudge of ink was there when we came into the room! All during the discussion period, I had carefully avoided getting my arm on the dried ink blot. I had meant to clean it off before I left but had forgotten.

Carter Kellogg insisted the ink had not been there. I asked to see where the ink had been removed from the carpet. There was no cleaned spot I could see. Carter Kellogg avoided my eyes.

That evening, I telephoned Jane Banneker. I could not understand his anger at the students and, obliquely, at me. Why would he want to blame my class for damage they did not do?

(166)

Jane sighed. "He wanted so much to be popular with the students. But he doesn't understand this kind of student and they don't understand him. We've had a lot of young white teachers who have all kinds of dreams about what they're going to accomplish. Some leave, some get bitter."

Unfortunately, Jane's words fit the facts. The first time we had met Carter Kellogg, he said he had dropped out of the Peace Corps because he believed urban education would be "more satisfying." Evidently, it was not. Perhaps he had tried very hard and in the end, his disappointment had turned into anger at the students.

My concern about Carter Kellogg was wiped out during the last weeks of school by an even more horrifying discovery. By now, I thought I knew my students so well. I was proud of the abilities I saw in them, of Donald's organizational ability that kept the dances going successfully, of Poncho's talent for fixing projectors and doing math in his head, of Gus's compassion for his classmates and even for the teachers. I had not realized that none of my students had ever shown me their report cards. No one, however, appeared to be worried about failing.

The first week in June, I asked Poncho whether he had finished reading the clipping I had given him. He silently pulled it out from his notebook. I asked if he wanted to read some of it out loud for the rest of the group. He said, "No, my throat's sore." Someone tittered. I asked Gus if he would read it. "Don't read too good without my glasses," Gus said.

Donald grabbed the clipping from the table. He began, "Uh . . . this guy . . . uh."

I said, "Matzeliger."

"Yeah, Matzeliger. When Matzeliger first went to . . . uh . . . work . . . in a . . . Hey, this is small type here. You read it, Mrs. Stalvey."

I felt sick as I took the clipping from Donald and began

to read out loud. Years of reading to my own children when they were small had taught me to read words while I thought of other things and now, as I mechanically pronounced the words in front of my eyes, I felt like screaming instead. These children could not read!

No wonder they had never taken my books home. But what on earth were they going to do when they got into the big junior high when they would get far less attention than they got here?

Poncho and Gus and Donald were giving me appraising glances. I made myself smile as if I had not guessed their secret. But how could these children get through eight years of the same school as Spike and be unable to read? How had I been so stupid as to miss this fact for eight months? No wonder my discussion group was so popular. I was giving them information they could get in no other way.

But how had they felt when I gaily discussed careers? I had talked in terms of college. Had I encouraged them to dream? If so, I was being more cruel than Miss Arnold or Carter Kellogg Unless some miracle occurred, these young men had no future whatsoever.

When I left the classroom that day, I felt as if I were leaving a sick room, trying to act as if I believed the patient was going to get well.

At home, I said to Spike, "Those kids can't read!"

Spike was rushing out the door to meet his friends, Tony and Dave. But he stopped, looked surprised and said, "Mom, didn't you know that?"

I waved him on. I could ask him later, rhetorically, how any child could go through eight years of school without learning to read. I had no idea he could tell me. That day, I just wanted to sit in my kitchen, trying to recover from what felt like witnessing the death of friends.

eleven

AFTER SPIKE LEFT THE HOUSE THAT BLEAK AFTERNOON, I sat numbly at the kitchen window, watching Sarah and Noah playing in the driveway. For a moment, I wished we had left the school with the other parents after sixth grade. If so, I would not have volunteered to teach, would not have got to care about children I did not know how to help. Then a phrase of Mrs. Jefferson's crossed my mind. During the frustrating times of Spike's worst study problems, she had said while mopping the kitchen, "What hurts most learns you most." Well, finding that Gus and Poncho, who seemed to have such potential, could not read had hurt. I had read statistics about low reading scores in big city schools, but looking into the faces of youngsters who did not know that their illiteracy doomed them was more painful than reading statistics. What could I learn from this hurt?

Even before Spike took me on a nightmare tour through eight years of school, during which he, but not others, had been taught to read, I was able to glean a few new insights. I had believed the students in my class were similar to my children and, of course, they were not. Gus, Poncho, Donald and Cephas were not from middle-class homes; they were from Taylor Street and Dorland Street, considered the "slums" of West Mt. Airy. Miss Arnold had once said to me, her thin mouth curled in disgust, "Why, the mothers of some of these children are *domestics*!" I had told her, politely but pointedly, that Mrs. Jefferson, who cleaned for us, would literally give her life for a decent education for her children.

The contrast between Mrs. Jefferson's home atmosphere or the homes of my eighth-grade class and mine was vivid. While Mrs. Jefferson cleaned five different houses each week to help pay for the family's frequent moves near "better schools," I had the leisure to read and to let my children see me reading. I had the time to drive Spike, Noah and Sarah to the library, the money to subscribe to children's book clubs and to stock our home library with reference books. Our children had grown up hearing Ben and me discuss the excitement, entertainment and information between the covers of those rectangular things piled around the house. When I had offered Mrs. Jefferson books that might interest her, she had taken them, but said, "Hope you don't care how long I takes to read it. Mos' nights when I gets home, can jus' make it through cleanin' my own house an' makin' dinner." Mr. Jefferson, employed as a laborer, was even more physically exhausted. If my own mother had not come home to a house cleaned by my grandmother and to an already-prepared dinner, she would not have had the strength to read to me as a child. I—and in their turn, my children—would not have learned to anticipate the wonderful day when we could finally understand those marks on paper that let us unlock reading adventures by ourselves.

Yet Ben and I had not tried to teach our children to read at home. It was important, we believed, for them to learn through the methods used in school. And the school had taught them to read well. Why had the same school failed to teach Gus and Poncho and Donald?

Spike returned early that afternoon. While I monitored the pot roast, I asked again, rhetorically, how these youngsters had failed to learn to read.

Spike sat on the counter, picked up the pepper grinder and as his long fingers began to dismantle it, he explained. At age fourteen, he had knowledge that "educational researchers" lacked. He had been in the classroom when no other adults were there to put teachers on their best behavior. His own struggles had given him empathy and insight into what had happened.

Spike said, "I thought you knew they couldn't read. All the other teachers do. They don't even bother to call on those kids. They kind of act like they're not there. That's probably why those kids liked you so much. Because you didn't treat 'em as if they were dumb."

They were not "dumb." Even I could recognize the slack features and dull-eyed look of low intelligence. These youngsters were bright-eyed and alert.

With his long legs now propped on a chair, Spike poured pepper corns into his hand and began at the beginning. "Look, Mom, these kids started out being put in the dumb class. Remember when Mrs. Peters took me out of Mrs. Grant's class and put me with Mrs. Schmidt? Well, Mrs. Peters said, right out loud to Mrs. Grant, 'I'm taking the bright students to Mrs. Schmidt.' Don't ever tell Gus Clifford that I told you, but he started to cry.

"I didn't see any of those kids in the so-called 'slow' classes until you had me put in Mrs. Othello's room that time, you know, for third grade when you didn't want me in the fast class for a while. Mrs. Peters made a big thing out of my not belonging there. And most of those kids couldn't read." My five-foot-eleven-inch eighth grader said seriously, "I was just a kid then, but even I thought it was dumb to put *all* the poor readers in one class. Mrs. Othello had me helping some of them during reading period, but, Mom, there were so *many* kids who couldn't read.

"I stopped doing my homework in fourth grade and lots of other kids did too. We all saw we weren't gonna flunk no matter what we did. Nobody ever had to repeat a grade unless their parents made them." Spike looked at me with a grin. He guessed somehow that Ben and I had talked to Vangie about Spike's repeating fourth grade. She had been aghast. According to her, "Children are scarred for life by the humiliation of repeating a grade!" Perhaps, but fear of flunking was primarily what had made me work on the boring parts of my studies—in elementary and high school.

"In fifth grade, Miss Banneker really worked hard on the slower kids. She was the only teacher who acted like she cared more about the slow kids than the smart kids. She used to have a whole bunch of them come over to her house after school."

In the sixth-grade cycle, according to Spike, only the English and science teachers "didn't make fun of the slow kids or send 'em to the office as often as they could. Some of those kids hardly spent any time in class! Mr. Kellogg used to let me get up and stretch my legs, but if Donald Welles did it, he got sent to Mrs. Peters. But Miss Grenelli was the one who was really nasty. One day Cephas raised his hand just a little bit, you know, like he wasn't *sure* he knew the answer, and Miss Grenelli said, real sneery, 'Well, look who thinks he can answer something!' Cephas called her a name and she took him out in the hallway. You could hear her yelling and it sounded like she tried to hit him or something. Cephas just walked back in the room laughing."

I shuddered. Cephas had learned a lesson that day. If he could not achieve intellectually, he now found he could control situations through his physical size.

"Mom, some of those teachers could make kids feel dumb without saying anything. And they kind of got across the idea to the rest of us that black kids were bad except for a few. Those teachers had a funny look on their face when those kids raised their hands. They didn't even call on some of 'em. One time, Poncho had his hand up and some other kid, I forget who, said, 'Don't bother. She'll call on Fineberg anyway.' She did."

"After a while," Spike continued, "teachers acted like those slow kids weren't even there—and then, if Mrs. Peters needed someone to help unload books or help the janitor, the teachers would send the slow kids instead of the smart ones. It just didn't make any sense at all."

If Spike had not suffered from being called "stupid" by his first-grade teacher, would he have developed the sensitivity to what was being done to other children? Yet Spike's "slowness" in academic subjects had been treated with tremendous concern. Was this because it was difficult for them to label and ignore the child of educated, middle-class parents? Spike, I knew, still carried the scars from first grade. Only recently, he had ripped up some drawings of carefully designed space capsules, saying, "I'm too stupid to do anything right." But Spike had got maximum attention from his teachers, from Vangie Peters and help from his parents. Children like Cephas, Gus and Poncho had had their belief in their own "stupidity" reinforced constantly by every conscious and unconscious act of teachers who could use their "backgrounds" as an excuse.

A deeply depressing thought about bussing suddenly came into my mind. I had supported the idea, wryly aware that my children were in the kind of school other whites were afraid to be bussed *to*. My children, I knew, would never be bussed out. Ben and I had often laughed over the fact that we could simultaneously support the neighborhood school concept *and* bussing. But why bother moving children's bodies around to achieve integrated education if, like the black children in our school, they could not escape teachers with segregating eyes?

Spike, as I expected, dropped the disassembled pepper grinder and as we picked up pepper corns from the kitchen floor, he said to me, "See, Mom, that's why I told you not to act mean with those kids in your class. They got treated mean for years." That moment, on the floor, I decided that, even though Spike was still not doing top work academically and even if he never did, he had learned things more important than what was shown on his report cards.

When we got most of the pepper corns picked up, Spike

said to me, "Remember when you said that reading was gonna be the key that opened all kinds of special doors? Well, it does, but I don't know what those other kids are gonna do in high school."

Spike left the room and I was glad because as he spoke a strange tension had been building up in me. A memory was being jarred loose and as I sat at the kitchen counter, I fought against some strong emotion. I knew exactly how those non-reading children felt and I did not want to remember why. But the emotion—a breathtaking mixture of shame and hate—burst through. No pictures came with the memory. I still cannot remember the teacher's name or face, but after all those years since my childhood, the emotion was as strong as ever.

I had always joked about my inability to do math and, all too casually, blamed my block on a third-grade teacher I didn't like, a substitute who finished out the last few months of a semester. I could not, I had always admitted gaily, memorize the multiplication tables past the sixes or get the same sum twice in adding a column of figures. But I had usually got by with paper, pencil, fingers to count on or people to ask. My success in a welcoming white world had helped me to suppress a memory that was too painful to examine and until that day, I had kept it at bay. I remembered now. In my mind, I was again standing in the classroom while humiliating words hit my seven-year-old ears. At the age of forty-four, the pain was still so acute that I could not recall the words—only the hate, the humiliation and the lifelong fear of working with numbers.

And I knew now that Poncho and Gus and Donald would feel the same as I had felt later in high school. I could remember my panic and loneliness when everyone but me understood algebra. I had tried, unaware of the block that was keeping me back, and though I was passed along, from year to year, I felt shame and isolation as I got farther and farther behind. At the time, I was relieved when I got a passing grade, relieved and surprised. Now I could guess why I had not been failed

(174)

and held back. Like the nonreaders, I was labeled "too hard to teach" and pushed along.

Yet my math block was not as serious as the inability to read. The doors to science had been closed to me, but illiteracy closed all doors. I knew enough arithmetic to function and could, slowly if necessary, figure out what I needed to know. Nonreaders could not. Even the reading of installment contracts, instructions on food packages and employment applications were insurmountable chores. It would be like trying to survive in a foreign country where people *spoke* English, but where every written word was unintelligible. Like Mrs. Jefferson's son, Ernie, one could not even read the street and bus signs and find one's way home.

Like Ernie and Poncho and Gus and *me*, pride would preclude progress. Pages of numbers made me feel scared, defeated and numb. I had never improved in math because I was too afraid to face my own stupidity. Nonreaders, with far less security than I, would feel the same. *Black* nonreaders with the myths of inferiority to haunt them would feel even worse.

That afternoon, sitting in my kitchen, prodding even so gently at the memories of my own childhood failures, I wished for the first time in my life that I had gone to college. If I had, it would mean only a few additional credits and I could be a teacher, giving help instead of merely empathy. As it was, it would take years—years during which children like Poncho and Gus and Donald would experience failure in junior high and in high school, would graduate to low-paying dead-end jobs if they graduated at all. While I attacked college math with a new motivation, these young men might be facing the reality of their limited futures, obliterating the pain with drugs or grabbing "success" in the violent ways open to them—robbery, mugging, burglary.

Ben had no more idea than I of what could be done immediately. He said he would help in every way if I wanted to go on to college. Meanwhile, he suggested, perhaps I should talk with the district superintendent. Perhaps the man did not know that children were being graduated from our school unable to read.

All right. But I wanted to have one more talk with Vangie before I did this. I said to Ben, "I know she tells me what she thinks I want to hear, but maybe she really doesn't know everything that goes on at school. Perhaps the teachers act differently when she's around."

Ben's outdoorsman's face looked concerned and tender. "Honey," he said, "I just don't want you to be disappointed. You know, you can't save the whole world."

I did not expect to. But Ben himself had pointed out the consequences of what I was seeing. In his job of trying to enforce the Philadelphia Plan and create equal job opportunities in the construction trades, he had known of several black men, highly qualified in their specialties but unable to pass the written tests that would admit them into the union. It was just barely possible that Vangie did not realize how far-reaching the consequences were.

Even though Vangie had been carefully avoiding me since my outburst over Lester Northrup and the condoms, she agreed readily to come to our house on Monday after school. In our living room, I listened resignedly to her flattery about my "inborn ability to handle *all* children" and my "loyalty to the school." "Lois, you're the only parent I can count on for honesty," she said.

When she stopped for breath, I pounced on the opening. "Thank you, Vangie. And I want to be very honest with you right now." I praised her imaginative, tireless efforts to prevent the re-segregation of the school. Her light lavender-toned skin turned pink with pleasure. I added, "But, Vangie, there are other problems I think are more important." I told her of all the sad episodes I had witnessed between Miss Arnold, Carter

Kellogg and the children, of Spike's description of how children had reached the eighth grade unable to read.

Vangie continued to smile as I said, "Wooing white parents is not as important as helping teachers teach *all* the children. If my three kids get the best education in the world, it's not going to be enough if children like Donald and Gus can't make an honest living. I don't want my children meeting them in ten years as muggers or welfare cases." Vangie's fixed smile brought a pleading tone to my voice. "Vangie, if you want to do something for Spike, Sarah and Noah, then give the attention you have been giving them to the children who don't have as much going for them in their homes. In the end, you'll be helping my children most."

By now, I was leaning across our white sofa, my hands on the center cushion that was between Vangie and me. Her orange linen dress looked beautiful against the whites of the sofa and the wall, but I wished I knew what was going on inside her head with its lacquered ebony hair.

"Oh, Lois, you're so right. If *only* all my white parents felt as you do! And our school *is* progressing! There's the most marvelous white family from the South . . . and they are sending their *four* children to our school next year. Isn't that *marvelous*?"

That evening, I told Ben, "This time it wasn't even like talking to a mirror. It was like talking to a television set. No matter what I said, she answered from some unchanging script."

The next morning, I telephoned for an appointment with Dr. Charles Kornreich, the district superintendent. After giving my name, I received an appointment for the following afternoon.

Dr. Kornreich was a short, round man who looked like a beardless Santa Claus. His little blue eyes twinkled and his chubby cheeks bounced as he came across his large office to meet me at the door. Ah, he had heard so much about me—

(177)

all my valuable time contributed to Mrs. Peters' school! He escorted me tenderly to a large, overstuffed easy chair across from his desk. I would not have been surprised if he had asked me to sit on his knee and tell him what I wanted for Christmas. Instead, he sat at his desk in a higher-than-average chair and beamed down at me. Now, he said, what was on my pretty mind?

I tried to be fair in my recital of the problems at our school. I began by assuring him that our three children had learned well, both academically and about people. I was concerned, I told him, solely about what I had seen being done to other children. I reported only the incidents I had personally been involved in.

Dr. Kornreich raised his white bushy eyebrows. "Breaking a window with a child's head? This was not reported to me." He made a note on a yellow pad, his thick pink fingers scribbling rapidly. I told him about Miss Arnold's verbal attacks on students, about Carter Kellogg's demeaning attitude.

Dr. Kornreich, scribbling away, said, "They treat *white* children like this?"

Oh, no. The children I had seen verbally and physically attacked had all happened to be black. Dr. Kornreich put down his pencil.

I continued, "Dr. Kornreich, Mrs. Peters has done a wonderful job of attracting new white families and trying to keep them happy at our school. The reputation she has established will continue to attract new white families. I think, though, that we need a principal with different talents now, someone to work with the teachers to help them teach children who can't get help at home. Mrs. Peters could be used so well in some other neighborhood that's just beginning to integrate."

Dr. Kornreich crinkled his merry little eyes at me. "Ah, Mrs. Stalvey, it's so refreshing to talk with you. Most parents come here only with special pleas for their own children. I am proud to be in the same district with a parent like you who cares about all the children."

Yes, thank you, I said, but could he please consider using Mrs. Peters' unique and considerable talents in some school area that was just becoming integrated? "Maybe Crestwood?" I suggested.

Dr. Kornreich's mind was probably on his next appointment. Still smiling merrily, he said, as if to himself, "Um. No, we've already written off Crestwood."

Dr. Kornreich obviously did not realize he had spoken his thought out loud. Mrs. Jefferson had just told me they were moving to Crestwood, futilely, it appeared. The schools and the children were already "written off" by the district office. I remembered how it felt when I found out grownups lied, that there was no Santa Claus.

At the door to his office, Dr. Kornreich patted my shoulder and chuckled, "Please remember to come to me with any problems." He patted my hand and said, "So *good* to meet you." He patted my back as I left. "If only we had more parents like you, my dear."

The meeting had been as productive as writing a letter to the North Pole.

Long before the summer of 1970, I had learned to understand the anger and despair of black militants. During the last two weeks of June, I realized I was acting out of the same belligerent hopelessness.

The day after my visit with Dr. Kornreich, I noticed the paperback book Noah was using in Miss Grenelli's reading class. It had ugly gouges in its back where Noah had used a ballpoint pen to obliterate several words. I looked closely. The words Noah had obliterated on his copy of *Huckleberry Finn* were "Nigger" in "Nigger Jim." At lunchtime, I was in Miss Grenelli's classroom, announcing coldly that I would not permit Noah, at the age of twelve, to read this book and would, in addition, take up the question with black parents at the next Home and School meeting. Miss Grenelli chewed her gum and sputtered about "classics."

True, but there were plenty of other classics that did not have words that hurt people. However, I shrugged, if she continued to use the book, Noah was to spend the reading period in the office and I would mention the subject at the parents meeting.

The books were collected after lunch.

In Jane Banneker's room, I reacted impetuously to another horror. Sarah had spent a calming year influenced by Jane, but one day I glanced up at the ceiling and saw the same sagging plaster I had noticed when Spike was in fifth grade. It was bulging even more dangerously. Jane said, no, it had never been fixed. She routed the children around the side of the room each day to avoid walking beneath it. "It worries me, but I'm even more worried about the stair railings that were removed and never replaced," she said.

I telephoned the director of school maintenance. I told him crisply that since my children's safety was at stake, I was calling my lawyer and the newspapers unless the ceiling and stairs were fixed by Wednesday. The man protested that this was impossible. I said, then I would make my phone calls to our attorney and the papers. He asked me to hold the line. In a few minutes, he came back to ask if I could give them until Thursday. Thursday noon, Sarah reported they had new railings and a "fixed ceiling."

On Friday afternoon, I went to "my" class. I felt bitterly angry seeing Donald and Poncho and Gus, knowing I could do so little for them. Althea, Poncho's girl friend, told me that the class had been denied permission to have a graduation party in their classroom. "Mrs. Peters says we're the worst class the school's ever had an' we don't *deserve* a party!" Althea said tearfully. I said, "Okay. We'll have it at my house after school." If I could give these youngsters little of what they needed, I could at least give them popcorn, punch and hot dogs. At the party, Lydia talked for the first time, telling me she was "gonna have a house like this when I get old." Near the end of the party, the youngsters suddenly surrounded me while Althea made a little speech and handed me a gift with a card each child had signed. They all thought they understood why I cried.

Vangie Peters telephoned the next day to thank me "for our marvelous new ceiling. How did those eighth graders behave at your house?" I told her that the Clean-Up Committee had found nothing to clean up. I added, "Vangie, I think you ought to know that I suggested to Dr. Kornreich that your talents ought to be used in another school that's just beginning to integrate."

"Yes, I know. He was so thrilled to meet you," she said.

The last Home and School Association meeting of the year was on June 23. Black parents who had heard about *Huckleberry Finn,* about the ceiling and stair railings came up to whisper their thanks. "Aren't you afraid she'll take it out on your children?" several mothers asked. The thought had never occurred to me.

On Spike's graduation day, Ben had to attend a meeting in Washington. I sat alone in the auditorium. It was an important day for Spike and I tried to focus only on him. He would not be getting any of the academic awards. Even on his medication, he had not been able to make up for six years of an undiagnosed handicap. I was happy that he would get a Service-to-the-School award for tutoring third-grade students all year.

Vangie began to announce the names of the students who were getting the Service-to-the-School certificate. From the front of the room, she looked directly at me and said, "And that's all."

On the stage, Spike looked stunned.

All the way home, Spike, who was usually unconcerned

about recognition, expressed simple puzzlement. "It's just weird, Mom. Honest, I went tutoring more than anybody."

I held back my tears until we were safely in the garage. I turned off the motor and said to Spike, "Honey, I think it was my fault that you didn't get the Service Award. All those things I did made Mrs. Peters mad. I think Mrs. Peters wanted to hurt me and she knew that hurting you would do it." And she had. When flattery had not kept me quiet, she had found another pressure point that worked. Tears flowed down my face, half because of Spike's being deprived of the one award he was able to earn and half because my actions had hurt my child.

I got out of the car, wiping my eyes. Spike followed me, looking worried. He touched me on the shoulder, "Listen, Mom. Don't cry. You did the right things. Anyway, I don't care about that stupid award. If Dad can lose his job because of you, I can lose some dumb award."

Spike looked relieved when my broad, heartfelt smile broke through my tears. Vangie had inadvertently given me something so much more valuable than a certificate we could frame. She had given me proof of what kind of man my son was growing up to be.

twelve

SPIKE'S GRADUATION FROM EIGHTH GRADE MARKED THE END
of one period of my education and the beginning of another.
My innocence about Willis School was over. I had learned how
bright children could graduate unable to read. Later, I would
become more intimately involved with two particular children,
but, during the summer and fall of 1970, the results of our
own children's unique education began to show.

All during Spike's graduation exercises, my distress over
Gus, Poncho, Donald—and, I suspected, too many other students in "my" class—was compounded by guilt. I did not know
how to prevent Gus and the others from going on to Irwin
Junior High terribly unprepared. Yet, because of our income,
we were about to give Spike the extra help other children
needed.

Spike was going to a private school and the decision had
been agonizing. With all my prejudices against private schools,
I could not refute the facts as Ben presented them. Spike's
Iowa Test scores which had jumped twenty points after he
began taking medication had slumped fifteen points at the end
of eighth grade. We did not know whether this was due to
lack of effort or lack of confidence. Ben pointed out that since
Spike would have spent only one year at Irwin Junior High
before going on to Germantown High School, this would be

the best year to try a private school. If the smaller classes and whatever other benefits private schools were believed to provide helped, fine. If not, he could then go on to Germantown High.

I had to admit that what I had heard of Irwin Junior High did not promise a serene and successful year for Spike. A black friend, Sybil Wheer, with a son at Irwin told me a disturbing story. Her son had been playfully scuffling with his best friend, who happened to be white. Sybil's son slipped, fell against a glass door which broke and cut him. The next day, the father of the white boy telephoned Sybil. The white principal, he said, had telephoned him recommending he take his son out of the school. "It's not safe for whites here," the principal had said. The father was outraged that the principal had made a "racial thing" out of two friends' horseplay.

If this was typical of the principal then I could understand other things I had been hearing and reading about the school. Irwin Junior High was situated in a neighborhood that realtors had succeeded in panicking. The school had changed from 35 percent black to 75 percent black in two years. The newspapers had printed confusing reports of "racial tension" the year before. According to Sybil's son, the problem began when a car full of white youths parked outside the school, and they called "nigger" to the students and brandished a gun. Sybil's son had seen it. The next day, older brothers of black students formed a group to protect their younger brothers. The following day, a unit of the militant Jewish Defense League literally invaded the school to protect white students (many of whom were Jewish) against the black protective unit! A policeman we knew had been assigned to the school. He told us that the principal "locked himself in the office and refused to come out." Irwin Junior High did not sound as if it would be the tranquil atmosphere Spike needed to progress.

On the other hand, I had many misgivings about private schools. The anti-Semitism Abby's children had experienced

—and the anti-Catholic attitude another friend described—would not be directed at Spike, but he would witness it. There was also an economic isolation at private schools; this, I feared, was the same handicap we had been glad to leave behind in the suburbs.

I had also recently had an unsettling experience with a group of private school mothers when Sarah was invited to the birthday party of a girl she had met at day camp. The party was a picnic at a far away spot and mothers were invited to stay during the party. All the other women had children in the same private school, William Penn Charter. We sat around a picnic bench having what I thought was an ordinary, pleasant conversation. Suddenly, one of the women turned to me and said, "I'm *so* glad you came! I haven't had such a fascinating, frank conversation in years!" The other women endorsed her remark. I must have looked startled because a lovely prematurely gray woman explained, "You just can't imagine, I guess, how uptight everyone is at Penn Charter. Why, I've known Sue for five years and this is the first time we realized we were both in favor of sex education at school. But, of course, we wouldn't dare bring it up at a meeting!"

The women had painted a pathetic picture of complicated social games, the rules and rewards of which were beyond me. A penalty, however, was being "a troublemaker" by criticizing a teacher or a school policy. "You're told your child's class is 'overenrolled this year. Sorry,'" one mother said. I had described the vitality and parent involvement at our public school and urged these women to consider it. Five polite smiles told me it was unlikely. Just as unlikely, I knew, as my giving up my habit of speaking my mind.

I hoped that Spike's eight years in our heterogeneous neighborhood had made him immune to a contagious snobbery. He was old enough to have explored the contrasting neighborhoods that adjoined ours: Roxborough to the west of us, a blue-collar neighborhood like the one in which I grew up;

Chestnut Hill to the north with its reputation for having more Social Register residents than any area in America and, to the south, the mostly black Germantown area. Our neighborhood was the stabilizer between them. Spike had had the opportunity to learn that blue-collar, blue blood or black—friends should be chosen on their characters, not on external labels. This he seemed to do. But could he change under the pressures of peer prejudice?

Ben and I finally worked out a compromise. We would try to find a private school that was not socially prestigious and that offered some mixture of students. Barbara Hamilton and several other friends whose judgment I respected had told me that St. Peter's Academy might fill our requirements. St. Peter's, I was told, was a relatively new school, unpretentious, sponsored by the Lutheran church and had a good mixture of middle-class pupils. The beautiful grounds, located ten blocks from our house, had been leased by St. Peter's when the private school that had occupied the grounds since George Washington's time moved to the suburbs.

When Ben and I came to St. Peter's for our appointment with the headmaster, Mr. Luetzow, I wondered how any school could have abandoned these lovely and historic grounds. The campus was studded with enormous oaks. The headmaster's office was in a building once occupied by a Revolutionary War general and, for a time, George Washington's two step-grand-children were students here, perhaps walking over the same flagstones we walked that day.

The headmaster was young, candid and enthusiastic. He was also from my native Midwest; his hard r's and familiar phrases made me feel instantly at home. He said, "Yes, the school is integrated . . . about thirty percent black. We've also got Jewish and Catholic kids . . . but I'm not going to tell you everything's peachy. The black and white students don't really socialize. And some of the white parents would have catfits if they did.

"We're a far cry from 'fashionable,' " he said, "but we try to run a strong academic school. We enforce a lot of rules that parents appreciate . . . shirts, ties and jackets to school and a gentleman's haircut."

I could not help looking at the picture of Jesus Christ on his wall as well as portraits of Benjamin Franklin and George Washington. We had never got involved in the battle of hair length with Spike or Noah. There were, to me, too many more important rules parents had to impose. Spike would follow the school rule, but I could not suppress a quiet laugh at the thought that Jesus was not considered a gentleman.

Mr. Luetzow laughed too. "Yes, you're right, but *most* of our parents like having us rule out long hair."

Ben and I left Mr. Luetzow's office. I learned that Ben had been as impressed as I. In Omaha, Betty Cohen had said, "A school is as good as the teacher your child has *that* year." Could that thought be carried one step further? Was a school as good as its administrator? We thought so. Spike took a test and was accepted as a student for September, 1970.

During the summer vacation before Spike was to begin private school, I explained to people who asked that, while Noah and Sarah were doing very well in public school, Spike still had problems and we were trying to find out if St. Peter's might help him.

What worried me most, however, was what effect the school might have on Spike. He was leaving a predominantly black school where many of the children were from low-income families; he would be in a mostly white school among children whose parents were at least affluent enough to afford the fifteen-hundred-dollar tuition. We had purposely removed our children from the white middle-class atmosphere of the suburbs. How would it affect Spike to make the return trip? I was proud of the values and sensitivity he had already acquired, but peer pressure was potent at his age. How would he respond if his private school classmates had values different from his?

The summer supplied us with an unexpected test of how our children reacted to an all-white world. The children had decided they were "too old" for day camp; they wanted to join a swim club. Ben inspected several swim clubs in the neighborhood and we finally decided on the one that was closest, least expensive and, we believed, integrated. The club we chose was operated primarily for the residents of a large apartment complex but accepted a number of neighborhood families. Since we knew that Judge William Hastie, a distinguished black federal judge, lived in the building, we believed it was surely integrated.

The children thoroughly enjoyed their first day at the pool. Spike met a pretty blond girl who apparently returned his interest; Noah found several girls to chase around the pool and Sarah jumped into the shallow end, determined to learn to swim. According to pool rules, we could bring a certain number of guests during the season and the children had already planned which friends they would bring.

On the second day, Noah said to me, "Hey, Mom, have you noticed that everybody here is white?" I had not. Unlike my children, I had grown up in an all-white world and unconsciously accepted it as "normal."

Later that day, I asked a friendly, deeply tanned elderly man if Judge Hastie came to swim often. The man said, "Oh, no. He's not a member. He'd feel funny, I guess, being the *only one*!" He finished applying oil to his own skin, ten shades darker than Judge Hastie's.

That afternoon, the college-girl lifeguard chatted with me during her rest period. She said, "You don't act as uptight as these other folks." She chatted about the "weird" attitude of the pool director. "Do you know he said to me, 'You can have two guests a week, but remember, no *colored*!" I had already asked Barbara Hamilton and her children to be our guests on Friday! I told the young lifeguard that many of my children's guests would be "colored."

"Oh, wow! They'll probably take away your membership. But it'll be good for these folks to get shook up a little!" she said.

I had no desire to shake up anyone. I had wanted a quiet, relaxing summer, reading in the sun while the children swam. I looked across the pool at Spike who was beaming down at Sandra, his first "serious" attachment. Noah was showing remarkable ability on the diving board, while in the shallow water Sarah splashed and sank alternately in her determination to swim. How would they feel if we lost our club membership? How would I feel if they showed they did not want to risk their summer of swimming by bringing black friends?

Ben felt we should be honest and specific with them. He said, "Kids, it's possible that if you bring Paula or Mike or Jimmy—if your mother brings Mrs. Hamilton or Mrs. Arthur —we could lose our membership. If that doesn't happen, some of the other kids at the pool might act funny toward you. Not be friendly."

Sarah looked horrified. "Would those people *hurt* Paula?" she wanted to know. Ben reassured her that there would be no physical violence.

I told Spike that Sandra might change toward him. Spike said, "Oh, she's all right. She used to be a *little* prejudiced, but we talked it over and she understands now." Understanding a principle and putting it into practice, I reminded Spike, were two different things.

Noah showed a belligerent determination. None of our children suggested we avoid the risk.

I felt Barbara should also know the truth about the climate at the swim club. "Don't worry. We're used to it," she said calmly, "but how do *you* feel?" I said, "Scared." In Omaha, I had blundered unknowingly into white hostility. Anticipating it was, I found, frightening. Only the alternative was worse.

Ben felt we should wait until our canceled check for the membership fee came back from the bank. One week later it

(189)

did. The following day, Barbara and her two children, Paula and Jimmy, drove with us to the pool.

The stairway down which we had to walk to the pool looked endless. Paula and Sarah walked ahead of Barbara and me, their arms draped around each other's shoulders. Spike, Jimmy and Noah raced ahead and into the water. Barbara joked as we walked along. "They're saying, 'Darn it! *They* found us . . . even behind those big old fences!' " I laughed, but for the first time in my Caucasian life, I had a small taste of how it must feel to be the only black person in a school, a neighborhood or an office. I felt suffocated by the real or imagined hostility and felt a new appreciation for Barbara's strength in having survived a lifetime of this. I wondered if my children were feeling—and learning—as much as I.

Barbara and I took seats at the edge of the pool; our children splashed away happily, uncaring or unknowing they suddenly had the pool all to themselves. I noticed Sandra had joined Spike. When the pool director marched toward us, I froze. He only wanted to say hello and tell Barbara he had once taught at an all-black high school.

That day—and for the rest of the season—our children, our guests and I were pointedly ignored or, if contact was inevitable, treated with a nervous geniality. The manager told me that applications for next season's membership were "ah . . . um . . . not being accepted yet. Call the office . . . uh . . . next . . . uh . . . June." But I enjoyed my sunny solitude; Spike had eyes only for Sandra while Noah and Sarah made friends among children who had apparently ignored parental admonitions. I read, rested and reflected. One of my worries had been dispelled; Spike was not likely to be confused or influenced by whatever racism might exist in his private school.

When Spike began his first day's class at St. Peter's in September, 1970, it was the first time our children were not at the same school. Noah and Sarah were scheduled to begin seventh and sixth grades at Willis School on September 10, but the first teachers' union strike in Philadelphia history would keep public schools closed for the first week. (The teachers' union would call a strike again in October and, once more, I would be a teacher. There would be more to learn at Willis School in addition to watching Spike's adjustment in a brand-new setting.)

Spike left the house for his first day at St. Peter's Academy on September 8, 1970. He wore his "gentleman's haircut," a shirt, tie, jacket and an air of resignation. Spike's best friend, jovial, chubby Dave Anderson, walked with him to the trolley stop. Dave, dressed in shirt and jeans, was to begin tenth grade at Germantown High School and I remember feeling an admiration for Dave's parents. They were obviously not afraid to send their white son into the enormous public high school with its thirty-five hundred students, 85 percent of them black.

That evening, Ben and I attended the parents' orientation meeting at St. Peter's Academy. Most of the hundred-odd parents in the chapel were white with a light sprinkling of black couples. (I wondered if the black parents were feeling anything similar to what I had felt at the swim club.) All the couples, black and white, looked more serious and formal than the parents at Willis School. Perhaps, I told myself, this was a good sign. Spike was here, after all, to be helped to do serious studying.

Mr. Luetzow, the headmaster, introduced the teachers with the same open warmth he had displayed in his office during our interview. All the teachers were young. With the exception of the history teacher, Mr. Rux, who seemed shy and nervous, they were as relaxed and outgoing as Mr. Luetzow himself. They were all, I noticed, white.

During the coffee hour after the orientation, we parents mingled with perhaps the same tentative friendliness our children felt among new classmates. While we waited for a chance to speak to Spike's teachers, we made it a point to speak to each black couple and to as many white couples as possible. The black parents—some friendly, some withdrawn—were all from the area; most of the white couples were from the nearby suburbs. I wondered why they had chosen St. Peter's over their suburban schools.

We finally had a chance to talk, for a minute, with each of Spike's new teachers. The young lady who would teach English was a natural ash-blonde, vivacious and eager for information about Spike. The math and science teachers, both young men, were also fair-haired, blue-eyed and friendly. Mr. Rux, the history teacher, a short, brown-haired man in his twenties, was as shy and nervous with individual parents as he had acted in front of the group. Since history was the subject in which Spike had shown most interest, it seemed fortuitous that his least-experienced teacher would be in that subject. Where Spike needed help most, I felt, was English, science and math.

For the first few months, Spike hoarded information about his school experiences exactly as he had done since he began nursery school. I knew I would only hear news of events that were extraordinarily good or bad. Otherwise, he told me, in answer to my questions, that the school was "okay"; his classmates were "all right" and as for his teachers, "Don't worry about it." Spike did not bring new friends home from his school, but this too was usual. Unlike Noah who brought crowds of children home at lunchtime or after school, Spike had always made one or two close friends, cautiously but then giving them his abiding loyalty. After school, he still spent most of his time with Dave and Tony.

What was new was Spike's difficulty in getting up and out of the house on time. His first-hour class was English and I soon got a phone call from the teacher. Could I get Spike to school on time? I would continue to try.

That fall, 1970, much of the nation's attention was on the rebellion of young people on America's campuses and so I was surprised that the subjects for the afternoon mothers' group at St. Peter's were hat-making and flower-arranging. On September 26, the President's Commission on Campus Unrest called on President Nixon to lead America to moderation on the part of students and law enforcement officers alike. On October 4, the same Commission condemned the National Guard for the "inexcusable" killing of four Kent State students. On October 14, an Ohio grand jury cleared the National Guard in the shooting and indicted twenty-five students for "criminal action." On October 29, nine hundred anti-war demonstrators hurled eggs, bottles and rocks at President Nixon's car in California. Since Spike could be on some turbulent campus or drafted into the Army in less than four years, flower-arranging was not topmost in my mind. I did not go to the mothers' club meetings.

Spike was already showing the disillusionment of America's young people. After school one day, he made the flat statement that I felt was the adolescent form of a question. "I'm not going to say the Pledge of Allegiance anymore, Mom. It's not true. We don't have 'liberty and justice for all.' "

Luckily I had once asked and answered that question for myself. I said, "It's not a declaration, honey; it's a promise. We're pledging to *make* this a country with liberty and justice for all."

He looked at me as if I had just shattered his faith in the generation gap. Then he looked pleased, if somewhat surprised, and said, "You're right!"

In November, Spike's first report card made us feel he was making academic progress. He got *B*'s in math, Spanish and science. In English and history, he had earned only *C*'s, but we hoped he would gradually bring these marks up. Spike had been talking about his math and science teachers with enthusiasm. On the parents' night following the report cards, we saw these two young men were indeed the "good guys" Spike said they were. They both surprised us by praising Spike's ability

(193)

in science and math. The math teacher said, "Bennett has a much better math background than the other students." Ben and I looked at each other. Spike's math background had come from neither of us. It could only have come from Willis School. The science teacher too commented on Spike's "good habits" in science. They too had had to come from somewhere other than our home.

The English teacher complained that she did not think Spike was actually reading *The Tale of Two Cities,* but trying to fake during class discussions. Unfortunately, that was something he *could* have inherited. I recalled, guiltily, how I had done exactly the same thing with the *same* book in my high school days.

Spike had tried to explain his *C* in history by confessing that the class was "so boring, I can't stay awake." When we visited Mr. Rux that evening, I was afraid I could understand how Spike felt. Mr. Rux's shy nervousness had now changed into a pedantic stiffness. "Bennett does not participate in class discussions," he told us. He nodded briskly in dismissal when we promised to persuade Spike to try harder.

By December, Spike had still said very little about his classmates except to ask us at the dinner table what to do about "a *girl* who keeps hitting and pinching you." Spike didn't think it was right to hit her back, but he was "sure getting tired of getting bruised."

Ben said, "You're right, son. You can't hit her back. Can you just stay out of her way?"

Spike said, "Not really. She's in all my classes."

I suggested that she was probably just trying to get his attention. Spike was now nearly six feet tall and, I thought, quite handsome. His jaw had lost its youthful roundness and acquired a square, strong look that balanced his long oval face. He had a well-shaped nose and large deep gray eyes. "I think the girl has a crush on you," I said.

"I don't think so," Spike said. "She's just more weird than the other kids."

Spike would not explain why he called the other students "weird." "Don't worry about it," he said.

Just before Christmas, at the school Christmas party, Spike nudged me as we sat at one of the long tables. "That's Linda, the girl who keeps pinching me."

I had already noticed Linda. She sat sullenly at the table, pouting, while her mother brought a tray for her. Her hair was bleached nearly white and her eyelids were heavy with bright green eyeshadow. Linda's pouting mouth was outlined in purple lipstick. I had noticed that many of the young girls were heavily made up. I wondered why the school policy of "a *gentleman's* haircut" did not extend to the girls' cosmetics and their short, *short* skirts.

When Linda's mother returned to the table, Linda had said, loudly, "Why'd ja bring milk? You know I won't drink milk. Take it back!" The mother sent me a "What can a mother *do?*" look before taking the milk away. I was glad it had not been a direct, spoken question.

After the dinner, Mr. Luetzow came up to us. "Hey, I'm hearing lots of good things about Spike!" he said. "The math teacher tells me Spike is teaching other students how to use a slide rule." Ben answered, pleased, but surprised, "I didn't know *Spike* knew how to use one!"

Mr. Luetzow said, "Well, he does and he's teaching other students." Then he added, "Can we look forward to having Spike's brother and sister in our school?"

I answered impulsively, "Oh, no. They're doing fine in public school."

With the same candor that had won us over originally, Mr. Luetzow said ruefully, "Yes, that's our problem here. We tend to get only the students who are having difficulties."

At the end of January, Spike got his second report card. He

had gone down from *C* to *C*– in English and history, from *B* to *D* in Spanish. I hated myself for saying angrily to Spike that his private school tuition meant we did without things and he should be using his privilege. Spike looked sad and ashamed. "Maybe I'm just not as smart as you think I am," he said. I protested that he was very smart, but he had to work harder.

In my own mind, I felt discouraged. We were back now into the same old struggle. The medication had unquestionably made Spike calmer, but how could he find the motivation or confidence to do the kind of work his IQ proved him capable of doing? The small classes and individual attention at private school had not made an appreciable difference. Once again, I rode the depressing seesaw between punishing and persuasion, feeling guilty and angry by turn. He was not allowed to leave his room until he had read the required pages of *Silas Marner*, a book I had disliked in high school myself. I prodded him through his history assignments, ignoring the fact that the book failed to treat the Egyptians as the dark-skinned Africans they were. This, I felt, was no time to worry about the book, only about Spike.

By March, 1971, when the world was discussing the My Lai massacre, I was still literally pushing Spike out of the door each morning and feeling sad about his obvious resignation as he plodded down the driveway toward the trolley. Perhaps next year, I mused, we could arrange for him to have math or science during the first hour instead of English.

We had no hint that anything else was troubling Spike about his school until he fell in the yard, cut his arm and had to be taken to the hospital for a few stitches.

In the Emergency Room of Chestnut Hill Hospital, a doctor prepared to close the wound while a swarthy orderly assisted him.

Suddenly the orderly said, in a slightly foreign accent, "Hey, wanta hear the latest Polack joke?"

(196)

To my astonishment, Spike, whose entire six-foot frame had been tensed waiting for the pain of the needle, said calmly, "No, thanks. I don't go for jokes like that."

The orderly looked at me. "You Polish?" he said. I shook my head, still smiling over Spike's directness. The orderly persisted. "You Jewish?" Again, I shook my head.

"We happen to be Protestant," I said, "but as Spike said, we don't go for jokes like that." The orderly shrugged and began to talk hospital gossip to the doctor.

On the drive home, Spike asked, "What would you have done if he'd gone ahead and told that joke?" I said I would have made it plain, by not laughing, that the joke did not amuse me.

"Well, that doesn't work at school," Spike said. "The other kids laugh and they just keep on telling jokes about Jews or Italians or black people. I've been wondering, Mom, if maybe I told an anti-Jewish joke after a Jewish kid told an anti-black joke whether he'd get the point."

Spike had obviously been worrying about this problem for some time. I told him quickly that I was afraid his idea wouldn't work. "Anyone who is so insensitive that he gets a kick out of jokes that put down other groups would probably be too insensitive to get your point," I said. Spike said, "Well, I can't think of anything else that would work." I said that perhaps the only thing he could do was to stay away from the kids who told ethnic jokes. Spike said, "Hah! The whole school's that way!"

My despairing attitude toward Spike's study problems now had a new layer of despair. We had so carefully avoided the private schools that reputedly had quotas for black and Jewish students and that were otherwise socially snobbish. We had carefully chosen a middle-class school, forgetting the middle-class custom of the ethnic joke. Instead of giving full concentration to English, Spanish and history, Spike was trying to combat this custom. I knew, however, that the only news more disappointing would be that he had ignored or gone along with the jokes.

As we drove toward home, Spike, reassured that I was not going to get visibly upset, revealed other aspects that had been bothering him.

"That's a real weird bunch of kids," he told me. "Some of the kids at Willis didn't behave in class either . . . but . . . I don't know . . . there's something worse about these kids at St. Peter's. Spoiled kind of . . . babyish, you know?"

Spike paused. "If you promise not to get all involved or talk to Mr. Luetzow . . ." I promised. "Well, the kids in math class don't like me or the teacher. They fool around all the time and they act nasty with him. He gets mad and tells them they should be working like me. Then they start poking me with pencils and pushing my books off the desk. But don't you get involved, Mom; I can handle it."

I felt overwhelmed by the irony: for eight years in a mostly black school, Spike had never experienced hostility because he was white; now, in a mostly WASP school, he attracted hostility because he was smart in math!

Ben could think of no solution to the problem. He pointed out that we should be proud of Spike for wanting to handle the situation by himself and for not trading popularity for math progress. "By the way," Ben said, "how *did* he learn how to work a slide rule?" "From the instructions that came in the box!" I told Ben proudly.

In the middle of April, Spike got his third report card. He was failing in English and history. By now, I felt as if I were seeing the same sad motion picture for the hundredth time. Homework time was once again a time of pleading, punishments and frustration. I confiscated Spike's beloved books on astronomy and space exploration until he demonstrated that he was reading English and world history assignments. It was sad to me that he had to be forced to read *Of Mice and Men* under the kind of pressure that made this enjoyable book a chore. In history, I sympathized secretly with Spike's feeling of boredom under the formal, pedantic Mr. Rux, but pointed out to Spike that learning to do what bored you was a part of growing up. "All adult jobs have boring parts," I said.

The day Mr. Rux assigned the chapter on Africa, Spike left his room and came down to the kitchen, his textbook open. "Look, Mom, read this!" he said. I was delighted he had found something stimulating enough to share with me. I read the chapter heading that Spike pointed to: "Africa Emerged from Darkness Late in World History."

"That's not true," Spike said.

I read the text under the heading.

> *We know very little about African history south of the Sahara before the tenth century when a Negro Empire, the Kingdom of Ghana, arose in West Africa . . . Moslem influence was very strong . . . many of the royal ministers were Moslems.* (Story of Nations, Rogers, Adams, Brown; Holt, Rinehart, Winston, 1965)

Not only had the book separated the Egyptians from African history and bleached them "unblack," but it had tried to credit Moslems with Ghana's culture and had ignored seven centuries of African history. The strange and destructive blindness to known African history that Basil Davidson had described in *African Past* (Little, Brown, 1964) still persisted in Spike's book. Quoting another white scholar, Melville Herskovits, Davidson had written that "the myth of the Negro past . . . (permitted) *rationalized discrimination.*" By pretending that Africa had no history, Africans could be seen as "retarded children" who "must be taken in hand by superior people." This made the European occupation appear necessary and ethical instead of the greedy rape for gold and diamonds that it actually was. It was to American-European interest to continue the belief that a people without a history were fit only for enslavement. Davidson, an Englishman, and a handful of other scholars had published the truth and were continuing to publish documentation of the rich civilizations in Africa's past. Spike's textbook not only ignored available information, but, by publishing "we know very little about African history," made an untrue statement.

Spike had remembered the African history we discussed around the dinner table and now wanted to share it with his class. I was pleased. I gave him a copy of the book Basil Davidson wrote especially for young people, *A Guide to African History* (Zenith-Doubleday, 1965), along with my folder of miscellaneous clippings.

That evening, Spike came into our bedroom with a clipping from a local, black-owned magazine, *Philly Talk*. "Hey, did you know Beethoven had African blood?" he said. Yes, we did. According to the well-documented article, not only Beethoven, but Haydn, Goethe and Martin Luther all had had African ancestors.

Ben explained to Spike that in Europe, black ancestry was taken lightly. At one time, black servants were considered "fashionable" by royalty and married freely with white servants. Many men of genius sprang from these unions and from marriages with Moors or with Africans in various European colonies. In America, however, intercolor marriage was condemned. Before we left Omaha, we had learned that a law against it still existed in Nebraska. In many states, laws also existed making anyone with more than one thirty-second African blood "legally a Negro" and subject to all Jim Crow laws.

Spike said, "You mean Beethoven would have had to hide in the back of the bus?" Yes. "And," Spike added, "he couldn't have bought a house in our suburb?" Probably not.

The next day Spike came home from school bewildered and angry. He had told the class about ancient African civilizations and had added that many geniuses had descended from these bloodlines; Beethoven, for example.

Spike said, his face flushed, "Mr. Rux said I was lying . . . that nobody should pay any attention to me. I told him I'd bring in the article. He said no article would say such a stupid thing."

Spike and I went to the public library where he used the Xerox machine and I checked the references in the article. Robert Haven Schauffler's book, *Beethoven, The Man Who Freed Music* (Doubleday, 1929), cited the description given by Beethoven's neighbor, Frau Fischer. On page one and again on page eighteen, she reported him as having a "blackish-brown" complexion. His nickname, "der Spangol" (the Spaniard) may have alluded to the Moorish blood of his servant-parents. Another Beethoven authority, A. W. Thayer, wrote that "Beethoven had even more of the Moor to his looks than (Haydn) his master." (Haydn, a collection of letters revealed, was called "my fine blackamoor" by his patron, Prince Esterhazy.) Portraits and a life mask in the Schauffler book showed Beethoven's broad nose, thick lips and curly hair.

Spike took the Xeroxed documentation to school. He came home in the afternoon, bristling. Mr. Rux had taken it, scanned it and handed it back to Spike without a word. "I asked if he could please tell the class I wasn't a liar," Spike said. "He said he wasn't interested in discussing the subject anymore."

"You know what I'm gonna do, Mom," Spike said, jutting his jaw forward exactly as Ben does, "I'm gonna do perfect history papers and on the bottom of every darn one of them I'm gonna write: Beethoven is too black!"

And so he did.

Ben reminded Spike that this gesture might cost him a lower history grade. Spike said it probably would. "Mr. Rux won't call on me anymore no matter how hard I wave my hand."

Ben said to me, "I guess fighting for what's true is what

(201)

education is all about." He made out a check for the last installment on Spike's tuition and added, "I wish he had picked a cheaper battle ground."

By June, it was evident that private school was not the solution to Spike's study problem. His work habits—except for math and science which he enjoyed—remained the same. It had taken constant prodding and punishments to make him work hard enough to pass (barely) English and Spanish. In history, he got a *B* on the exam, a *D* for "class participation" and a *C*– average. The school, as I once feared, had not warped his values. Instead, he had spent much too much energy coping with ethnic jokes and a racist teacher.

"Look," Spike said, "why can't I just go to Germantown High?"

At that moment, I could think of no rational reason to say no.

thirteen

DURING THE YEAR THAT SPIKE WAS IN PRIVATE SCHOOL, NOAH and Sarah kept me closely involved with Willis School. For Noah and Sarah, school opened a week late. The first teachers' strike in Philadelphia history kept the public schools closed until September 15, 1970.

I was instinctively on the side of the teachers in their strike. If the teachers' union succeeded in forcing increased salaries, the public schools could attract higher quality people to replace those who allowed children to graduate from eighth grade hardly able to read. If bad teachers like Carter Kellogg, Miss Arnold and Miss Grenelli benefited temporarily, so be it. At least Jane Banneker and other devoutly concerned teachers would also get the salaries they deserved.

When school opened, the strike had not been settled. The teachers' union had merely answered the request of the governor of Pennsylvania to go back to the classrooms while the bargaining continued. Noah and Sarah went off to school; Noah to seventh grade, Sarah to sixth. At noon, they brought home some startling news.

"We've got a new principal," Noah said. "Mrs. Peters is on a sab . . . saba*th*ical."

Sarah said, "Mr. Levine is our new principal and he smiles at everybody!" Sarah, I noticed, had developed a sensitivity to subtle racism recently. When Paula Hamilton cut her finger while at our house, Sarah had got out the adhesive strips and noticed they were labeled "Flesh-toned." She had written the company, protesting that her friend's flesh was not pink. She had received no answer. Mr. Levine, however, passed her newly close inspection.

In our neighborhood, there was speculation over whether Vangie Peters was really on a sabbatical or whether she was using this absence as a graceful way of leaving our school. Ben suggested this might be her way of dodging the emotionally charged strike. We could only guess and I could hope that Mr. Levine was permanent.

During my first brief encounter with him, I was impressed. He was a short, round man with gray hair, gray eyes and a gray suit. I had introduced myself to him on the playground and he had smiled pleasantly, but his attention was on two youngsters who were quarreling a few feet away. He said to me, "Very nice to meet you," and excused himself to go to the two angry students. A few smiling words from him and they went off cheerfully in opposite directions. He then moved off quietly, calmly among the children. His air of tranquillity seemed contagious. I watched him, relieved to find that my whiteness, rare as it was becoming in my children's classes, was not going to get any special attention from Mr. Levine.

Jane Banneker, who would no longer have my children in her classroom, had remained a friend and she reported that Mr. Levine was organized, hard-working and "has the same rules for everyone. I mean all students and all teachers!"

As the month of September moved along, I understood what Jane meant. Sarah said she had overheard Miss Grenelli complaining that Mr. Levine had sent her home to change clothes. "But, Mom, she used to wear such short skirts that we could see her panties when she sat on the desk," Sarah said. "An' Miss Grenelli gets to school on time now too."

I had also noticed that the male sixth-grade teacher, a young white man with swollen eyes and the posture of a pretzel, suddenly abandoned jeans and began wearing a suit to school. Noah and Sarah and the friends they brought home at lunchtime all talked about "how nice it is not having Mrs. Peters yelling in the hallways anymore." Jane Banneker told me that supplies were now being ordered and evenly distributed among the teachers. The only complaints I heard about Mr. Levine were from parents who were accustomed to special privileges. A new calm settled over the school and I was surprised at how much difference one quiet man made.

On Thursday, October 15, negotiations between the school board and the teachers' union broke down and union leaders called for a walkout. I read the details in the newspaper, trying to understand the strike issues. Salary demands were being made and for the first time I learned that Philadelphia teachers were the third highest-paid in the nation. The other important issue was the length of the senior high school day. During the Depression, senior high school teachers were given a shorter day in lieu of a raise. Even though there had been many raises since, the shortened day (illegal, according to state law) was still in effect.

The teachers' union also asked for smaller classes. I had never been concerned about small classes for Noah and Sarah, but with what I had learned the year before, I believed that smaller classes might help other children get the attention their homes could not provide.

My main concern, however, was the anger that had shown itself between the union leaders and the school board. The school board announced that the schools would remain open and asked teachers to remain on the job; the union promised to throw picket lines around the schools. Violence between teachers or between teachers and students would once have seemed impossible to me, but by now, I had seen and heard enough to worry. I decided to walk to school with Sarah, to see how much tension existed and, if necessary, to bring my children back home if the school was not able to remain open.

(205)

Sarah and I walked together along our attractive street, still beautiful with its fading fall foliage. Noah had run ahead. I was almost entirely indifferent about whether my children would stay in school that day. I agreed with the teachers' salary demands and with their demand for smaller classes. If Noah and Sarah missed some time in school, this sacrifice, in the end, might benefit children like Gus or Poncho or Donald by giving them better teachers and more attention.

My narrow attitude lasted until we were a block from school. It was unimportant to *me* whether my children were at school or at home, but what about the mothers who worked? And at our school, there were many mothers who worked, not by choice, but by necessity. Where would their children go if the school was closed? I decided I had better volunteer my time to Mr. Levine if he needed someone to cover a classroom.

I had already made the decision when we turned the corner and I saw the picket line. My conscience had begun to bother me about crossing a picket line for the first time in my life. Then I saw the pickets. Marching in the line were Carter Kellogg, Miss Arnold, Miss Grenelli, Miss McGregor, the swollen-eyed male sixth-grade teacher and the bewildered-looking blond art teacher—all the least competent teachers at the school and each one of them white. There was not one black teacher in the line. I took Sarah's hand and, with no compunction whatsoever, walked between Carter Kellogg and Miss Arnold into the school.

As I walked down the corridor to Mr. Levine's office, a long forgotten incident involving unions came back to me. During my advertising days in Chicago, one of my clients had taken me to lunch with one of his old classmates, a former Capone gang member and now a union official. In the middle of our lunch, the union official decided that my high forehead denoted "brains" and had said, "Girlie, I'm gonna do you a real favor. How'd you like to have the hairdressers' union?" I asked what problems hairdressers had. "Oh, honey," the man had said patiently, "you tell 'em what problems they got! Then you sign 'em up. It's a sure twenty-five thou a year. My son—the bum—he don't work at all an' he clears thirty thou from a union that should break fifty." I had found some cautious way to say no to a former mobster and had pushed the disillusioning episode out of my mind. I recalled the incident only when I saw which teachers carried signs reading "Teachers In Defense of Dignity."

I knew nothing that implied the teachers' union officials were exploiting teachers for their own financial gain. I still believed in the right of workers to strike against powerful employers, but this strike was not affecting some large corporation; it was affecting children and their parents. This strike would not "punish" a big commercial company whose customers would go to a competitor; it punished the children. And, I realized as I walked to the office, it punished mostly black children. Since we had moved from Omaha in 1961, the Philadelphia schools had gone from 49 percent to 60 percent black.

In the principal's office, I noticed that every black teacher had reported for work. So had the white eighth-grade math teacher and the second-grade teacher who had prayed for Spike. These caring teachers knew what I had almost ignored: that most black mothers worked and had no place else to send their children.

In his office, Mr. Levine looked sad but unruffled. When I offered to help, he consulted a list in his hand and asked, "Could you handle *two* seventh grades?"

Probably not, but I would try. If I was all he had to throw into the breach, the situation was serious. I went upstairs to where the room dividers had been thrown open and seventy teen-agers were milling around in the enormous area.

My first job was to get the students away from the un-screened second-floor windows where, incredibly, they were holding shouted conversations with picketing teachers. Josh Pitt, one of Noah's frequent visitors at lunchtime, was halfway out the window, responding to Carter Kellogg's remark, "We're striking for better conditions for *you!*" Josh, a stocky black tree trunk of a fellow, was laughing. "No, man," he said, "it's for the bread! Don't jive me!" I got to the windows, closed them, put Josh and the second toughest youngster in charge of keeping the windows closed.

Surveying the large group of youngsters (of which Noah was one), I decided that my contribution to education that morning might consist solely of keeping children from falling out of windows. Yet, in spite of the double class, the confusion and the excitement of a strike, the students were exceptionally cooperative. From their questions and comments, I began to sense a feeling of Them (the pickets) against Us (those inside) and, in the children, a sad sense of betrayal. Aggressive youngsters like Josh Pitt expressed their feelings directly. Josh said, "Those ones don't care about us. Coulda tol' you who'd be picketing and who'd be teachin'!" A small ebony-hued young man said sadly, "I did my homework real good last night. Ain't nobody gonna look at it?" (I did, marked it *A* and marked all the other papers given me.) Children wanted to know if the schools were going to close, why the teachers were striking and when the strike would end. I tried to answer as reassuringly and fairly as possible. No child in this 90 percent black class asked what must have been as obvious to them as to me, why all the pickets were white. At the end of the morning, four sober-faced young ladies surrounded me at the door of the classroom. One said, "We want to thank you for coming in to take care of us." I was very glad I had.

By the time I reported back in the afternoon, Mr. Levine had organized the school and teaching was to be at least attempted. The seventy seventh graders I had supervised in the morning were divided between the science and math teachers and the administrative assistant, Mrs. Spain. Mr. Levine asked if I would take a third-grade class.

I went to look for the third-grade classroom with misgivings. Teen-agers I enjoyed, but I could hardly remember what my own children were like in third grade. One fifty-minute period with my eighth-grade class had been pleasant; how would I handle a class of eight-year-olds for an entire afternoon?

In the end, I would have this class for four days. I would learn that panic too can be the mother of invention. I would learn why my emotions were different from a "real" teacher and I would begin to understand the kind of help a new teacher needs.

When the third graders filed into the classroom, I realized, first, that this time I was bigger than the children and, second, that this was not necessarily an advantage. I crouched constantly to hear and answer questions from soft little voices; the small bodies seemed harder to keep track of and the children all looked up at me as if I knew what I were doing. I could not, as I had done with the eighth-grade class, confess my feeling of ineptness. These children still believed in Santa Claus and in teachers.

I could, however, use the technique I had used with the seventh graders that morning when I put Josh Pitt in charge of the windows. I looked for and picked out the biggest, most hostile looking child I could find. I asked if he would be my assistant. His name was Caleb and, by turns, he looked surprised, pleased and rapt with thought. He even knew where the teacher kept her lesson plan.

While Caleb got the lesson plan and the roll book, a tiny girl with a soft miniature Afro beckoned me to her desk. "You gotta watch that Caleb," she whispered anxiously. "Mrs. Honeybacher says he's *bad, bad clear through.*" He did not look so bad to me, I lied. Anyway, I told the child whose name was Jacqueline, sometimes bad people turn good.

Caleb proudly presented me with the lesson plan. Instead of something specific like reading, it called for one hour of "creative activity." I whispered to Caleb, "What does that mean?" Caleb whispered back, "Means everybody do their own thing!" Somehow this did not sound promising.

Sure enough, when I had called the roll and gingerly announced creative activity time, the class fragmented. Six little girls giggled together in a corner; one of the three white boys in the class pulled out a comic book. For three other boys, Their Own Thing was experimenting with a flashlight battery, a bulb and some wires; for several others, it was grabbing the battery and bulb away.

Two pint-sized pugilists began to slug it out in another corner. I separated the fighters and was told by each, "He hit me first!" With an inspiration I wish I had had when my own sons were that age, I said, "Okay. You each pretend I'm him and hit me. I won't hit back and that'll end it." Two small brown faces looked gleeful, two hands tapped my arm and everyone settled down for the moment.

Soon everyone's Own Thing became noisier again. I called the class to attention. Perhaps publicity would work. I announced that I was beginning two lists on the blackboard. I wrote at the top of one section: *Our Best Workers.* I wrote *Not Our Best Workers* on the other. From then on, I was shown notebooks, drawings and mysterious objects that were explained at length by their creators. *Our Best Workers* list covered two sections. I needed only to write the first letter of a child's name on the *Not Our Best Workers* list and misbehavior magically stopped.

By Monday morning, the strike was still on and I reported to the third-grade classroom again, but by noon, I no longer felt as if I were rowing us all out to sea in a leaky boat. The children had become people with predictable behavior patterns and I felt involved with each one. Some of the youngsters had a wonderful inner security; they worked, made mistakes, corrected them and went on. Others mispronounced a word in reading period and stood, head down and crushed. Carola, a raggedy little girl with large sad eyes, simply sat. (Jacqueline, class informant, said, "She's new.") Caleb's exemplary behavior disintegrated during arithmetic. "Won't do that jive," he said belligerently. Somehow I knew instinctively that Caleb's ego could not stand being the second—or sixteenth—best. "All right, Caleb, but could you go help Carola?" I said. Caleb puffed up and walked off to help Carola, apparently sure he knew more than she did.

I was congratulating myself for some lucky guesses when Jacqueline came to me to whisper, "Mrs. Honeybacher always hits Caleb's hands with a ruler when he won't work." I said, well, all teachers do things differently.

While the class did the exercises in their arithmetic book, I had a quiet moment to wonder once again why some teachers used methods on children that could only create hostility. Surely all children wanted to learn as well as their classmates. Some obviously needed different kinds of help, but no child—or adult, for that matter—responded to humiliation or pl.ysical pain. Long ago, a neighbor who was a teacher had told me, "A good slap is the only thing some children of this type understand." Yet in my extremely limited experience, I had never once *wanted* to hurt a child.

That persistent inner voice that blasts our hypocrisies reminded me that I had occasionally lost my temper and hit my own children. In the middle of my "Yes, but . . ." reply, I realized that I had found the difference between me, a volunteer, and a real teacher. I did react emotionally to my own children. Many factors, including my own ability as a mother, were involved. And for a real teacher, there were similar emotional involvements with her class, emotions from which I was entirely free. I was not in the classroom, testing long expensive years of education against reality. I did not have to wonder why handling a class alone was more difficult than practice teaching, whether something was wrong with my preparation or with myself.

As a mother, I had learned that my own feeling of ineptness could change to frustration and anger. Certainly the same dynamics could operate with a teacher. While I in my role as mother could forgive myself and try to avoid my destructive responses next time, it would not be that easy for a teacher. She had colleagues to keep up with and a supervisor to please. It would be wrong, but all too human, to become angry at the children who increased your own self-doubt.

Just then Mr. Levine stuck his gray head through the door. "Looks like you're doing just fine," he said quietly. I remembered the many times I had been with Vangie Peters when she entered a teacher's classroom, flinging open a door to glare silently at a noisy class or interrupting the teacher with some spur-of-the-moment speech to the class. Mr. Levine's words made me feel warmly reassured, for myself, but even more for what he could do for real unsure new teachers.

On the evening of my fourth teaching day, the strike was settled. The school board had agreed to a $53.2 million two-year wage increase and had given up on the issue of the legal-length school day for the senior highs. These teachers would be paid overtime for the extra class time required by state law. I was glad Sarah and Noah's classes would be back to normal, but I knew I would miss the twenty-eight children I had got to know so well in the short time.

At noon the next day, I went up to school to say good-bye to my third-grade class. The children were lined up in the hallway to be dismissed for lunch. We said good-bye to each other while their real teacher ignored us. To her, of course, I was a "scab" and I understood her hostility. I wanted to tell her of the bits of insight I had gathered about some of her pupils. Her glare told me it would be risky to try. I left the school, hoping the scars of the strike would not take too long to heal.

With Mr. Levine in charge, the scars of the strike and the other concerns I felt about Willis School seemed to be gradually disappearing. Jane Banneker told me Mr. Levine had held a meeting with the nonstriking teachers. He reminded them that their colleagues had acted on what they believed was right and urged renewed friendships.

"He's a wonderful change," Jane sighed. "I trust him. The other day one of my students told me that Pat Grenelli kicked his brother in the back. It felt good to tell him to have his parents talk with Mr. Levine. He'll follow through. He supports his teachers, but he'll work with Pat Grenelli too. Or get rid of her."

I thought of Mr. Levine when I read an article in the December 13 Bulletin about a white male teacher who was fighting a forced transfer out of an all-black school for two episodes of slapping students. The fifty-seven-year-old man had been transferred from two other schools (the first, 70 percent white; the second, 100 percent black) for hitting children. Vangie Peters had always told me "the union would get me if I try to get rid of a teacher," but the black principal of this man's school had filed an Unsatisfactory Service Report. I had learned recently that this act did indeed take courage on the part of a principal. According to a friend with the Board of Education, a principal must document his charges in exhaustive detail as well as his attempts to help the teacher improve. The union provides counsel for the teacher. "If a principal's skirts aren't absolutely clean," our friend said, "they'll drag out any dirty linen they can find. Even if the principal's above any kind of criticism, it's still a long, messy process. A principal really has to put the kids ahead of himself to do it." I felt Mr. Levine would. The prominence of the newspaper article made me wonder how seldom other principals did the same.

Ironically, newspaper and magazine articles were now appearing on "increasing assaults on *teachers* in big city schools."

I read the pieces carefully, hoping to find that some reporter looked for the connection between teacher brutality and student revenge. Not too surprisingly, no reporter made the connection. After all, it had taken six years of close contact before I learned what was being done to children in our far-from-worst school and to understand how this affected mine. But I had recently come across a disturbingly well-documented book in the library, *The Mentally Disturbed Teacher* (Shipley, Chilton, 1961). Surveys in 1934, 1943 and Dr. Shipley's own research revealed that emotional imbalance was high among teachers; higher, one study proclaimed, than any other occupation. This information had been met with anger by the teachers, evasion by officials and helplessness by parents. It had been swept under the bulging rug. Newspaper and magazine reporters had not looked under that rug for the causes of student assaults; only the results were reported.

In our neighborhood, the result was soon to be murder, but before this event stunned Philadelphia, Ben and I had weekend visitors from the suburbs of Detroit. Ben's college friend brought his wife and three children, the ages of ours. We would have the chance, I knew, to compare life-styles and to guess what might have happened had we never left our Omaha suburb. Naturally, we discussed schools.

Ben's friend George said, "Sure the suburban schools are overrated. We found that out. If a kid asks a searching question, he's shushed unless it's directly connected with the Iowas or the SATs. [Standard Achievement Test for college acceptance] They gear the whole thing to preparing the kids for those two tests. There's more to education than passing certain tests!"

George's wife, Beth, a slim, pretty woman with a bubbling manner, added, "And if anyone thinks vandalism and juvenile delinquency is only a city problem, they're crazy. Last week, some bored kids set fire to the junior high! That stuff never makes the papers though!"

We suspected as much, but both Ben and I were pleased to hear praise from our visitors for our children's "amazing self-sufficiency." We considered our children average in most ways, but they did seem to be a bit less dependent than the suburban-raised children. Our children were used to traveling where they wanted on buses and trolleys; Beth sighed that she had to drive the children "everywhere" and she felt it was not good for them.

The suburban children, not unexpectedly, showed their inexperience with black children. Noah had arranged with his friend, Mike, to bring our visitors' son along to Mike's birthday-dance party. The afternoon before the party, Noah took the boy to Mike's house "so he won't feel he doesn't know anyone." The boy developed a sudden headache and refused to go to the evening party. Noah said, "He acted funny when he met Mike. Like he was scared or something." By contrast, the oldest son formed an immediate friendship with our neighborhood's young black con-man. "Wow!" Spike told me privately, "he thought Skit was just great! Skit talked him out of a dollar he'll never see again! How could he be so dumb!"

Beth asked me about the drug problem at our school. I had to confess that up until then I had heard nothing concerning our school except for a glue-sniffing episode Noah had told me about. Two friends of his, he said, were sniffing glue after school. I had told him of the dangers and learned he had passed my words on to his friends. "They wanna know, Mom, if they'll be okay if they stop right now," Noah had said.

Beth said, "*If* that's all you've got here, you're lucky." A classmate of her oldest son had died from an overdose and she said, "I just cross my fingers and pray."

When the family left, Spike confided to me that the older son was very concerned about his younger brother. "He said he got busted for ripping off stuff in a sporting goods store.

This was the *second* time and it's on his record now," Spike said. Then he added, "Gee, I'd hate to live in the suburbs and have to worry about Noah!" I explained that the suburbs were not exactly a corrupting influence that could make good kids bad. With Ben, I could speculate on whether any of these problems might have affected our children if we had stayed in Omaha. It was hard to know, but it was interesting to learn that the suburbs were not the problem-free areas some of our white neighborhood parents seemed to believe.

In January, 1971, the long bitter school strike began in Newark and would be settled only after eighty thousand students (almost all of them black) had missed three months of school. The 70 percent white teachers' union demanded that paraprofessionals be hired to take over playground and cafeteria monitoring. Beneath this modest demand, there were bitter emotions ranged against the teachers, most of whom lived in the suburbs outside Newark. According to a *Newsweek* report, one-third of the graduates of Weequahic High School in Newark were graduated functionally illiterate. White teachers were accused of drawing pay and running home, uncaring about black and Puerto Rican children. "Paraprofessionals," to the black community, meant black mothers hired to keep the kids in line for teachers who feared and disliked their children. By contrast, our two short strikes seemed minor and I felt sure Philadelphia schools would not have another. Our union had got their demands.

At the end of January when Spike was demonstrating that private school was not solving his study problems, Willis School appeared to be thriving under the conscientious direction of Mr. Levine. On my visits to school, the hallways were quiet. Even Miss Grenelli appeared calm. Miss Arnold had suddenly retired.

There was only one depressing episode in late January over which Mr. Levine had no control. At lunchtime, Sarah mentioned that her class had a substitute for the day. After school, when I picked Sarah up for a dentist appointment, she walked out of the school door with a pretty young red-haired woman, small and expensively dressed. Sarah introduced her to me as Miss Ross, the substitute.

Miss Ross smiled at me broadly and said, "Oh, Mrs. Stalvey, Sarah is such a smart little girl. You really ought to put her in a private school. She'll never learn anything *here*. I couldn't even get those children quiet enough to call the roll!"

I was silent for a moment, amazed at this young person's incredible bad luck. Of all the mothers she could have chosen for her destructive remark, she chose me! My reply, I knew, would be rude, but she had earned it. I said, gently, "Please. Do not blame our children for *your* inadequacy."

To her credit, she was willing to hear me out and to answer my questions. No, she had not been taught techniques for controlling a class at college; she had, she confessed, chosen teaching because "I wasn't sure what I wanted to do." She had, however, been taught the excuse I had heard for so many years. "But," she said, "most of these children come from such bad backgrounds that the school can't do much for them!"

By now, the poor thing was frantically looking at her watch while I explained that children from homes where their parents were poorly educated were exactly the children for whom the school must do *most*. To my delight, Sarah added earnestly, "Honest, Miss Ross, some of the kids they call 'dumb' try harder than the others."

Miss Ross, looking worriedly at her watch, said she would love to stay and talk but she was taking a course at the university and was late for her class. She said, "I won't be in a classroom anyway. I've been promised a job in a special program to teach ghetto teachers to teach." That, I thought bitterly, would be just dandy. As she prepared to walk away, I had one last question. "Why have you chosen public rather than private school work?" I asked. She smiled as if at my innocence and said, "Oh, but private schools don't pay as much."

On Monday, February 1, 1971, two dismaying pieces of news followed each other. At noon, Sarah and Noah announced that Vangie Peters was back. In an assembly, she had told the children, "All right, your five-month *vacation* is over. I'm getting this school back in shape." I was still reacting to her return and her deplorable slap at Mr. Levine when the kitchen radio broadcast the news that a white teacher at Irwin Junior High had been shot and killed on the steps of the school by a fourteen-year-old Negro student.

Irwin Junior High was the school Spike might have attended, where "my" eighth-grade class had gone. For one horrible moment, I felt certain that Gus Clifford had met another Miss Arnold and had not controlled his emotions. I was wrong. It was not Gus or Poncho or Cephas, but it was another ninth grader who had brought his father's .45 caliber mail-order gun to school and shot Samson Freedman, a fifty-six-year-old ceramics teacher, in the head. A playground full of children had witnessed his death.

During the next few days, I watched the press and the public react to a tragedy I had feared was inevitable, in a way that was sadly predictable. The head of the teachers' union asked teachers to stay home on Tuesday "to protest the school superintendent's indifference to violence in our schools." The superintendent, Mark Shedd, then officially closed the schools for a day of mourning. In downtown Philadelphia, Ben heard white people muttering about "those nigger animals." At the train station, he heard a woman say, "I don't blame those teachers for striking. They risk their lives every day with those nigger bastards." One man suggested a public lynching.

(218)

Almost exactly one year before, a University of Pennsylvania student had shot two of his professors, killing one. There had been no public outcry about "violence in the colleges," no city-wide day of mourning for the dead professor. The college student, of course, was white.

On Sunday, the *Bulletin* carried a detailed article on the murder, and it was impossible for me to read it without adding my own knowledge between the lines. The fourteen-year-old murderer (whom I will call Johnny Smith) had gone to eight schools in nine years. His parents would not speak to reporters, but his grandmother said that the Smith family moved each time to "try to do a little better for their children." (And, each time, as Mrs. Jefferson found, whites fled the schools and they were "written off.") Johnny was known as "quiet and withdrawn," yet several paragraphs later, the article revealed that his teacher at another junior high the year before reported an incident. The teacher had been lining the children up when Johnny told him, "I'm not going to listen to that ————." (Had this teacher said, as I had heard Carter Kellogg say, "Move your dumb asses, you bunch of apes?") The teacher admitted he had slapped Johnny across the face. Johnny's father had come raging to the school that afternoon, threatening to "kill that teacher with my bare hands." (I remembered my own rage at Vangie Peters over her lie about Lester and the condoms. Had she slapped my child, I felt sure I could have made the same threat.) The principal had called the police and Johnny had seen his father taken away. The school reported that the incident "had no noticeable effect on [Johnny] . . . he was quiet and polite."

Johnny's parents transferred him to Irwin Junior High, a "better" school (where white youths brandished guns and the white principal urged whites to leave?). On Friday, January 29, two days before the murder, Samson Freedman, according to school records, had suspended Johnny for cursing at another student in the halls and for cursing Freedman for giving him another pink disciplinary slip. On the day of the murder, Johnny had sneaked into the school, apparently to steal the pink slips that could send him to Daniel Boone Disciplinary School. (Boone School had a terrifying reputation that scared even the toughest youngsters I knew. "They don't teach you nothin' an' they *really* beat you," Josh Pitt had told me.) When Samson Freedman caught Johnny with his own and a friend's pink slips in his pocket, he took Johnny to the principal's office.

Shortly after three o'clock, Samson Freedman, who had no children of his own, finished discussing a new gang control program he was planning with a fellow teacher. He walked out the door of the school. Johnny, who said later he wanted only to "scare" the teacher, lifted the heavy gun, yelled, "Look out, y'all," and fired. Samson Freedman who had been a leader in school and neighborhood human relations activities died. A young human bomb, triggered by other teachers, had killed someone who was trying to help.

On TV panels and radio talk shows, no one seemed to want to know why a fourteen-year-old child decided he must resolve his problems through murder. Instead the recommendations were for "more discipline" in the schools.

Jane Banneker came to our house on the Monday after the murder, her soft face tightly set. Vangie Peters, she told me, had announced a "get tough" policy at the school. "Lois, you won't believe whom she put in charge of school discipline, Pat Grenelli, the building union rep."

Anger had also splashed over onto the entire black community. Jane told me that a white woman at the supermarket hissed at her, "You're all killers," and walked away. Barbara Hamilton had had the same kind of experience in another part of the city. I remembered that no black person had called me "killer" when a white Protestant killed Martin Luther King.

Before Jane left, she took a battered Philadelphia *Inquirer* clipping from her handbag. "I've been carrying this around as a . . . well, perhaps as a good-luck piece. Read it if you want and then throw it out."

That evening I read the clipping. At first I was thrilled. A prominent black Philadelphia judge of Juvenile Court, Judge Charles Wright, had denounced the illiteracy "fostered by Philadelphia schools" and shown the clear correlation between illiteracy and crime. Finally someone was speaking out.

Judge Wright had released a fourteen-page report to the press. This was not one of the endless expensive "studies" that white "experts" had made for decades; this was the unpaid research by an angry man distressed by what he saw and determined to find the answers. He found them. He found that 78 percent of the juveniles brought before him were "functional illiterates," that 90 to 95 percent were retarded readers, and 12 percent absolute illiterates. He cited specific cases where youngsters fifteen to eighteen years old *with normal IQs* were reading on first- and second-grade levels.

"How can a judge punish a truant," he asked, "who is in the tenth grade and cannot read? What person would go to school regularly under these circumstances?" They could only wait, he said, to drop out of school, unprepared for anything useful and to haunt us all as adults.

Judge Wright made ten specific and practical recommendations. Among them was the immediate closing of Boone Disciplinary School . . . "staffed by . . . inexpert and non-education specialists." He urged an end to the automatic promotion of children who had not mastered the basic skills. His other recommendations were actually requests that the school system do what it is supposed to do: understand the problems of the children and teach them basic skills. He asked for "a higher degree of professional dedication and performance," warning that "four years of observing juveniles as truants . . .

(221)

burglars and even . . . killers lead to the conclusion that an overwhelming number of these . . . can be retrieved, or even better, their delinquency prevented."

I finished the article with a vast feeling of relief. Perhaps now our city would get to the Johnny Smiths before they killed. I wondered how I could have missed this important article in the newspaper.

Then I looked at the date at the top of the clipping: March 8, 1970, almost one year before. None of the judge's recommendations had been implemented. None of the reporters writing of "assaults on teachers" had explored the judge's clear indictments. Last March, there would still have been time to keep Gus and Poncho and the others in Willis School until they learned to read. There would still have been time to close Boone Disciplinary School and perhaps to have saved Samson Freedman's life.

fourteen

BY THE END OF FEBRUARY, THE MURDER AT IRWIN JUNIOR High was replaced as a topic of conversation around town by two serious drug incidents at two all-white high schools. At one, students were caught stealing drugs from the school's civil defense supply to sell to other students. At another, thirty-nine children were found under the influence of drugs in their classrooms. In March, about the time Spike was trying to cope with ethnic jokes at his private school, Germantown High School made the news with a story headlined: Germantown School Violence Is Blamed on Public Apathy. Gang activities in the school were blamed on "parental neglect" and lack of funds for gang control. The illiteracy documented by the juvenile court judge was not cited as a possible cause. Yet this mostly black high school was where Poncho and the other nonreading students of my eighth grade were slated to go after leaving Irwin Junior High.

At Willis School, Vangie Peters was again in the principal's office, and I could take pleasure only in the fact that Sarah and Noah appeared to be doing well in their school work and in their maturity. They had gone together to visit a friend in a New Jersey suburb, witnessed a mugging at a train stop and while other passengers milled about, Sarah and Noah had helped the mugged woman (who was black) to her seat. While Noah brought her water, Sarah had comforted the distraught woman. Ben and I were proud of their calm compassion.

Academically, Sarah was earning *A*'s and *B*'s on her report cards while Noah, who was becoming dedicated to sports and girls, was skimming along with *C*'s. Noah's happy-go-lucky attitude toward studying did not concern us greatly. He had proved in the past that he could apply himself seriously when necessary. As for qualifying for Central High, Philadelphia's selective academic high school, we had never pushed him. Neither Ben nor I was sure whether intellectual segregation was any better than color segregation. Noah was clearly capable of qualifying for Central, but it should be by his own effort. If he did not choose to work hard enough, then he could go to the new Baldwin Junior High soon to be completed in our area. Noah now believed he wanted to be a lawyer and go into politics. If so, Baldwin Junior High would be an advantage. It was supposed to serve a cross section of northwest Philadelphia. Politicians should know all kinds of people.

Noah's outgoing personality was also an advantage. Unlike Spike who formed a small number of close friendships, Noah brought literally dozens of classmates home at noon. Our driveway and our basement were usually teeming with seventh-grade youths whom Noah had invited home to play basketball, Ping-Pong or to box. I thoroughly enjoyed having the youngsters around. Many would drift into the kitchen and we would talk. Vangie Peters had not asked me to take a class again and Noah's friends gave me the contact with teen-agers that I had missed.

No clairvoyance warned me that I would become even more agonizingly close to products of a badly functioning school system or that I would bump painfully into new obstacles I did not know existed.

The boxing matches at our house—with Noah's set of gloves and my strict rules—needed a referee. (I tried to fill the spot but was inclined to close my eyes if anyone landed a blow.) I used the same technique that had worked well in my classes; I chose the biggest, toughest lad to enforce the rules.

My unquestionable choice was Joshua Pitt. Josh was built like a stunted tree, short, but bulging with muscle. His face looked as if it had been roughly carved from stained walnut, but his mouth was generous and usually wide with a grin. Beneath his outward toughness, Josh had an open manner that I liked. When Josh and I talked, his large brown eyes always held mine and he seemed to have a precocious maturity.

Josh and the other youngsters Noah brought home at noontime came from the low-income streets in our school area. None of them went home for lunch either because their parents worked or because the area was too far away to walk to during the lunch period. They all lived near each other, and there was no question that Josh was the neighborhood leader, either through his maturity or his muscle. According to Noah, no one "messed with" Josh—in his neighborhood, at school or at our house.

My own playful challenge to Josh had literally shocked the group into sudden stillness. During one of the conversations in our kitchen someone began a discussion about which it was better to have: "no mother or no father." Of the four young men in the group, each was missing one parent, two through death. Jimmy, a small thin fellow with light brown skin, said, "You eat better if you got a Ma." Fish, as slim and always-moving as Spike, stuck his chin out and protested, "Yeah, but mothers don't let you *do* things." Josh's brown eyes turned ice-cold above his perpetual grin and he said, "Fathers is best." The group hastened to agree. Yes, fathers were best. The sad picture of children without complete families reactivated my own childhood yearning for my own missing father. I covered my feelings by saying indignantly to Josh, "Well, thanks a lot! You sure make me feel useful!" Josh grinned. "Ain't your fault you ain't a man." In mock anger, I put my hands around Josh's neck. The other fellows stiffened in apprehension. Josh laughed and pretended to collapse. The others relaxed with nervous smiles.

Later, Noah asked, "Did you really grab Josh's neck?" According to Noah, Josh was no one to "mess with." "Even Mrs. Peters is scared of him," Noah said. I truly could not understand why. I told Noah that I liked Josh and Josh knew it. Josh had known I was teasing.

It was hard to explain to Noah, but I was able to understand Josh's swagger and toughness. Vangie Peters had told me that Josh's mother had left her husband and son when Josh was six. Like Josh, I had used a similar pseudoconfidence to cover the hurt of my own father's desertion. As a white female, I had found ways to excel that were intellectual rather than physical, but Josh and I had similarities I could feel.

Josh and I had also started a verbal game, the significance of which escaped me for a long time. In what undoubtedly began as a test, Josh sauntered into the kitchen one day and said, "Hey, Mrs. Stalvey, can I have a cigarette?" I said, "Certainly *not!*" and began the same lecture I gave my own children. I told Josh that I had started smoking before people knew it was harmful, that I had begun as a teen-ager because it made me feel grown up and that now, my habit was, so far, unbreakable. "I care too much about you, Josh," I said, "to let you get like me." Josh had grinned, swaggered off and, as the weeks passed, Josh seemed to enjoy our unchanging dialogue. I saw it as a friendly game.

In early March, 1971, Noah came home after school, his face wrinkled in anger. "Guess who I'm teamed with for the social studies report! Your pal, Josh."

I asked what was so terrible about that?

Noah said, "Oh, Mom! We gotta do the report together and share the mark! Josh never did homework in his life. He won't do anything and we'll get a lousy mark. I don't want to do it all by myself. That's not fair."

(226)

Noah was in no mood to hear that a lot of things in life were not "fair." He with his educated parents, his home well-stocked with books and his future college education insured, got the benefits of other unfairnesses in life and in our school. Noah had been four years old when we moved to Philadelphia. He had grown up without Spike's memories of our suburban misadventure. The word "nigger" in his *Huckleberry Finn* book had offended him, but he had apparently missed other unfairnesses that racism and poverty brought to a child like Josh.

Noah was pessimistic about my suggestion that we solve the problem by getting Josh to work on the report at our house. I said, "Listen, he doesn't have a mother to help him, you know." Noah said, "He won't work. You'll see. All he ever does in class is act tough."

Noah was wrong. Josh accepted the invitation and arrived at our house with a brand-new notebook and a mechanical pencil.

The subject of the report assigned to Noah and Josh was "The Belgian Congo." I tried to find an up-to-date account and had chosen the *New York Times Almanac* in addition to other books. I suggested we all read it together around the kitchen counter.

I read the text slowly to myself, trying to keep pace with Noah and Josh. When I came to the word "chaos," I asked the boys if they knew the meaning of the word. Josh and Noah both said yes. The next sentence described Patrice Lumumba as "charismatic." Did they know that word? Josh said, "Yes"; Noah said, "No." I told Noah it meant having a strong personality, having something about you that people liked and trusted. Josh turned to Noah. "Like John Kennedy," he said, paternally.

In the following four columns of print, Josh said he knew the meaning of "succession," "mercenaries" and "neo-colonialism." His grin had disappeared. I watched his eyes. They never left the first paragraph of print. Like the others, Josh could not read.

I said, "Look, fellows, let's do it this way. I'll read out loud and kind of summarize it and you can write down some notes. You see, the Congo was like America when we fought for our independence. Lumumba was sort of like our George Washington. Want to write that?"

Noah scribbled away. Josh opened his notebook, carefully erased a smudge on the page, adjusted his mechanical pencil, readjusted it and finally said, "Uh, Mrs. Stalvey, how do you spell 'George'?"

It took the entire lunch hour for Josh to write a dozen words. Each word was laboriously formed as I dictated every letter. Over Josh's shoulder, I saw Noah's face look shocked, then sad. When our time had nearly run out, Noah said, "Listen, we've got most of it, Josh. I'll copy the rest after school."

Josh said, "Right, man. I did the thinkin', you do the writin'. That's fair."

Noah's pink face looked pale and he glanced at me with pain and understanding in his blue eyes. He said, "Yeah, man, that's fair."

As Josh and Noah walked down the driveway, I remember sitting at the kitchen counter, shaking my head—in despair for Josh and in amazement over my own incurable ignorance. How long would my middle-class mind assume that all bright children could read? Josh had undoubtedly gone through our school under the same conditions as Gus, Poncho, Donald and the others, conditions that Spike had described vividly. If Josh had been labeled "slow" because of his home background and treated as if he could not learn, it would not take long for him to cover his own shame with defiance and toughness.

I had, however, discovered Josh's secret earlier than I had discovered that Gus and Poncho could not read. This time, there was something I could do. Jane Banneker had been angered enough by the reaction to the murder of the teacher to press hard for a reading specialist for our school. She had got a group of parents to demand a specialist and, to avoid the delay in finding one, had reluctantly left the classroom to take the job herself. I was sure she would be willing to work with Josh.

I telephoned her immediately. Jane said, "Of course, I'll help. I've always felt guilty about Josh. You know, when I had him in my class, seventeen out of the thirty children had reading problems and I was allowed *one* hour a day for reading instruction. I wanted to keep Josh back. He's been very much underestimated in our school and I thought if I had a little more time with him. Well, Peters said no. I have always wished I had fought harder to keep him." She said she would be delighted to work with him now. Did I think he would agree? Either the teacher or the student had to request the time out of class.

I said I would talk to Josh. I did, using every bit of psychology possible. With his ego, I could not say directly, "You can't go to junior high unable to read." Instead, the next time Josh was at our house, I said, "Hey, listen. I just heard that Miss Banneker is working with kids so they can get through high school faster. Maybe she can help you get all *A*'s and get a scholarship to college or something."

Josh leaned against our refrigerator, inspected his fingernails and said, with his usual grin, "Naw, I get all *A*'s already." Noah had come into the room just then, heard Josh and, behind Josh's back, tried to signal me that this was not true. "Yeah," Josh repeated, "get all *A*'s."

By April, I had thought of no way to get through Josh Pitt's terrible pride in order for him to get the help he needed. Then, one day in front of the school, Vangie Peters stopped me. "I've just arranged the most marvelous opportunity," she said. "Noah's class will be spending a *weekend* in May at

(229)

Longville State Teachers College. Can you imagine the new vistas this will open up for the children?" The weekend sounded like fun for Noah, but he would be going to college eventually. The children for whom it could open vistas would be children like Josh. It was just possible that being on a college campus could awaken Josh to the kind of future available to him and could break through the pride that kept him from having it.

I asked Vangie if all of the seventh graders were going. She said, "Oh, yes! All the children to whom it would be a 'meaningful experience.'"

"Fine. Then will you do me a favor, Vangie? This could mean so much to kids like Josh Pitt and Fish and Jimmy. If someone has to stay home, would you see that it's Noah?" Noah, I told her, would understand and, if necessary, we could make it up to him somehow. From what I had heard at lunchtime, none of the other youngsters had parents who had gone to college or, for that matter, brothers, sisters or relatives who were college trained. The trip could be truly important to them.

"Oh, you're so right, Lois. But don't worry. There will be plenty of room for all the children who want to go."

Farther down the block in front of the school, Hallette Spain, Vangie's assistant, also rushed up to me. "Did you hear that Longville State Teachers College has asked us to send our seventh graders to them for a weekend? They want to get to know inner-city students." Her dark brown face took on a conspiratorial smile. "Don't worry, I'll see that Noah goes," she said in her high-pitched nasal voice.

Once again, I explained that there were other students who could get more from the experience.

Hallette Spain wore a yellow pants suit almost identical to Vangie Peters' red one. She smoothed the jacket of her suit and said, "Oh, you're so right, Mrs. Stalvey. Of course, my family is all college trained, but you're right that these lower-class children should know what a college is."

(230)

I said, "Yes, *children* should know, so please put Noah *last* on the list."

At home, I telephoned Ginny Arthur to ask if she had heard about the college weekend. She had and her reaction was the same as mine. Ginny's father was a college professor and her daughter, Amy, had spent most of her holidays on campus visiting her grandfather. I learned that Ginny had also asked Vangie Peters to include her daughter only if *all* the other children were able to go.

During the weeks before the trip, Noah's lunch-hour gang talked of little else. Each child had been asked to write an autobiography to send ahead to the college. I was asked how to spell "laborer," "sanitation department," "digging crew." (Josh asked how to spell "corporation executive" and, straight-faced, I spelled it for him. I had met his father a few weeks before. He was one of the most defeated-looking men I had ever seen. Even his work clothes looked limp and spiritless as he sat outside Vangie Peters' office with Josh. I had introduced myself and said, "Josh is a pleasure to have around our house." His father said, "Firs' time I ever heard any good about him!" I had stuck my head into Vangie's office and said I hoped Josh's problem got straightened out. She chirped, "Oh, you know I adore Josh!" That had as much truth to it as Josh's "corporation executive" label for his father.)

The other children were resignedly honest. Fish asked, "What's that other name for 'cleaning woman'?" Domestic? Yeah. Fish asked whether I didn't think that sounded better than "cleaning woman." I said I guessed he was right. Fish's short brown fingers struggled to form the words. I had never seen Fish—or any of the other fellows—hold a pencil before. If it accomplished nothing else, the trip was motivating these children to write as well as they could.

Noah had proved understanding when I explained that many of his classmates needed the trip more than he did.

(231)

His realization that Josh ("and a lot of the other guys") could not read had given him a lot to think about. He told me he had seen the seventh-grade Iowa Test Scores when his teacher left them on the desk. "Lots of those guys don't have anything but twenties, Mom; that means they're working like second graders!" Noah told me. Noah was quite willing to trade off the trip for a chance to go to overnight camp in the summer.

As the day of the trip moved nearer, I felt unusually optimistic. The college students at Longville had, I felt, shown imagination and common sense in wanting to get to know the kinds of children they would be teaching. According to Noah, Vangie Peters was using the trip as a disciplinary threat, but it seemed to be working. Noah said, "You wouldn't think they were the same kids! Are they being *good*!" Ginny Arthur and I had continued to remind both Vangie Peters and Hallette Spain that our children were not to crowd out any other child. We were assured there was no problem.

The bus was to leave after school on Friday, May 7. Ginny and I were both there on the sidewalk in front of the school with our children and their suitcases. Other parents and the entire class of children were also milling around waiting for the special bus to arrive. Vangie and Hallette were not there, but when the bus came, four college-student chaperones got off and greeted the children. They began to call off the names from their list and the children named boarded the bus.

As the bus pulled away, Ginny said, "I don't know whether to cry or scream." All the white children and the children of the black professional families had boarded the bus. Josh, Jimmy, Fish, T.D. and half a dozen others stood on the sidewalk, waving good-bye.

The day Noah returned, I wrote a note to his college-student sponsor, thanking her for Noah's interesting weekend and asking the reason for the project. I received a long letter in return. The project, she wrote, was originally planned so that the college students could get to know "deprived children" from the inner city. When the autobiographies of the children came to the college, they realized that Mrs. Peters had not understood "we were sponsoring a project for underprivileged children." "Mrs. Peters informed us that it was too late to arrange for underprivileged children . . . instead of the ones her faculty had picked."

I showed the letter to Ben. It was useless for me to have another confrontation with Vangie. The trip was over. But, I told Ben, if I could just understand why the children who needed the trip most had been left home.

Ben read the letter and said, "Well, Peters probably wanted to use the trip as a treat for the white kids she's trying so hard to keep at school—and she probably didn't want anyone to know she's got seventh graders who can't read." Ben, always more a realist than I, added, "But you can't let someone like Vangie Peters get you upset. There's only a certain amount you can do. There's too much wrong with the whole school system."

Ben now told me of a recent experience involving the Neighborhood Youth Corps high school students he was using part-time in his office. Ben and Mrs. Chambers his secretary, were training these youngsters, as the government-funded project required, for jobs after graduation. Mrs. Chambers, a young black woman with preschool children, was outraged at the inadequate education the Youth Corps students described. They all attended a black high school and one promisingly bright youth told her that he literally could not understand his English teacher, a man with a thick Italian accent. From other students, Ben had learned that some of the high school teachers simply read newspapers during class, leaving the students to do as they pleased. When the Youth Corps counselor made his obligatory visit to Ben's office, he had tossed a rating sheet on Mrs. Chambers' desk, saying, "Don't bother to fill this out, girlie. You can't expect much from these kids anyway. You know how they are . . . poor in spelling and grammar." Mrs.

Chambers, usually calm and quiet, told the "counselor," "Then why didn't your school do something about it?" She had taken the rating sheet in to Ben. They found the top rating was "Average." Under Mrs. Chambers' patient instruction, Ben said, these teen-agers were doing much better than average work. Ben and Mrs. Chambers added their own category of "Excellent" to the rating sheets. The "counselor" read them and shrugged. "Well, just don't forget to watch your purse, girlie," he said as he left.

Ben's story was hardly comforting, nor was Noah's report that, since the college trip, "the kids who didn't go aren't friends anymore with the kids who did." I had been wondering why Josh, T.D. and Fish no longer came home with Noah at lunchtime.

The college trip was to leave even more ripples in its wake. Ten days after the college weekend, Noah asked me at lunchtime if "anybody" had telephoned me. When I said, No, he gulped and said, "Well, I got in trouble in mechanical drawing class today. Mrs. Spain said she'd have to call you."

The trouble, as Noah described it, occurred at the nearby school where our seventh graders were bussed each week for industrial arts. Noah had been complaining that the industrial arts teacher, a Mr. Muchinski, was "prejudiced." "He treats the white kids different than he treats the black kids. He never yells at us and he gives us better marks. I tried to tell him we notice this, but he just told me to go back to my seat." That day, Noah explained, a new group of papers had been graded. Noah's work had been marked $B+$ and put up on the board; "Josh's paper was just as good as mine and he got a C and it wasn't put on the board," Noah said.

Then he looked down at the table, paused, took a breath and said in a rush, "So I just lost my temper and I ripped my paper down and told Mr. Muchinski he was a bigot."

My immediate reactions were so mixed, I could only look at Noah silently while questions tangled themselves in my mind.

Had I projected a disrespect for teachers that Noah had picked up? Was Noah trying to emulate Spike who was fighting the battle of Beethoven at his private school? Was Noah using this method to win back Josh's friendship?

The first question I asked Noah was whether he could not have found a more polite way of dealing with Mr. Muchinski's alleged prejudice. Noah said he had tried for weeks. Mr. Muchinski had ignored his polite words.

I said, "All right. Now, I want you to be extra-honest with yourself. Did you do this so that Josh would like you better? Because if you did, I don't think it's going to work. Josh isn't the kind of guy who wants other people to fight battles for him."

Noah paused before he answered. He was, I noticed, looking troubled instead of triumphant. If his motive had been to get attention or to feel big by challenging a teacher, he would, I believed, have shown some trace of satisfaction. As it was, he looked more ashamed and frightened than proud of what he had done. And by the focus of his eyes, I could tell he was trying hard to think about my question.

"Mom, I don't think I was trying to get in good with Josh. I think . . . I think it was because it's no fun getting good marks if the teacher's cheating for you. I think I did it for *me*."

In one sentence, my twelve-year-old son had described in simple terms a feeling I had been trying to identify for years. Ever since discovering that white and black people were treated differently in America, I had often wondered why I cared so much. I sensed too that my caring had a strange selfishness about it, that it was not to *my* interest that people were judged on the color of their skins. Now, Noah had expressed this haunting feeling perfectly. It was "no fun" enjoying all the privileges of life when I learned the cards were stacked in my favor. When the schools "cheated" in favor of my children, I —and Noah too—missed the joy of fair competition.

I said, "Noah, honey, I know *exactly* what you mean!"

Just then, Hallette Spain phoned to give me the details of the incident. Noah had indeed torn his paper from the board and accused Mr. Muchinski of being a bigot. Mr. Muchinski had bypassed his own black principal to call Vangie Peters demanding that Noah apologize for calling him prejudiced. Vangie had turned the problem over to Hallette Spain.

Hallette Spain lowered her nasal voice and said, "Just between you and me, Noah is right about that teacher. I talked with other students in his class and all of them—black and white—said that he has a double standard for grades and behavior. But he says he won't allow Noah back in his class until Noah apologizes. He said he didn't mind Noah's ripping his paper down, but Noah must apologize for calling him a bigot. What would you like me to do, Mrs. Stalvey?"

It was fair for Noah to apologize for disrupting the class and for being rude, but it was not fair to make him apologize for the one issue on which he was apparently right. I suggested that we have a meeting with Mr. Muchinski, his principal, Mrs. Spain and me.

Next morning, the tall, spare black principal attempted to lead the meeting in his office. Mr. Muchinski, who was a great deal older than I had visualized him, ignored everyone but me. He was a pale man in his sixties with sparse, straight colorless hair and faded eyes. He immediately began shoving Josh Pitt's drawings into my hands, proclaiming them "poor" work. He had not brought Noah's work for comparison and I could only look at the drawings dumbly. This finished, Mr. Muchinski began a passionate speech on his inborn lack of prejudice and his lifelong practice of "tolerance." "Your son must apologize," he said in a high, quavering voice. "I do not have one bigoted bone in my body."

I glanced at Hallette Spain who was examining her hands. I said to Mr. Muchinski, "Noah *will* apologize for being rude, but perhaps we can all learn something from this experience." As gently as I could, I told Mr. Muchinski that *I* did not believe I had no bigoted bones in my body. "Because of the way in which I grew up, sir, I believe I have plenty of hidden prejudices I haven't discovered yet. Perhaps our generation will never be able to rout out all the unconscious racism we've absorbed. I know I discover new prejudices in myself constantly." Mr. Muchinski looked at the ceiling in elaborate boredom. I continued, "Mrs. Spain tells me that most of the children in your class believe you treat black and white students differently."

Mr. Muchinski rose to his feet. "I do not," he said in his quavering high-pitched voice. "You may be bigoted but I *am not*! And I have a class to teach." He whirled and walked out of the office.

Hallette Spain was still examining her hands. The principal appeared to be as speechless and surprised as I. To break the silence, I asked him, "How long has Mr. Muchinski been teaching?" I expected to hear that this tired-looking man was close to retirement. Instead, the principal surprised me by saying this was his first year.

But, I asked, what had he been doing all his other years? The principal tried, loyally, to obscure the facts, but I finally got the truth: Mr. Muchinski was one of the many engineers who had been laid off by industry. He had once got a teacher's certificate, as Ben had, "just in case." Mr. Muchinski, in addition to losing his job at an advanced age, also had to drive a long distance each day from his home in a New Jersey suburb. I felt sympathy for this tired, disappointed man.

I asked, but only rhetorically, why he had been assigned to a mostly black school instead of an easier white middle-class school where he could feel more comfortable during his last working years. The principal shrugged, but we both knew that the easy middle-class schools were taken by teachers with seniority and connections. Also, white middle-class parents might object to an inexperienced sixty-year-old teacher and their objections would be taken seriously.

The principal changed the subject briefly; then, as if introducing a new topic, he said, "By the way, when a principal rates a teacher as unsatisfactory, the teacher does not leave the school system. He is merely transferred to another school —often to the *same* kind of school he leaves. You don't feel right sending your problem to another principal. Sometimes it's best to do what you can for a teacher yourself." He rose now, tall, thin and determined-looking, and said, "You will ask Noah, won't you, to apologize for being *rude?*"

As soon as I got home, I wrote a note to Mr. Muchinski, wishing him success in what I had just learned was his new career (my note was never acknowledged) and the following week, Noah received a cold nod to his apology in class. Noah added, "And you were right about Josh, Mom. He said, real tough, 'I don't need nobody stickin' up for me!' "

This seemed a good time to explain to Noah that, in this complicated world, you did what you believed was right— and you did it without expecting thanks for it. Noah nodded soberly, "Yeah, I figured that out."

Josh Pitt, I believed, had taken himself permanently out of my life. I missed seeing him. He was never among the youngsters who had gradually returned to our backyard at lunchtime. Then, near the end of May, I had to go to school to pick up Noah's homework assignment when he was in bed with a bad cold. I heard a familiar voice behind me. "Hey, Mrs. Stalvey, you got a cigarette for me?" I turned and grinned back at Josh. "No, I care too much about you to have you get like me!" Josh seemed to be pleased I remembered our dialogue. He waved and went to his class.

The tall, bewildered-looking blond man who had taught art but was now Noah's English teacher was writing down the assignment. Suddenly I heard Carter Kellogg's gravelly voice vibrating through the hallway. "You smart-ass bastard . . . you get the hell out of my sight!"

I heard a muffled, unintelligible reply. I stepped out into the hallway. Josh, fists cocked, was standing with his back to me and in front of him was a red-faced Carter Kellogg, yelling at the top of his voice. With each screamed "smart-ass" or "bastard," Josh advanced and Carter Kellogg retreated. Kellogg shouted, "Jerk . . . stupid jerk," and Josh's fist moved back to strike.

I grabbed Josh's heavy arm from behind and held on, saying into his ear, "Don't hit him. If you hit him, he wins." Kellogg had retreated inside his classroom, slamming the door. Josh tried to shake me off to go after him. I grabbed Josh's shirt to hold him back. I said, frantically, "If you hit him, they'll send you to Boone. Josh, don't let him win."

By placing myself in front of his every escape, I maneuvered Josh into the empty teachers' lounge. I asked over and over, "What happened? First tell me what happened?" Josh's eyes were wide, the whites showing. He looked like a wild horse about to bolt. I crowded him into a corner of the room and he allowed me to hold on to his thick wrists. Then he pulled away and turned his back for a moment. I said again, "What happened?"

Josh threw down a crumpled note he had been holding in his hand all this time. It landed on the table. As I picked it up, Josh said, "Kellogg don't never put up Fish's drawings. He do real good ones. I got a note from Peters sayin' Kellogg should put up Fish's drawings."

He had indeed. The crumpled note was in Vangie's handwriting. It read: Please put up Arnold's drawings, V. Peters.

Then, like a fist in my face, it hit me that Josh was trying to do for Fish what Noah had tried to do for him. Josh had even gone about it through more responsible channels. Vangie had written the note, probably as an easy way to get Josh out of the office. Josh had undoubtedly swaggered into Carter Kellogg's room. Carter Kellogg did not suffer student egos gladly.

Even Josh, in his fury, could not quite hide the bewilderment on his face. Was he wondering why, every time he measured himself against Noah, he came up short? Reading, college trips, protesting unfairness—Noah won; Josh lost.

I said, "Oh, Josh. I know it's not fair. But you've got to be the *man*. You know what Mr. Kellogg's like and you've got to be smarter and stronger than he is. If you hit him, that's it for you. You've got to be strong enough to hang on and be more of a man than he is."

What I said did not matter. I think I could have recited the alphabet as long as I blocked Josh's exit from the room and kept talking long enough for him to get control of himself. He knew as well as I what hitting a teacher meant. Josh paced the floor silently; I talked. The bell finally rang.

Josh said, "I'm too smart to hit that fool. Too smart." Somehow the grin was back on his face, though his eyes were hard and cold as frozen mud. He said, "I gotta go now," and waited to see if I would stand aside. I did and he walked past me into the hallway now full of students.

I saw or heard nothing about Josh for the next week. Then, the first week in June, Noah said at lunchtime, "Josh told me to tell you he's being transferred to Fox Junior High." I asked whether Josh acted as if he wanted me to do something about it? Noah said, "I don't know, Mom. He just said to tell you."

Fox Junior High was an all-black junior high just outside our district. It was notorious for gang wars and low standards of achievement. To me, it was the worst possible place for Josh to be. Josh, blocked from any other kind of achievement, was a perfect candidate for a gang. He was old enough now to do with his muscles what he had not been helped to do with his mind. Also, as the "new kid" in a school, he would spend the last weeks of the semester proving himself in battle after battle, battles in which dozens of children his age had died.

I went to the school at the end of the day, determined to find Josh and learn what his message to me meant. Josh was in front of the candy shop and when he saw me, he came across the street.

I said I had heard he was going to Fox next week. Did he want to go there? Did he want me to talk to Mrs. Peters so he could stay here?

Josh's wide grin never slipped. He said, "Nobody gonna send me to no school where I don't want to go."

Somehow I was missing a clue. Josh had sent the message home with Noah. Why? I said, "Josh, are you *sure* you want to go to Fox?"

Josh laughed. "Hey, don't worry. I can take care of myself with those dudes. No sweat."

Fish strolled across the street and joined us. Josh said to me, "Hey, Mrs. Stalvey, you got a cigarette for me?" I said, distinctly and slowly, "No, Josh, I care too much about you . . . to have you get like me."

Josh gave me a playful poke on the shoulder and grinned. "Hey, I'll be seeing you," and he walked back across the street.

I watched him go, feeling helpless. As his stocky young body moved across the black asphalt pavement, it felt to me as if I were watching him cross a river and the river was sweeping him away. I did not know how to pull him back.

The school year ended on June 24. From his private school, Spike got his *D* in history. Noah's mechanical drawing papers were returned to him, the grades on half of them very carefully erased and lowered.

Ben looked at the boys' report cards. He said, "Well, fellas, I guess it's just as well that you're learning now that fighting some of these things cost you something. You don't always win. But I'm proud you tried."

I was proud too. Ben was right. You did not always win. The boys paid through lower grades on their report cards; I paid through a huge aching sense of having failed a proud young man whose pride was both his protection and his prison.

fifteen

I SPENT THE SUMMER OF 1971 IN AN ELABORATE CAMPAIGN of self-deception. By August 30, when school buses in Pontiac, Michigan, were being fire-bombed to protest a court-ordered integration plan, I was well into my own unconscious plan to avoid facing a fear I was ashamed to admit.

It took me over a year to understand my sudden interest in moving to Denver. While I could admit that part of it came from my feeling of helplessness over what our vast public school system did to children like Josh, the move seemed mostly to be for Ben's benefit. Over the past few years, Ben had occasionally mentioned openings in other cities for area directors of the Department of Labor's Office of Federal Contract Compliance, the job Ben held in Philadelphia. Each time, I told Ben how much I would hate leaving our house and our neighborhood. In early July, Ben looked astonished when I agreed he ought to apply for a new opening in Denver. In Philadelphia, Ben had been unable to get the Philadelphia Plan adequately enforced. Rumors were that a powerful Pennsylvania politician did not want the construction industry "bothered" by the requirement of hiring minority group workers. Ben felt that perhaps in the Denver area, he could finally get the necessary staff and the cooperation of the administration in enforcing sanctions.

I said, "I think you ought to have the chance to find out.

And a new part of the country might be a good experience for the children."

Ben's bushy eyebrows shot up. "Are you *sure* you want to move?"

I said casually, "Look, honey, I read somewhere that people, like plants, benefit from occasional repotting. I think it would be good for all of us."

At that moment, I sincerely believed what I was saying.

It is now obvious that I was frantically submerging my fear of Spike's entering Germantown High School. The cost of another year at St. Peter's Academy was simply not justifiable. Spike had done well in math and science, but his English and Spanish teachers had made the same comments I had heard for years: "He's not living up to his potential." He had barely passed both subjects and his relationship with the history teacher was obviously beyond repair. Trying other private schools was an expensive gamble and Spike wanted to go to Germantown High School with his friend, Dave.

Dave, a year older than Spike, had been one of the few white students in tenth grade the year before. According to Spike, Dave had had no "real" problems in the thirty-one-hundred-student school where 89 percent of the students were black.

I said, "What about the kid who kept threatening to beat Dave up if he didn't bring him a quarter?" Spike said that Dave had never brought the quarter and the fellow had never done more than threaten.

I had talked with Dave's father one day when we waited in line together at the post office. He was enthusiastic about Germantown High. "Dave's getting a good education there, academically, and he's getting something more—experience with people. Listen, someday someone's going to have to bridge that abyss between blacks and whites. It's going to be an issue in a lot of fields. Who knows, Dave's years at Germantown High might be the most valuable experience he has."

This conversation had taken place while Spike was beginning his year at private school. Admiration for Mr. Anderson's attitude was easier when I was not about to try to emulate it. Even while talking with him, I had some unexpressed doubts. Dave, after all, was a stocky, placid fellow with a cherubic face, not the kind of boy to attract hostility. I knew too that Mr. Anderson had been caught in the rash of industrial layoffs and was now trying to establish his own business. Private school was beyond their resources. Was he, I wondered, rationalizing a choice he did not have for Dave?

All during the past year, Dave had told Spike of the "cool" science department, the good teachers and the equipment. Spike told me, "Dave says they've got their own computer terminal at Germantown." Spike was itching to get at it. By the first part of July, Spike was getting more and more information from Dave and planning his first year at Germantown High.

By the middle of July, I told Ben I was sure I wanted to move to Denver.

Ben requested and received the transfer to the Denver area. We contacted a realtor who put a big red "For Sale" sign on our lawn. We anticipated no problem with selling our large house. West Mt. Airy, our neighborhood, was a model for successful integration. New white families were moving in constantly. Many, unfortunately, were planning to send their children to private schools, but property values had increased astonishingly. The house which was across the street was actually a bit smaller than ours and had sold two years before for over *twice* what we had paid for ours. The realtor had advised a price I considered almost greedy, but she said that even during the notoriously bad selling seasons of summer and fall, she would be able to get that amount. We would make a large profit, it seemed, but I was surprised at the almost physical pain I felt when a stake with a "For Sale" sign was driven into our lawn.

(244)

Ben made his first trip to Denver on July 26 and brought back news of an integrated neighborhood there, Park Hill. Park Hill's schools, he said, were not as predominantly black as those in our present neighborhood: their largest minority group was Spanish-speaking students. Fine, I told Ben, our children could learn Spanish. We decided to buy our new house in Park Hill, but I felt depressed by the pictures of houses Ben brought back with him. There were no towering oaks, no lush rhododendron; nothing resembled the wonderful house in which our children had grown up.

It is now possible for me to understand the special anguish I felt during the six weeks between the end of July and September 9, the day Spike was scheduled to enter Germantown High. Each time the phone rang, I prayed it would be the realtor. There were distressingly few appointments to show our house. The realtor who had talked so optimistically in July now explained that families with children, the prime customers for our large house, usually did their buying in spring. "They want to be settled," she said, "by the time school starts." I was not aware how frantically I wanted to do the same.

In August, Ben was approached downtown by two different men, both white Protestants, who had heard our house was for sale. Both men expressed disappointment in not having heard this a few weeks earlier. They had wanted to buy in our integrated neighborhood, but had been told by *our realtor* that there was nothing that size available. Each family had bought a large house in Chestnut Hill.

While trying to understand this disturbing information, I suddenly realized that every prospect our realtor had brought had a Jewish name. From our own experiences in 1962 when we had to insist on a mixed neighborhood, we pieced together the reasons why other WASPs were still being steered to all-WASP areas. As WASPs, we could "safely" be sold houses in areas like Chestnut Hill—all-white and virtually all-Protestant.

(245)

Jewish families, unwelcome in Chestnut Hill, were shown our house while two likely Protestant prospects were literally kept away. Apparently it still took determination and knowledge for WASPs who were interested in integration to combat real estate tactics. Depressing as this news would have been at any time, I felt overcome with anger and frustration. Our exclusive contract with the realtor still had two months to run. Challenging the realtor with this discovery only brought fervent denials—and no new prospects.

In spite of my mounting panic, I could not combat Ben's common sense decision that buying a house in Denver before our house was sold was risky. We could not afford to carry two mortgages and our house, empty of furniture, would look overwhelmingly larger to prospects. Yet on September 7, it would be necessary to register Spike for school; on October 19, Ben had to take up full-time duties in his Denver office. I recalled my calm acceptance of a three-month wait in Omaha while Ben had gone ahead to Philadelphia. Then, I had coped with showing the house and with two preschool children. What, I wondered, caused such panic now?

On Tuesday, September 7, after an unexpectedly sleepless night I drove Spike and his friend Dave to Germantown High School. I was to take care of the paper work while Dave showed Spike around the empty school. (Classes would start on Thursday, September 9—the day that prisoners took over Attica prison, the same day that the ex-Grand Dragon of the Michigan Ku Klux Klan was arrested for fire-bombing buses in Pontiac.)

On that warm, sunny Tuesday morning, I parked the car at the corner of Germantown Avenue and High Street—a corner I was to know intimately during the next month. Dave, Spike and I walked toward the immense empty yellow-brick building. I reminded myself, reassuringly, that Germantown High looked very much like the high school I had attended.

(246)

As we got closer to the building, its walks deserted except for two other parents also bringing their youngsters to register, I saw the walls and doorways were scrawled with graffiti. I told myself that in my day we had only chalk and crayon available to us, not these permanent inks.

Inside, the corridors echoed with emptiness The school seemed well cared for and clean. A uniformed security guard nodded politely and pointed toward the office. Dave and Spike said good-bye to me at the office door and proceeded on their tour of the school. As they walked off, I again grasped at the similarities between these wide hallways and high ceilings, and the high school I had attended.

In the office, I took a seat along the wall to wait my turn. The office was large, well lighted by big windows and staffed, I noticed, by women, all of whom were white. All the other parents waiting in line were black. A burly black man had gotten up to give me his chair. I looked up at him now, attempting to start a conversation to pass the time.

I asked, "Are you registering a son or a daughter?"

He looked down at me and smiled. "Lady, I'm registering me. I'm in twelfth grade. We just moved here from Chicago."

Oh. The young man was obviously flattered; I was astonished. Were there many students this size at Germantown High?

Just then, another young black man walked into the office and spoke to one of the clerks. She called him "Mr. Gresham." Good heavens, he was the principal and he looked younger than the twelfth grader I had mistaken for a parent! He was of medium height, with Caucasian features but deep copper skin. His face looked smooth and young. The picture of Mr. Gresham dealing with gang members was difficult to conjure up. It was also difficult to assess whether he had been given his important job because he could handle it, or because *he* was easily handled as a black token in a mostly white bureaucracy.

When my turn came to register, the information was taken by a blond middle-aged woman with an intricate hairdo and unasked questions in her eyes. Her brusque, impersonal attitude with the black woman ahead of me changed immediately. She had muttered directions to the mother before me; when she completed Spike's form, she carefully wrote down a name and room number and added smiling directions to the counselor's office where Spike's roster would be made up.

Spike and Dave appeared just as I left the office. Spike's gray eyes were dancing with excitement; he had just seen the computer. As we walked down the hall to the counselor's office, I glanced at the slip of paper in my hand. Spike's counselor would be a Mrs. Saxon, but, I decided, it could hardly be Sonny Saxon's mother. Spike's old friend from Cub Scouts was now college age, and we had not seen him for some time. It would be too much of a coincidence to find his mother here —and Spike assigned to her.

Coincidence or not, Ilka Saxon was indeed Spike's counselor. When we walked into her private cubicle, I watched Spike's face and hers light up with pleasure. Spike even allowed her to give him a hug. She had always been one of Spike's favorite adults and a woman I admired. Born without conventional prettiness, Ilka looked like a brown-skinned version of a Modigliani painting, but her sensitivity, warmth and outgoing personality made her look—to me and others—thoroughly beautiful.

To Spike, she said, "Sonny will be so glad to hear you're at *his* old high school! Do you remember the night you settled that fight between Sonny and Neal? Sonny kept saying, 'That Spike, he understands me!' "

I remembered that evening. Then, Spike had looked up at Sonny's father and Neal's, explaining that Sonny was only teasing them. Now, Spike looked down from his height of six foot two. And Sonny was away at college.

Ilka quickly filled Spike's roster with teachers she felt were good. Then she said, "This school is better than people believe. Sonny got an excellent education here. And don't believe all the scare talk about gangs. Some gangs tried to recruit Sonny because he's so big, but he just ignored them and never had any problems. They're not going to try to recruit you, Spike, because you're white. And they're not going to bother you either."

Spike was less interested in gang problems than in being sure that computer math was on his roster. He leaned on Ilka's file cabinet, folding and refolding his roster card and beaming at Ilka.

Ilka turned to me, "Lois, don't worry. There are a lot of good teachers here and Culver Gresham knows what he's doing. He's the kind of principal this school needs. Don't worry about Spike here."

I changed the subject to Sonny. I was not yet willing to concede that I had worries. As we left the school, I tried to people the corridors with students. I put that out of my mind too.

As was to happen during other crucial times, Ben was in Washington on Thursday, September 9, when I drove Spike to his first day at Germantown High. Even Spike's friend, Dave, was not with us. Classes for the eleventh and twelfth graders did not begin until later in the day; Spike was to report in the morning for tenth-grade orientation. With Spike sitting next to me and unusually quiet, I drove the car as if I were on a conveyor belt that moved me involuntarily along the twelve blocks toward the school.

As I turned the corner onto Germantown Avenue, I saw the school building, not as I had seen it during registration day, but looming out of an immense crowd of students. Among the students, there must have been some girls and some short boys. There must also have been a few white youngsters. But, as I was forced by the traffic to pull up in front of the main doorway on High Street, I could see nothing but hundreds of tall, muscular, hard-eyed black males. Not one of them looked anything like the soft-faced, friendly and familiar black eighth graders Spike had known in Willis School.

All the self-deception I had employed until that moment fell away. I took a breath in panic before beginning to shift gears and drive away. In that moment, Spike opened the car door and got out. Exactly as he had done on that safe, serene day in Omaha when he strode blithely off to nursery school, he did not even stop to say good-bye. I sat, numb with terror, as Spike disappeared into the mob. My last glimpse of him was of a slender white birch swallowed up by a forest of weathered, storm-scarred black oaks. By the time I opened my mouth to call him back, he was gone.

A car horn sounded behind me and I knew I had to move my car down narrow, one-way High Street. I drove as slowly as I could, one eye on the sidewalk. Even more huge dark brown *men* were sauntering along toward the school. The mark of gang members—small gold earrings—glinted on many of them. As my car crept along the remainder of High Street, I did not see one white face or one brown face I knew.

I reached the cross street. It looked unexpectedly familiar. Then I remembered. I had driven Spike along High Street, across Baynton, nine years before. This was the route I had taken every day during our first summer in Philadelphia when Spike went to day camp at Germantown Settlement House. Spike had been the only white child at the Settlement House, but his six-year-old playmates from the low-income projects nearby were no longer six years old. Nine years of poverty had affected them differently than Spike's nine years in an untroubled middle-class family. The eerie coincidence of retracing a nine-year-old route only increased my determination to rush back and rescue my son.

As I turned left onto Baynton Street, I thought bitterly of my words to Noah's bigoted mechanical drawing teacher. I had not lied; there were indeed many layers of unconscious racism in my generation of whites. I had just found a new one. It was expanding inside me as if to stifle my heartbeat. All right, I conceded my racism. Now, how could I get my child back out of that school?

At the end of the block, I waited impatiently for the traffic to clear so that I could turn onto Walnut Lane, complete the third side of the square and get back to Germantown High. I tried to control my panic, reminding myself that Spike's friend Dave had had only one threat during one year of school. But was this the truth? Or did Dave want the company misery loves? Dave's father had said he wanted his children to bridge the abyss between black Americans and white. I thought I did too—until today. When Spike disappeared into a mob of toughened young people, many of whom could not read, did not want to be in school and had no illusions about their futures, my idealism had sputtered and died.

I was finally able to turn left onto Walnut Lane. At the end of the block, I could turn left again, go back to the school and take Spike home.

As the traffic on Walnut Lane inched along in sickening slowness, I suddenly confronted two problems I had chosen to ignore. How could I find Spike in that vast, crowded building? And when I found him, what would I say? Could I look up at this tall young man and tell him, "I am afraid for you. I am taking you home." Spike was fifteen years old, executing those complex steps between childhood and manhood. Would he let me take him home? Did I dare to insist that he—and I —still needed more years of protection? In that moment, I wished desperately that the years had not gotten out of control, that Spike was still small enough for me to pick him up in my arms and put him again in the safety of a playpen.

My unconscious mind completed the connection it was trying to make. I had been sitting next to Spike's playpen the day I read *Life* magazine's account of the riot at Little Rock's Central High School. In September, 1957, with my pink and blond baby laughing and trying to climb out of his playpen, I had looked at the pictures and read the text describing the mob of more than a thousand white adults, jeering and threatening to lynch nine Negro students. I had felt shame for my fellow whites and gratitude that my little boy would never have to fight for an education. And, for just one moment, while I watched my son who was so precious and special to me, I tried to imagine what those Negro mothers felt as they sent their children through that mob of hostile whites.

Now I knew.

But I also knew there was no mob of a thousand *black* adults outside Spike's high school yelling, "Lynch the honkies!" My child was not the opening wedge for an unpopular Supreme Court decision; he was merely one of the last white students in a sad example of Northern-style segregation.

How many of those black mothers in Little Rock whose children were as special and precious to them as Spike was to me had said, as I was saying to myself, "I agree with the idealistic principle, but why does it have to be *my* child?" Why indeed. Perhaps their young people too had made the choice as Spike had made his; perhaps for those black parents, as for Ben and me, it was too late to alter a course they had deliberately chosen long ago.

I reached Germantown Avenue. I did not turn the corner. I drove straight ahead on Walnut Lane and went home.

The mothers of those nine black students at the high school in Little Rock—and the mothers of all black children who have been the first in white schools—certainly walked the floor and watched the clock as I did for the rest of the day. I concede they had more reason for fear than I did—no national guard had had to be called to enable Spike to enter the building. It is hard to concede that these other mothers worried more. At 1:45, I saw a flash of the gray-green trolley through the trees a half block away and then Spike's tall figure coming up the street. For the first time in an endless day, I breathed naturally again.

Spike came through the door. I asked, "How did it go?"

"Okay. Got lost a couple of times. That's a *big* building!" Spike said. But he knew what I wanted to ask. "Mom, *no* problem. A couple of kids said, 'Got a quarter?' I just told them, 'No, thanks.' They laughed and I laughed."

When Ben came home from Washington that evening, he thought Spike's method was both hilarious and effective. "The kids probably test each other the first few days. If they thought Spike was scared of them, it might have been different." I was not ready to tell Ben how scared I had been.

My fears did not fade. Each day at 1:30, I took up my post at the window, feeling like Bluebeard's wife calling to her sister, "Sister Anne, do you see anyone coming?" I was not looking for a cloud of dust; I was looking and listening for the gray-green number fifty-three trolley.

Over the next few days, I learned that, in spite of the fact that Germantown High was allegedly 10 percent white, Spike was the only white student in most of his classes. Of his eight teachers, five were black. In several classes, Spike was the only white person in the room. For Spike, this was nothing unusual. He would not feel—or show—discomfort. I reminded myself that the daughter of Mark Shedd, the superintendent of Philadelphia schools, was also one of the few white students at Germantown High. Surely the superintendent of schools would not send his daughter into a situation he believed was dangerous. Would he?

On Monday, September 13, Governor Nelson Rockefeller gave his approval for state troopers and national guardsmen (all of them white) to storm Attica prison where prisoners (most of them black) were still holding hostages in a protest against prison conditions. Thirty-two prisoners were killed in a storm of bullets and—after conflicting reports were investigated—the world learned that the eleven dead hostages had died from the bullets of their "rescuers." When Spike went off to school on Tuesday, I tried not to think of the emotions created by this white slaughter of black men.

That day, my wait at the window seemed even longer than usual. When Spike finally came home, I asked, "Kids talking about Attica at school?"

Spike was again dismantling the pepper mill as he munched his sandwiches. "Not really," he said. "Oh, yeah, some kid in biology class said, 'I hate all whites. I'm gonna kill you, boy.'"

What happened then?

"Oh, I just told him, 'I guess I know how you feel!'"

And *then* what?

Spike was under the table now, looking for the piece of the pepper mill he had dropped. "Oh, he just went back to his seat. Never came near me again."

When Ilka Saxon called me to ask how Spike was doing ("He hasn't been in to the counselors' office," she said, "so I guess he's okay."), I told her of the incident. Her warm, deep laugh came through the phone. "That's my boy! He's really somethin' else! And that kid knew Spike *did* understand."

Until October 6, Spike reported no new incidents. He had begun to talk enthusiastically about his computer math class ("It's really cool! We've got our own computer terminal.") and his geometry teacher ("She's really okay! Little tiny thing —but is she tough!"). Spike's friend, Dave, was talking to the chemistry teacher about getting Spike into the Saturday ACS (American Chemical Society) program. "It's really only supposed to be for eleventh and twelfth graders," Spike said. "And it's sort of for 'underprivileged' kids, but the teacher says they've got extra room and maybe I can start now in tenth grade."

On October 6, Spike told me, somewhat nervously, that a *white* student ("and a *big* mean-looking guy at that!")

had threatened to beat him up if he did not bring a quarter to school. Spike said it was "stupid" to start paying money; he would just try to stay out of the fellow's way. Spike's smile was wry. "At least he's white, Mom. Makes him easier to spot in the halls."

On October 7, a neighborhood tragedy made the threat to Spike seem minor indeed by comparison. A neighbor had taken her son out of the fifth grade at Willis School. She was afraid of the "rough seventh and eighth graders." I had tried to re-assure her that Sarah and Noah, who were now in seventh and eighth grades, reported no unusual roughness. She had, how-ever, transferred her son to a private school. On October 7, he was found drowned at the bottom of the private school swimming pool.

Ben and I talked of the special grief these parents must be feeling. Ben said, his face creased with concern for the be-reaved parents and for my worry over Spike, "I wish there were some way to guarantee our children will always be safe —but there isn't." Ben reminded me now of two suburban incidents we had heard about recently: the son of a friend in St. Louis whose jaw was broken during an unprovoked beating by a white gang; a friend in Philadelphia's all-white Northeast who was harassed constantly for his parents' antiwar activities.

"I don't have to wait for Spike to come home everyday the way you do, honey," Ben said, "but maybe you can make yourself see that the best way to keep our children safe is to let them learn independence and self-confidence. Look, all young people are attracted to the cities—and some of the top colleges are in urban areas. In the end, I think our kids are going to grow up better able to take care of themselves than if they'd come to the city after being raised in some isolated middle-class atmosphere. Does it help to look at it that way?"

It did, but I felt sorry for Ben, trying so hard to reassure me. Our house had still not been sold. He had to leave on October 19 to begin full-time work in Denver. I did not want him to know how desperate I felt about all the weeks ahead when I would be without him.

On October 14, while Ben was in Washington for a last briefing, I went with Dave Anderson's father to the first Germantown High School Parents' Association meeting and, for the first time, was able to form an opinion of Mr. Gresham, the principal.

This young-looking man with his moderate Afro and handsome features attacked the gang question head-on. "I grew up in a neighborhood a whole lot tougher than this and these gang kids don't fool me for a minute. They've finally come to understand that I am not their social worker and that I'm running a *school*—not a playground or a battlefield. I don't care how tough they are outside the school. Inside, they're just another bunch of students." In spite of his pleasant smile, his dark brown eyes were glinting with their no-nonsense message. "There are a lot of rumors around that aren't true. Some young white teacher comes in here, is basically scared of black kids, can't control her class and calls the newspapers to talk about student hostility. And if a serious incident does occur in an all-black school, it gets much more space in the newspapers than one in a white school."

I was impressed. Neither gang kids nor teachers nor the newspapers fooled this man. I wondered if he was alluding to an incident at an all-white school that had been suppressed completely. A friend who was a counselor there told me that one of the students had landed a karate kick on the chest of an elderly security guard who then died of a heart attack. The death was never reported in the papers and hushed up in the school.

Mr. Gresham invited the parents to "come to school; walk through the halls; see what really goes on here. It's not what the rumors would have you believe." Then he said, "And I'll say this even to this mixed group . . ." I glanced around. In the group of about one hundred people, Dave's father and

I were the only people who made it "mixed." Mr. Gresham continued, ". . . that even though this school has gone from 30 percent black to 90 percent black in ten years, we do not need white students in order to make this a good school. We need only good teachers and the *determination* to make this a good school." Culver Gresham sent a direct, level gaze to all the parents. His jutting Cary Grant-style chin left no question about *his* determination.

I left the school with Dave Anderson's father and a new feeling of reassurance about Germantown High School. Culver Gresham was no Vangie Peters. He was honest, direct and totally unimpressed with my color. He ran a school, it appeared, on the old-fashioned principle of basic education.

Ben left Philadelphia on October 19 for what we knew would be a separation of at least seven weeks. I felt less panicky now about Spike's high school, but it was hard for me to hide the desolation I felt about Ben's being gone. I told cheerful lies. I did not want him burdened with worrying about me while he organized his new area.

On October 20, Spike came home from school while I was in the midst of a telephone conversation with a woman who had asked me to recommend some "affluent Negro families" who might send their children to the boarding school her son attended. "We'd like to give our children a more rounded education," she had said. I was in the process of telling her that my own son was getting a *well*-rounded education right here at Germantown High. She gasped, "But aren't you terrified?" I admitted that I *had* been and I quoted some of Ben's sensible theories. Spike listened and I noticed a small smile on his face, as well as a red blotch on his cheek. I made my excuses and ended the conversation on the telephone.

As soon as I put the receiver down, Spike said, "Mom, I got beat up today." My mouth was still open with shock when he added, "By that white kid."

Spike said, "Close your mouth, Mom. This is what happened." While my eyes searched his long frame for any other sign of injury, Spike talked, but with a forced attempt at his usual casualness. He said that the same white student who had threatened him two weeks before had come up to him in the hallway, demanding his payment of a quarter. "This guy isn't much taller than me, but he's heavier, you know, broad, kind of." Spike had tried to ignore him and walk away. He had grabbed Spike, hit him in the chest and then, Spike said, "I guess he hit me in the face. I guess I got knocked out because the next thing I knew, some other kid was helping me up and another guy was picking up my books for me."

Spike had gone on to his next class, but when it was over, he said, he was still feeling "kind of shook up." He had gone to Ilka Saxon, his counselor and friend. (I learned later from Ilka that she had immediately recognized his need to be alone for a bit "to get himself together." She had let him sit for a while in an empty office and had then taken him to Mr. Gill, one of the vice-principals.)

Spike, who had been taking his ball-point pen apart as he talked, looked across the kitchen at me and said, "Mom, you're supposed to come to school with me tomorrow morning. Mr. Gill wants to tell you how they'd like to handle this."

I had listened wordlessly to Spike's description of the episode, but my mind had been filling up with outrage and pessimism. I had no intention of seeing Mr. Gill. Spike had been beaten up in the halls of his school, whether by a black or white student, it did not matter. Private school had its disadvantages, but at least Spike was safe there. No matter how strong and determined Mr. Gresham was, it was also clear that supervising nearly four thousand students was impossible. Whatever valuable things Spike might learn in his vast public high school, they were not worth what had happened to him that day.

I said to Spike, "You don't have to go back there. You can go somewhere else . . . anywhere you want."

(258)

Spike kept his eyes on the ball-point pen he was now putting back together. He never looked up at me until he finished what he had to say. "Well, I was thinking about that . . . all the time I was in that next class. That guy really scared me. He's got a funny look on his face. But, you know, while I was walking to Mrs. Saxon's office, I started to think. If I run away from something now, maybe I'll get in the habit of running away from things. I decided it's better if I stay at Germantown."

Now Spike looked at me. He knew how concerned I had always been for his safety; he knew, by my wordlessness, how shocked I felt about what had just happened to him. I could see the plea in his eyes, a plea for permission to fight his fear.

If I had gone back into the school on his first day there, this is what I would have faced from my fifteen-year-old child-man. With a sick feeling, I knew that then—and now—I had no choice. My son was already man enough to admit his fear and strong enough to fight it. I had to find the courage to match his. I wished desperately that Ben were home, but even that was a useless hope for rescue. I knew exactly what he would want me to do.

In a voice that sounded unfamiliar to me, I said, "Okay, Spike, what time does Mr. Gill want to see us?"

When Ben telephoned from Denver that night, I said everything was "fine."

"Then why are you crying?"

"Because I miss you so much, Ben." Much as I wanted his comfort, it seemed unfair and cruel to tell him what had happened. There was nothing he could do out there in Denver except worry even more helplessly than I.

sixteen

EARLY ON THE MORNING OF OCTOBER 21, SPIKE AND I walked into the office of Mr. Gill, one of the four vice-principals at Germantown High. Mr. Gill rose to greet us. He was a slender man with a thick neat Afro lightly touched with gray. He had the contemplative look of a pipe smoker and on his light tan face I saw laugh lines etched at the corners of his now-serious dark brown eyes. Apparently in his late forties, Mr. Gill gave me what seemed to be a look of appraisal as Spike and I took our seats.

Mr. Gill leaned forward across his desk and said, "First of all, we know who this fellow is who attacked Spike. He's a much bigger kid than Spike . . . taller and a lot heavier."

Spike sat up straighter as if his fears had been vindicated. (The night before Spike confessed that he was not sure what the youth looked like. "It's funny, Mom, but I was too busy ducking to look!")

Mr. Gill continued, "Now, you've got a right to press charges, but we'd like to try handling it in a different way. This student has shown problems already. Bad truancy record. He's only been in school two days this year. Rather than just having him arrested—he'd be out of custody in no time anyway—I'd rather try to get to him and see if we can't find out what's bothering him."

Mr. Gill, I realized, was not choosing the easy way of

(260)

handling a problem that had begun to take on improbable color dimensions. Spike, attacked by a white student, had instinctively gone to black Ilka Saxon. Now, Mr. Gill, black himself, wanted to help the troubled, violent white student instead of passing the problem on to the police. Worried as I was, I could not help wondering whether a life—two lives—could not have been saved if the white administrators had shown the same concern and compassion for the troubled black student who killed his teacher.

Mr. Gill was waiting for my answer. I told him we did not want to press charges, that his approach sounded much more productive.

"I'm very glad you feel that way, Mrs. Stalvey," he said. "Now there's only one more problem. I don't want this fellow —Bernard Ludenheiser—to get to Spike before I get to Bernard. Spike, *inside* the school, you can just point the guy out to any teacher or NTA (nonteaching assistant), but I'm going to ask your mother to drive you to and from school for the next few days until I can get to this Ludenheiser."

Spike groaned softly. Mr. Gill said, "I know how you feel, but it's best." To me, he said, "We always have the most problems with the tenth graders. These kids come from junior highs or elementary schools where they were big shots—they feel they've got to prove themselves here. And too, by the end of tenth grade those who don't want to stay in school are old enough to drop out." Mr. Gill, relaxed now that he knew I preferred help for Bernard rather than vengeance, grinned at me. "Well, at least Bernard was easy to pinpoint! We just don't have that many white kids here!" I returned his grin. Mr. Gill had made me feel as reassured as anyone could—which wasn't much, but it was something.

The next morning, as I drove Spike to school, he reassured me that he knew where the NTAs were stationed. I reminded him of the gang-leader student he had made friends with in biology. Weeks before, Spike told me that this fellow had sug-

gested, "You help me with biology; I help you with muscle."
I asked whether this friend could give Spike a little extra protection in the halls. "Forget it, Mom," Spike said, "I only see
him once a day and anyway, I don't want to start any wars in
school."

As I dropped Spike off at the same entrance as on his first
day, I hardly noticed the tall black lads. I was looking only
for a white face this time. I arranged to meet Spike at dismissal
time, two o'clock, at the corner in front of the school.

At home, waiting for the day to pass, I cut out the fabric
for a plaid skirt and forgot to match the plaid; at noon I tried
to make toasted cheese sandwiches for Noah and Sarah without plugging in the sandwich toaster. By 1:30, I realized I was
apprehensive about standing on the corner where almost four
thousand students would pour out of the school. I recalled
a black supermarket clerk telling me she avoided this block
at dismissal time; a hairdresser told me that none of his customers would accept appointments that put them on the trolley
passing the school at the end of the day. I decided not to take
my handbag, to put my keys and change in my pocket. Nothing
but Spike's safety could have made me overcome my anxieties.

Of course, I arrived early. I parked my car in front of the
church across from the school. I realized I had to get out of
the car. While I felt safer inside, I had to be ready if Bernard
appeared. Ready to do what, I wondered. Bernard was no
small Jelly Stowe I could hold onto; screaming for help was
the only course. *Would* anyone help? At that moment, the
street near the school was deserted. Only half a dozen students
sat on the long stone wall surrounding the church. None fit
Bernard's description. I noticed with relief that all the youths
sitting on the wall were black.

A bell rang and suddenly the school doors exploded with a
stream of young bodies. I ignored the brown faces, searching
only for two pink ones—Spike's and someone who could be
Bernard. Spike still had not been able to give me a detailed

description; he could not tell me the color of Bernard's hair, eyes or describe his features. "All I can remember is that funny look on his face . . . real mean." I superimposed a mean look on the few white males I saw. One carried a violin. Were violinists ever violent?

Suddenly a deep voice boomed in my ear, "Hi, Mrs. Stalvey!" I turned and looked up at a dark brown giant. Good heavens, it was Poncho! He had been the biggest in my eighth-grade class; he was even bigger now.

He said, "Watcha doin' here?"

I said, "Some white kid beat up Spike. The vice principal said I should pick Spike up until they can talk to the other guy."

Poncho said, "White kid, huh? That's kinda funny, but I know it ain't funny to you." He said he'd keep an eye out for Spike, but he had not even seen him once so far.

I asked how he was doing. Poncho looked down at the sidewalk and said, fine. I asked about Donald and Gus and Cephas. He looked back down at the sidewalk again. "Jus' fine. All jus' fine."

Just then, Spike and Dave appeared in the throng of students. They said hi to Poncho and we three got into the car.

For the next two weeks, Spike and I followed what would become an increasingly frustrating routine. I drove Spike to school each morning; he reported to Mr. Gill's office where Mr. Gill checked to see if Bernard had come to school that day; each afternoon, I picked Spike up, both of us hoping that perhaps tomorrow Bernard would have been reached and our routine could end.

For a while, I had enjoyed my daily waits outside the school. I had found that, up close, these students who frightened the supermarket clerk and the hairdresser's customers stirred up pleasant memories for me. Except for their richer pigmentation, these teen-agers were reassuringly similar to my classmates at Bay View High in Milwaukee. It was fun to watch them and to recognize the similar traits and types I remembered.

Just as Bay View High students had in the 1940's, Germantown High students in the seventies congealed into easily identifiable groups. The tall handsome young men walked hand in hand with pretty girls while the short, the fat, the less-mature pretended indifference. Plain girls sneaked wistful looks at the big fellows with athletic letters on their jackets; shapely confident girls glided past the shy, hungry glances of small, runty boys. Some students, bespectacled and loaded down with books, bustled between groups of laughing, carefree boys and girls, pretending their aloneness was by choice. Here and there I saw physically unattractive youngsters who had twinkling eyes, broad warm smiles and groups of friends around them. They were the lucky ones—not born beauties and forced to make the valuable effort to be interesting, interested and nice to be with—who were developing the personalities that would never fade with age.

Strangely, I saw none of the hard-eyed hostility I had noticed that first day of school. Had my own imagination placed it on those faces? Or, I thought, remembering my own teen-age reactions, were these faces relaxed because school was finally over for the day? Then, with the sadness of too much experience, I knew another answer; hard-eyed hostility would be on the faces of youngsters who could not read and who were steeling themselves for another year of failure.

Midway between the two weeks of driving Spike to school, I had telephoned Mr. Gill to ask if the school could perhaps contact Bernard's parents by telephone. Bernard's records, Mr. Gill said, showed the family had no phone. Could a note be written? One had been; there was no reply.

Mr. Gill said, "I've put his name on the list for a home visit by the attendance officer, but to tell you the truth, it's a long list and we have only *one* attendance officer." For nearly *four thousand* students? Mr. Gill asked if I could possibly continue as we were for a little while longer.

At that time, driving the dozen blocks to Germantown High twice a day was no problem for me. Fate was allowing only one kettle to boil at a time. Sarah and Noah were having an uneventful two months at Willis School and it was easy to drop Spike off each morning, get back in time to make breakfast for my other two children and then pick up Spike after Noah and Sarah had gone back to school after lunch. In fact, I considered myself lucky that I had a car and the time to provide the protective service Mr. Gill felt was necessary. It was only Spike's impatience with this restrictive routine that began to concern me.

The last day I was to drive Spike to school was November 2, 1971, the same day Philadelphia elected ex-police commissioner Frank Rizzo as its new mayor. Rizzo, a tenth-grade dropout himself, had caused controversy in 1967 when he allegedly commanded a busload of policemen to attack a group of Philadelphia high school students who were demonstrating at the Board of Education building for more Black History and the redress of other grievances of black students. According to eyewitnesses inside the building—one of whom was former Mayor Richardson Dilworth, then president of the school board—the police attack was both unwarranted and brutal. On television, I had seen films of individual students attacked by two or more policemen wielding clubs, and I shared ex-Mayor Dilworth's anger. To my amazement, Dilworth suddenly backed off from his threat to file a complaint against Commissioner Rizzo. Now Frank Rizzo was to be elected mayor. Philadelphia's black community had fought to prevent this, but although our schools were now over 60 percent black, the city population was 67 percent white. Frank Rizzo had put together a coalition of high- and low-income whites from both major parties and by evening would be announced the winner.

(265)

Early that morning, however, I cast my own vote and then drove back to the house, concerned about Spike's increasing impatience with my daily escort service. Mr. Gill was doing all he could, I knew, and in the enormous school, Spike's problem was the most important only to me. Was there, I wondered, anything more I could do to solve it?

As I turned in at our driveway, it suddenly occurred to me that Bernard's name, Ludenheiser, was certainly an uncommon one. Mr. Gill had told me that Bernard's parents did not have a telephone, but if any other Ludenheiser were listed in the book, they might be related and could perhaps get a message to Bernard's parents about his continued absences.

There was indeed a Ludenheiser listed in the phone book and at an address only three blocks from Germantown High. I sat, my hand resting on the telephone, wondering if it would be terribly unethical if I telephoned, pretending to be Mr. Gill's secretary checking on Bernard's many days away from school. I decided it would not be *too* unethical and that anything was better than more weeks of waiting.

The thin quavery voice that answered the phone was that of Bernard's grandmother. She was apparently lonely and anxious to talk with anyone, especially about her family problems. Her first words were: "But didn't my son tell you the family moved?" She went on without stopping, telling a pathetic story of Bernard's mother running up bills and then deserting the family, of Bernard's strange moods and of her son's inability to control *his* son. She finished the sad tale with, "And so my son decided to move to the Northeast to get Bernard out of that school with all those *bad colored*." She paused, perhaps wondering if I were "colored."

For the first time in my life, I did not defend integration. I said, fervently, "Oh, he'll love his new school. It's marvelous, absolutely marvelous!" It was an all-white school and, most marvelous of all, far, far away from our neighborhood.

Mrs. Ludenheiser, Senior, said, "Well, it's better than going to school with all those niggers . . . animals, they are, I always say."

I interrupted her to ask if she would please have her son notify our school officially so Bernard's records could be sent to his new school. She sure would. I said good-bye, with heartfelt good wishes for her son and her grandson in their new neighborhood.

And then I telephoned Mr. Gill. "Maybe I shouldn't have done this, Mr. Gill, but . . . well, you have a new secretary . . . and this is what I did." I gave him a word-for-word report of my conversation with Bernard's grandmother.

At the other end of the phone, Mr. Gill was silent for a moment. Then I heard a sputter and finally, a whoop of laughter. Mr. Gill said, "Well, I'll be a son of a bitch!"

If this were a book of fiction, it could close neatly one month later with a nearly incredible ending to Spike's long struggles in school. I could simply ignore the people and events that were soon to involve Sarah and Noah and end this book on a note of optimism. It would be a happy ending but foolishly fraudulent.

Exactly one month after my telephone conversation with Bernard's grandmother, I did, however, have an evening of almost unbearable joy that repaid me in full for the anxiety of the first two months. On November 29, Spike had brought home his first report card of the year; on December 2, Germantown High School had its Parents' Night and I visited his teachers.

Spike's report card had given me a cautious joy. It contained the first A's he had ever gotten—an A in (accelerated) geometry and in computer math. He had got B's in Spanish and English and, of his C in biology, Spike had said, "I know how to raise that." I could remember when C was a high grade for Spike.

When Ben phoned from Denver, Spike read him his

marks with shining eyes. After Spike had left the line, Ben said to me, "I don't care *why* he got those *A*'s. I'm just so darn happy for him, even if he only got them because he looks good compared to those kids who can't even read." I had had the same thought and I told Ben that Parents' Night was the next Thursday and I would try to find the answer.

On the evening of December 2, each teacher contributed to what would grow into my feeling of intoxicated happiness. Spike's biology teacher, a young man with a huge Afro, said, "I gave Spike that *C* because I don't want him to get over-confident. He's got real talent in science and I want him to stretch himself." The geometry teacher, a tiny black woman with enormous soft eyes, said, "You must be Spike's mother, but why are you here? Spike couldn't be doing better!" The computer math teacher, who Spike insisted was named Mr. Gainesborough, turned out to have the slightly less romantic name of Ginsburg. He smiled at me and said, "What can I tell you? He's one of the best students I have."

I could not hold my emotions in one minute longer. I said, "Mr. Ginsburg, let me tell you what Spike has been through since first grade." When I finished the long, frustrating history of Spike's *D*'s and *E*'s, the psychological examinations, the private school, Mr. Ginsburg shook his head. "I find it hard to believe," he said. "This is not an easy course and few of my students work as hard as Spike. And, believe me, his prominence is *not* due to 'the flatness of the surrounding territory!' "

On my way to the Spanish teacher's room at the other end of the big building, I felt like a middle-aged Tinker-bell, floating and glowing as I walked. No more, "I don't know how to reach him" or "He's not living up to his potential!" Spike was working and succeeding. I wished Ben were here to share this evening; much as I had missed him during the sad and scary times, I missed him even more on this wonderful night.

As I moved through the hallways, my coat billowing out

behind me and my feet feeling as if they were moving to music, I passed other parents, some sad-eyed and with defeated-looking students in tow. I knew so well what they were feeling, the confusion, the anger and the guilt. I wanted to stop them, to reassure them, to tell them that changes can come from unexpected places, to somehow share our good fortune. As I passed, I sent them silent wishes for their children, wishing I could explain the miracle to them and to myself. What had happened? Plain chronological maturity? Had Bernard Ludenheiser helped? Had Spike's battered self-image been healed as he found the courage each day to risk meeting Bernard? Or had this big, crowded school given Spike a privacy to work out his problems?

Spike himself could never explain. "It's a good school," he said. "I had good teachers." He told us too about the Saturday when he and Sarah were in a record shop near his school. Two young ladies, not knowing Spike's sister was standing behind them, whispered together. One said, "That's Spike Stalvey. He's in my class and he's a real brain." Sarah had proudly reported the comment to Spike. "I liked the way that made me feel," Spike said.

That night, when I reached the Spanish teacher's room, he gave Spike the same kind of praise I had heard from the others. I beamed and drank it in, letting each word heal the painful sores of all those years of worry.

Any of our doubts about the quality of instruction Spike was receiving at Germantown High were dispelled by the end of that summer. Spike had seen an announcement at school of a college-credit summer computer math course at De Pauw University in Indiana. Spike asked to be allowed to go there. As one of the youngest in the group and competing against a 99 percent white suburban group of students, Spike's Germantown High background enabled him to earn a *B* in the college course. One year later, Spike's scores on the national PSATs (Preliminary Standard Achievement Tests) ended any lingering questions. Germantown High, with its reputation as a "bad" school, had performed a genuine and lasting educational miracle.

By February, 1972, our house had still not been sold and the man who had been given Ben's former job in Philadelphia decided to go back to Washington. Ben was finding, in Denver, that he was getting no more staff or cooperation than he had got in Philadelphia. Ben was home on a weekend early in March. I said, "Can we change our minds about moving?" Ben said that fighting the Philadelphia Plan battle in Philadelphia, with all his years of experience, might be best after all—and he knew it would be best for Spike. Yes, he said, we could change our minds.

Our conversation took place late on a snowy March night. I put on a coat over my nightgown, put on my boots and tramped through the snow to pull up the "For Sale" sign from our front lawn.

seventeen

FROM THE TIME SPIKE ENTERED GERMANTOWN HIGH SCHOOL until we learned Bernard Ludenheiser had left the area, Fate had indeed been considerate. It had kept Noah and Sarah's school life uneventful. Then, as if on signal, my attention was pulled back to Willis School, to Sarah, to Noah and to a child who affected me even more than Josh Pitt.

For the first part of the school year, I had avoided Willis School as much as possible. I felt I had seen all of the problems and none of the solutions. Nothing at Willis School had changed for the better. Even Jane Banneker had given up. Her Reading Clinic, pathetically underfunded from the beginning, had never gotten more than token cooperation from Vangie Peters. Jane was offered a job in a new project: teaching teachers to teach ghetto children. Jane said, "Maybe I can do more for *more* children this way." I did not want to discourage her by pointing out that the director of the project was a white woman who had taken her daughter out of our school to put her in a private school.

It did not seem possible that I could witness a tragedy more affecting to me than Josh Pitt's. Since Josh had left our school for the gang-infested junior high far from our neighborhood, I had heard nothing about him. All I could do was read every newspaper report of gang killings—eighty-four in two years, according to a black columnist—hoping I would not see his name. If there were other youngsters like Josh, I did not know them and, ostrichlike, did not want to seek them out unless I knew how to help. When a child sought *us* out, it was impossible to run.

For the first months of the 1971 school year at Willis School, I was preoccupied by Spike's problems and grateful for the strengths Noah and Sarah were showing. Sarah was fulfilling the traits she had shown since babyhood. She looked so pink-and-blond-and-delicate, but beneath her fragile appearance was an armature of steel. One Sunday afternoon when she and Noah were strolling around the neighborhood, they heard a crash and saw that an elderly woman had driven into a tree in front of her own house. Noah had run into her house to tell her maid to call the police and was asked to make the call by the distraught servant. When he came out, some men, passers-by, had decided to pull the woman out of her car. "You should have *seen* Sarah!" Noah laughed. "She looked at the men, real fierce, and said, 'You don't move injured people!' And she held 'em off until the cops got there."

Sarah had just turned twelve that October when her newly feminine figure produced a frightening incident with an equally frightening backlash. After leaving the house following lunch, Sarah was back home again, trembling with fright, to tell me that a man in a car had followed her, trying to lure her into his car. I drove her to school and it seemed important to report the incident to Vangie Peters so that she might perhaps warn the other children. Instead, Vangie phoned the police. A young white policeman arrived to take the information from Sarah. After getting her name, the time and the locations, he said, "It was a colored man, wasn't it?"

Sarah said, positively, "No, sir. It was a white man with straight black hair and glasses." The officer wrote down a few words, and Sarah added to the description of the car and the man. The officer scribbled some more and then said, "A *light-skinned* colored man, you say."

I may have gasped out loud. Sarah again shook her head and said firmly, "No, sir. He was white, just like you, but shorter."

I shuddered at what I had heard the policeman say. What if Sarah had not been accustomed to black men as family friends, as teachers or as the fathers of her friends? If "black" represented danger to her, she might easily have been persuaded that the molester was black. I wondered how often this happened with frightened, suggestible children—or adults.

Noah carefully escorted Sarah to school for the next few weeks. They never saw the man again and he was never apprehended.

Noah still brought his friends home at lunch time. Big, bear-like T.D. had replaced Josh as arbiter of arguments and enforcer of rules. But by now, Noah had grown to be nearly as big as T.D. Noah did not, however, have the temperament to enforce rules. He was happy-go-lucky, friendly and enjoyed being part of the crowd. His baby chubbiness had thinned out to a tall, heavily muscled frame. It was important to Noah to clothe his large frame with the latest "in" clothes. Happily, what was "in" at our school was inexpensive, sturdy denim jackets, jeans and heavy work shoes.

My only anxiety concerning Noah was whether his desire to be "in" could also lead to drug experiments. So far, we had heard nothing of drug abuse at our school. A social-worker neighbor who headed a drug abuse program had told me that the problem was much more severe in the suburban schools. "These suburban kids have more money to spend and the pushers know it," she insisted.

The social worker may well have been right, but to me there was no such thing as an excess of caution. Noah, I reminded myself, had talked three friends out of glue-sniffing, but time had passed since then. Each time the subject of drugs came up, I had encouraged a full discussion. During one of them, Noah admitted, "I worry sometimes that if someone called me 'chicken' for not trying, maybe I'd be afraid to say no." It seemed a good omen that Noah could be honest with himself about his fears. I told him that admitting a weakness was one step toward conquering it. There seemed little else I could do but try to give my children facts and a feeling that they could come to us with their worries. And hope for luck.

I remembered—but did not understand—that while teaching my eighth-grade class, there had been no questions relating to drugs. Toward the end of my year of volunteer teaching, the children had approached me privately with many personal problems—sex questions, difficulty in communicating with their parents, problems with brothers or sisters—but not one question concerned drugs. Either drugs were not a problem in their lives, I decided, or they considered me too inexperienced to give good advice on the subject. They were right. In my high school days, "reefers" were whispered about, but no one I knew ever tried them.

Almira Stampp came into our lives, therefore, literally from another world. I would never have invited her in. There were already too many other youngsters whom I did not know how to help. I was thinking seriously of investing four years in becoming a teacher, but in those early autumn months of 1971 the move to Denver was still planned. I could not take the first steps. In the end, had I been a teacher, it might not have made any difference—to Almira or to most of the children who were to leave our school when they graduated with Noah in June.

I had been aware of Almira since she and Noah were in third grade together. She was the blank-eyed, silent child whom Miss McGregor had made stand in the wastebasket and had then called attention to Almira's wetting her pants. Almira had changed over the years into another of our school's infamous "bad kids." Unlike Jelly Stowe and Josh Pitt, Almira had stirred up no sense of identification in me.

She looked unrelievedly hostile and as appealing as a belligerent black porcupine. In sixth grade, she had taunted one of Sarah's fifth-grade classmates, a white child with long straight black hair, and had threatened to set fire to the child's "honkie hair." (The child's parents had put her into private school the next day.)

By the time Almira and Noah were in seventh grade, I had learned more about Almira through Ginny Arthur. After Almira walked abruptly up to Noah in the hallway and slapped him for supposedly laughing at her, I tried to explain to Noah. "Almira has a pretty bad homelife. It was wrong for her to slap you, but I think the best thing you can do is stay as far away from her as possible." I tried to explain the word "paranoid" to Noah—"when you're very unhappy and you think everyone is laughing at you or dislikes you." From what Ginny had told me, the conditions under which Almira lived could easily produce abnormal behavior.

Ginny had visited Almira's home after Almira had begun harassing Ginny's daughter, Amy. She had come away saddened and had given Amy the same advice I gave Noah. Ginny had told me that the thin, leathery woman who answered the door proved to be Almira's grandmother who was raising her. "She took me into the living room where there were two mattresses on the floor. On one of them was a very old woman, obviously blind and senile. And on the other, there was a child about four or five years old, I guess, and it just lay there, Lois, and made kind of a humming noise. While I talked with Almira's grandmother, she moved the child to a different position several times."

Ginny shuddered. "And there was another sick person upstairs, because Almira's grandmother had to go up there twice when a young woman's voice called."

Ginny had quickly abandoned the ideas of complaining about Almira's behavior. "Instead I just kind of weakly said I hoped Almira and Amy could get to be better friends." And

(275)

since Ginny's visit was near Christmas, she had tried gently to find out if the family would accept a Christmas basket from her church. "Almira's grandmother said, 'Oh, no, thank you. I work and my husband works, but there's a family next door who could use one." Ginny said that apparently Almira took care of the three invalids when her grandparents worked. "What a terrible life for a young girl!" Ginny said.

From then on, I became more aware of Almira when I saw her around the school or school yard. Once, our eyes met and I said hello. She turned a disdainful shoulder. Yet I could remember when she was silent and staring. Her belligerence seemed healthier.

That fall of 1971, she and Noah were in eighth grade and I had noticed a few changes in her when I saw her on the sidewalk near school. Her clothes, once worn, rumpled and drooping, were now neater. Her chin, once thrust out constantly, had lowered. I even saw her laugh with a girl friend; her almond-shaped eyes, sparkling and pretty. Several times, she had given me a quick, muttered "hello" when she passed me.

Two days after I had learned that Bernard Ludenheiser had moved far, far away—after my daily escort service was finally over—I was waiting outside the school to take Sarah shopping. A group of girls from Noah's class came out of the school, surrounding one young lady who was crying. Mark Smith, a usually quiet, studious young fellow, rushed up to me. "We had a substitute today, Mrs. Stalvey," he said excitedly, "an' he called Claudia a 'bitch.' He hit a couple of the guys with his key chain."

Just then, an obese man with dishwasher-colored hair waddled down the school stairs. Mark Smith said, "That's him." As the man was about to pass me, I said conversationally to him, "Did you hit children with your key chain and call one young lady a 'bitch'?"

The man sneered at me. "Yeah. So what's it to *you*?"

By now, I had long since spent my anger on this kind of

teacher. I said, mildly, "Oh, well, I have children in this school and I feel the district superintendent should know when things like this go on." I had taken out my red leather notebook and I smiled. "May I have your name, please?"

The substitute's manner changed abruptly. Now he looked fearfully at me, searching my face as if trying to read my background and position. I kept smiling, my pencil poised. He said with a whine, "Well, they wouldn't keep quiet." I said, "Uh-hum. But if you can't find better methods tomorrow, it would be good to have your name."

A car drove up to where we were standing. The man muttered his name and got into the car driven by a stout woman and containing four chubby children. As they drove off, he shot me a nervous look.

As I wrote his name in my notebook, a low but feminine voice whispered almost into my ear. "They *told* me you was on the side of the kids." I looked up from my notebook and into a brick-colored face with almond-shaped eyes. It was Almira.

From the soft smile on her face, I knew it was a compliment, but it gave me a sudden, sick feeling. Her conspiratorial whisper made it sound as if there were a war between adults and students. I replied quickly, "*Lots* of grown-ups are on the side of the kids!" Almira smiled knowingly as if I had made the proper cryptic code reply. She walked away before I could argue persuasively.

I watched her go. Almira had indeed changed. Her carriage had always been naturally graceful, her figure slim and well-proportioned. Now she had developed a stunning figure and she walked regally. Her once-sparse hair was now a glossy halo. She was immediately surrounded by friends, all of whom appeared to be vying for her attention. Almira moved silently in the center of the group as if her mind were somewhere else.

The incident with the substitute teacher (who had, according to Noah, stopped swearing at the students for the remainder of the week) had occurred just after Frank Rizzo was elected mayor of Philadelphia. Mayor Rizzo had promised, if elected, to "get rid of" School Superintendent Mark Shedd. The teachers' union had long been demanding his ouster, charging him with "permissiveness toward students" and denouncing the student Bill of Rights that Shedd and the board of education had approved. It seemed to me as if law-and-order were an issue with both the teachers' union and the voters. Mayor Rizzo began immediately to set in motion the buying up of Mark Shedd's contract. I felt dispirited. Mark Shedd had demonstrated his sincerity by living in the city and sending his own children to the public schools, one of them to Germantown High. (The new superintendent, a suburban resident, would not.)

I was still reflecting on why Mark Shedd had antagonized the union when Sarah came home from school at noon to proclaim, wide-eyed, "You'll never guess, Mommie! Almira Stampp came up to me and put her arm around me and she said she's coming to our house for lunch! She isn't, is she?"

Ever since Almira had threatened to burn the long hair of Sarah's former classmate, Sarah was terrified of her. Sarah had taken to hiding her own long yellow hair under her hat or tucked into her coat whenever she saw Almira.

I told Sarah that I had not invited Almira for lunch, but that Almira had changed. "And, Sarah honey, I think this is Almira's way of saying she'd *like* to come for lunch." I had missed whatever subtle signal Josh Pitt had tried to give me before he left our school, but I did not miss Almira's signal.

Sarah said, "Well, I'm not inviting her. I'm scared of her."

By now, Noah had come home and learned the news. "I'll invite her," he said. And, of course, Sarah now decided she would.

It took three lunches before Almira told me what she wanted from me. The first day she sat stiffly, glancing at Sarah before picking up a spoon or fork. That day, Sarah complained to her that "some of the big girls never let me play jump rope. They say I'm not good enough." Almira, chin up now, said, "We'll fix that."

When the girls finished eating, Almira directed me to turn one end of the rope while she turned the other and instructed Sarah in the techniques of Double-Dutch. I was deeply moved by Almira's patient, maternal manner with Sarah. When Sarah improved, the pride in Almira's eyes made her beautiful.

Almira said, "Now, can I braid your hair, Sarah?" Sarah said, "Sure!" She sat quietly while Almira brushed and braided her hair. I felt like an eavesdropper as I saw the hungry look on Almira's face as she handled Sarah's heavy, truly golden hair that now reached almost to her waist.

When the three youngsters left for school, I told Almira to come back "anytime." "We've always got enough soup and sandwiches." Almira nodded soberly.

Four days later, Almira returned. This time she looked up from her sandwich suddenly and said, "I used to hate white people. But I got over it last year." She went on to some other topic.

Noah was clearly fascinated by having "the toughest girl in school" as a family friend. She adopted an advisory attitude toward Noah. Two fellows who had been suspended from junior high were hanging around our school. "George is okay," she told Noah, "but watch out for Skeeter. He lives on my block and there's something wrong with him. He'll just up an' hit you for no reason. Give him *lots* of room."

There was a sudden silence around the table and I felt that everyone was remembering that Almira herself had once hit Noah. Noah turned red and looked down at his sandwich.

Almira said, "Yeah, I hit Noah. Noah, I apologize, okay?" She turned to me. "I used to think everybody was laughing at me. Then my mama—she lives in New York—she didn't come home like she promised. I didn't want to be mad at her, so I got mad at everybody else."

I marveled at this child's self-knowledge. "Almira, you

understand yourself better than some grown-ups. How did you figure that out?"

Almira shrugged. "Jus' knowed it. Sometimes you jus' know stuff."

Sometimes you did. And I knew that Almira's visits had a purpose, but also that Almira was fully in charge of revealing it. In addition, she seemed to be trying to give *me* something before she asked whatever she wanted in return. She said to Noah and Sarah, "You two don't know how lucky you all are, havin' your mama and daddy. If I was lucky like you, I'd be good all the time and never do nothing naughty. You gotta 'preciate what you got!" Her voice broke and her jaw tightened. She turned to me, "My ma and pa . . . uh, they live in . . . New York." To Sarah and Noah, she said in a firm voice, "You two be good to your ma, y'hear?" Noah and Sarah nodded obediently; Noah looked at me as if he had never noticed me before.

While I knew what Almira was trying to do, I could not let the subject stop there. I told her that I too grew up without a father and that for many years I believed there was something wrong with *me* that made him leave. "Children get funny ideas like that," I said.

Almira suddenly had a dozen questions. Where had my father gone? Was my mother all right? Did I like my grandmother? Did my father ever come back?

As I answered each question, she gave a quick nod and went on to the next. I told her that my father had gone back home to his family on a farm in Indiana; that my mother had been all right. ("Not sick?" No, I said, not sick.) I told Almira that I did not really like my grandmother very much because she seemed not to like me; that my father had not come back, but that I had gone to find him when I was eighteen and we had become friends before he was killed in an accident. Almira wanted to know what kind of job my father had before he left. I said, "Well, lots of different ones." Almira laughed companionably, "Yeah, mine too."

Before the three children left for school that noon, Almira had another question. "Where did Sarah get that dress she's got on?" Sarah heard and answered, "It used to be Amy Arthur's, but it got too small for her." Then Sarah added vehemently, "And I *wish* she'd hurry up and grow out of that pantsuit!" Almira looked at me. "I remember the dress when Amy wore it. You don't care she wear black kids' clothes?" I laughed. Of course not. "Mrs. Arthur makes beautiful clothes for Amy. We just wish Amy would grow a little faster," I said.

Almira came to lunch the third time on the day after my exhilarating visit to Spike's teachers at Germantown High. As she and Sarah came up the driveway, I noticed that Almira's chin was again up and out, but not, I decided, in belligerence. I was right. It was determination.

Before we sat down, Almira said, "I want to ask your ma to do something for me and I hope none of you don't laugh."

Noah said, "We won't laugh."

Almira stood erect, her chin up and her hands clasped in front of her waist. "I want you should help me write a book. Some bad things happened to me, but it's better now and maybe it'd help other kids to read about what happened."

I was so proud of Almira. To me, the only good reason for writing a book was to help people understand others or themselves. But I believed too that merely putting feelings on paper could be a healthful, healing outlet even if a book never reached print. I told Almira I would be happy to help her. Her quick nod showed she had more to say.

She sat down at the table, took a sip of milk and then leaned forward, her hands clenched. "Mrs. Stalvey, I gotta tell you something about why I gotta write a book. Maybe you know, but my mama is a user, a addict, an' my daddy, he's in prison." My eyes certainly told Almira that I did not know this. She held onto the edge of the table and began to talk. For the next fifteen minutes, neither Sarah or Noah or I said a word, but occasionally, I had to blink, to clear my mind and to remind myself that this was no television drama, this was real and it had happened to the slim fourteen-year-old child sitting at our table.

"Yeah, my mother's a user an' we think that's why there's something wrong with my sisters. Blanche—she's my big sister—she can't move her arms, and she can't stand up." Then Almira's face showed the same pride I had seen when she taught Sarah to jump rope. "But Blanche can almost write real good now with her toes! But my little sister—she's Dorrie an' she's five—can't move at all. Can't talk neither." (This, I thought, must be the child Ginny Arthur saw on the mattress.) Almira shook her head in a kind of wonder and apology. "Nobody knows why, but I'm the only one that got born okay."

Almira continued. "My mom was carrying a big habit when Dorrie was born. Just brought Dorrie to Granma and left. Dorrie didn't move at all, but she could scream all right. Oh, my lord, she screamed all the time. Then Granma knew. She said this baby's born hooked."

I felt Noah's hand on my arm. As Almira continued, he pressed his fingers harder and harder around my wrist.

"Granma said the baby hadda go 'cold turkey' and we hadda walk her till she got through it. We walked her, seem like a year we walk her. An' got lil' sips of sugar water down her throat. An' all the time, Granma's lady—the lady she cooks for—kept callin' up and yelling cuz Granma didn't come to work." Almira looked directly at me and said, "That's why I used to hate whites so much, but they ain't all like her. Granma tol' her we got a sick baby. She say to put her in the hospital an' come to work. But no hospital gonna walk that baby like we walk her. Granma got so tired, she

(282)

cursed the lady out. Tol' her, 'You don't know my troubles! You don' even know my last name!' The lady stopped callin' and pretty soon the sugar water stayed down for Dorrie and she stop screamin'. *Then* we can take her to the doctor. He says she's messed up real bad. Never gonna walk, never gonna talk. Blind, too, like *Old* Granma. But my granpa says Dorrie knows us, me and Blanche, an' she knows we love her."

"My granpa, he works on the trash truck an' he couldn't help too much with Dorrie, but he's who taught Blanche to write. Blanche can read real good too. But can't walk. Somethin' didn't grow right in her back."

Almira's face changed when she spoke of her grandfather. Her chin tilted up with pride. "Granpa says nothin's so bad some good don't come from it. He says when I was bein' so bad in school, I was fightin' my demons young. If I beat 'em now, I wouldn't need to fight 'em with the needle like my ma."

"See, in my book, I wanna write about my granpa and how everybody got somebody like my granpa who can help. My girl friend, she's got a neighbor lady she talks to. I got Granpa. An' he says he got me to let him fix up the mistakes he made with my ma. He says his ma did right by him. She lives with us too. She can't talk no more or see even. But Granpa talks to her and she smiles sometimes."

Almira paused for a moment and for the first time in fifteen minutes, I noticed with surprise that we were all sitting in a quiet room in a spacious house. We—Noah, Sarah and I— had all moved closer to Almira. Sarah had her hand on Almira's arm; Noah's hand was hard and tight around my wrist. His chin was quivering.

"So," Almira said, "I wanna write my life story and about my granpa and about when I knew I was *actin'* bad because I was *feelin'* bad. And I want for you to help me about the commas and that. I think because I'm lucky, I oughta help somebody else, you know, like kinda pay back because I was born okay."

I said, in a voice that cracked, "I'll get you some paper," and I ran from the room. I thought that if I could just keep thinking about tangible things like paper and pens, I could hold back feelings that were about to overwhelm me. In the library closet, I tried to see through a blur of tears to find paper, a handful of ball-point pens and a bright red notebook cover. I wanted to give Almira so much more. By offering us the story of her life, she had shown my two children the tragedy that drugs cause and she had also helped them see how people can and do survive through simple loving. What on earth could I give Almira in return? Only more paper, an eraser, a box of paperclips?

At the table, I found that Sarah had given Almira her ladybug paper clip; Noah had added his favorite pencil. I told Almira that, for now, punctuation was not important "except for periods so you can tell when the sentence ends." I said not to worry about spelling yet. "Just write down what you know and how you feel and just write it *all* down. You can take out things you don't want in later, honey. Every writer does a lot of rewriting, so in the first draft, just you write and let everything you think of come out. And I'll help you in any way you want."

I watched Almira, Sarah and Noah go off to school and, while watching, formulated a crazy plan. I must have known it could not work because instead of discussing it with Barbara Hamilton, I headed for Ginny Arthur's house. My two closest friends were predictably different; Barbara, with her Harlem street wisdom, would be too realistic—Ginny had been raised on a black-college campus and just might encourage the wild idea that had formed in my mind.

But perhaps no black person of intelligence can afford sentimentality. Ginny heard me out. I retold Almira's story. I said, "Ginny, if Almira lived with us, she could have her own room. She could have peace and privacy. She's earned that and more." Ginny shook her head. "You weren't listening hard enough to what she said, Lois. Almira is a giver, not a getter. She would never leave her sisters."

I had forgot that Ginny, with all her patrician background, was also a highly trained, experienced social worker. I was so ready to tell Ginny—and Ben—why it would be easy for *us* to give Almira a better life; I had not thought of why it would be impossible for Almira. Ginny's insight was irrefutable. "She could never leave her sisters without a lifelong feeling of guilt for having deserted them. Lois, think of how grateful you feel for Spike's success—for everything your family has. Almira feels the same gratitude for having been born whole. She said she wants to do something—write her book—to 'pay back.' The last thing she would do is leave her sisters."

My face must have shown my disappointment and my acceptance of the truth. Ginny said, gently, "Lois, don't worry. Almira is a strong, wise and determined child. She's got to make it in her own world. With any kind of luck at all, she will."

I walked home from Ginny's, resigned, but reflecting that, in Almira's world, even a little bad luck went a long way.

As I passed the school, Vangie Peters' big car pulled up and she got out. I called to her. Without much hope for help, I still told her that Almira seemed to be at a turning point in her life. "Vangie, whatever you can do . . ."

Vangie smiled, but glanced between me and the building. She was apparently in a hurry. She said, "Oh, we have always tried, Lois. But after all, she did see her father kill a man with an axe." I simply held onto the bright green sleeve of Vangie's suit until I got the story behind Vangie's casual bomb. Almira had been about five, Vangie said, when her father had been playing cards and drinking with friends in their kitchen. There had been a quarrel. Almira's father split a man's head open with an axe. He had been in a penitentiary "for years."

Vangie Peters smiled cheerfully, "But, of course, we have always done our best with Almira." I watched as she hurried away into the school; I remembered her bland indifference the day I told her that Miss McGregor had made Almira stand in the wastebasket. It seemed that all of Almira's bad luck had to be behind her.

On Monday, December 20, the week school was to close for Christmas vacation, Almira brought me five pages of her book. In small, neatly formed handwriting, she had begun by describing her parents' childhoods in Georgia ("when farmers bought machines, no more field work for anybody"), their decision to move north and her own first memories. "I was always scared on Friday nights. That's when the men got paid and they would come to our house and play cards and drink. My daddy liked me to sit on his lap. He called me Li'l Luck. Then people got talking loud and I felt scared."

Almira then described the food her mother cooked for the cardplayers. ("Greens, peas and pig-feet . . . if she wasn't sick. I was too little to know about habits. I just figured she was sick lots.")

As I read Almira's detailed description of those Friday nights, I wondered if she would—and could—describe the terrible scene she had witnessed. It was not on these pages. They ended with: "Sometimes my daddy would yell at my mama. I was always glad when Friday nights was over."

I told Almira truthfully that she had written this well. She had used simple sentences and her descriptions were realistically specific. She had made me see that kitchen ("linoleum that used to be blue," "sitting under the table, feeling the places where the paint got hard in drips," "the stove we had to feed with wood"). "Just keep on this way," I said.

That day, Almira said she would bring me more pages

"tomorrow" and that her mother was coming home for Christmas.

I did not worry when Almira did not come to our house for the rest of the week. Christmas, after all, was a busy time and Almira was also expecting her mother. When school began again after the holidays, Noah said he had not seen Almira. I telephoned her house. An operator said the phone was "temporarily disconnected." This was, I knew, the euphemism for an unpaid phone bill. A few days later, I asked Noah to find out from Almira's homeroom adviser if he knew why Almira was not in school. He told Noah, "Oh, the family moved." Noah asked where. The tall blond male teacher with the vague expression had told Noah, "Who knows!"

Ginny Arthur and I drove to Almira's house where a moving van was unloading the possessions of another family. A neighbor told us she did not know Almira's family was planning to move. "But the daughter came home Christmas . . . 'n there was some fuss. Couple days later, they was all gone."

Driving back to our house, Ginny said, "I'm afraid I can guess what happened. If the mother came home—well, you can hardly imagine what an addict can do to a family, Lois. Almira's grandparents may have been forced to disappear from their own daughter!"

My note to Almira came back marked: Moved. No Forwarding Address.

The deep sense of loss over Almira's disappearance deadened my response to the news that Vangie Peters had abruptly retired, obviously on the very day she was eligible. I met the new principal when I went to school to ask if Almira's records had been requested by another school. He was a handsome man in his middle forties with darting blue eyes, gray-blond hair and the kind of pink skin that proclaims unremitting care. His name was Robert Kaufmann. "Please call me Bob, Lois," he said, and promised to tell me if a request came through for Almira's records.

So far none has.

My hopes for change under Robert Kaufmann began their death at our second meeting. He had called together all eighth-grade parents to discuss a class trip to Europe initiated by Hallette Spain. At the meeting, I expressed concern that, once again, certain children could afford the trip while others would once more be left behind.

Our new principal smoothed his gray-blond hair and fixed me with a wide, sincere smile. He said, "Oh, you're so right, Lois."

The European trip went off as scheduled—and predicted.

On June 21, 1972, Noah was graduated from Willis School. I sat in the crowded auditorium alone. Ben was in Washington as he had been for Spike's graduation. I sat stoically through Mr. Kaufmann's patronizing compliment to the mostly black audience of parents for their "orderly behavior" and I clenched my teeth harder when Vangie Peters, the guest speaker for the day, reminded the graduates of how much they owed to "our marvelous school." I could not look at her or at Mr. Kaufmann. Instead I stared at the back of the heads of the graduates seated in the front of the auditorium.

It was time for the class song. The children stood up and turned to face the audience. Noah looked unfamiliarly young in his shirt and tie. T. D., Jimmy and Fish looked younger too. I searched for Josh Pitt's face, for Almira's, knowing I would not find them.

I knew which song the children had chosen to sing, but I was unprepared for the impact of watching their faces as they sang what was a heart-wrenching lie.

They began. "We've only just begun . . . to live. White lace and promises . . . a kiss for luck and we're on our way." Tears welled up in my eyes and streamed down my cheeks.

Too many of these children had *not* "just begun"; along with Poncho, Gus and Josh Pitt, they were on their way to nothing —nothing but a bigger school where they would get less than they had got here.

I could not even raise my hand to wipe my eyes. I watched T. D. singing, head up, eyes alight: "We start off walking and learn to run." I had had to read the instructions to him when he filled out a form for the library card demanded of all eighth-grade students. Fish, beaming out over the audience, could not spell the word "woman," let alone "cleaning" when he tried to write the autobiography for the Longville college trip he did not make. Yet he sang, "So much of life ahead." Not for Fish.

Through the mist of my tears, I saw Noah's face, saw a flash of concern and then a tender smile of what he thought was understanding. It was just like mothers, his smile seemed to say, to cry at weddings and graduations. I managed to return his smile, wishing he were right, that my tears were for such innocent and sentimental reasons.

But with Noah reassured, I did not need to struggle to hold back the tears that streamed down my cheeks. I was weeping for Almira, for Josh and for all the bright-faced children who were leaving their last chance behind. So many adults had failed them. So had I. Nothing I had done— nothing I knew to do—could change the failure that lay ahead for too many of these hopeful young people. I wept for their failure and for mine.

The graduates finished their song. I knew I could never hear "We've Only Just Begun" without aching for these cheated children. The newspaper statistics of school achievement tests in all big cities would forever have this sad song and these young faces behind them.

The graduation exercises were over. I wiped my eyes and went out into the school yard to say good-bye to Noah's classmates. Somehow I made myself smile.

eighteen

DURING THE SUMMER OF 1972, BEN, THE CHILDREN AND I
watched the telecast of the Democratic convention at home
in Philadelphia; we watched the Republican convention telecast in a rural area of South Carolina. Between the Republican convention and the reelection of Richard Nixon, two
long-held beliefs of mine were demolished. One was a prejudice I was well rid of, but one was a slim hope it hurt to
watch die.

The summer season had already begun with senseless violence. In May, a disturbed young man from my hometown
of Milwaukee shot Governor George Wallace, leaving this
proud active man a prisoner for life in his wheelchair. In
July, my favorite uncle was murdered in his yard in rural
Wisconsin by a gang of white teen-agers who had robbed him.

My uncle's death only increased the bleakness with which
I looked forward to a trip to South Carolina. Ben's parents
had retired and moved back to the farm community where
they had both been born. Ben's parents had responded ad-
mirably to the schools their grandchildren attended and to
our black friends, but I had qualms about the attitudes of
Ben's aunts, uncles and cousins. They were nearly all tobacco
farmers and, in my mind, I saw them as the kind of small-town
Southerners made famous in the telecasts of the 1960's—the
hate-filled people who had rioted, killed and fought bitterly
against integration. At the very least, I feared, I would hear

talk of "niggers" and "race-mixing" and (black) "crime in the streets." My uncle's murder by whites and the events of the last school year would not help me remain silent.

I considered staying home while Ben and the children made the trip. I said to Ben, "I don't want to upset your parents. And if someone says something bigoted, I won't be able to ignore it."

Ben said, "Honey, I wouldn't expect you to ignore it. I wouldn't want the kids to see us let something ugly be said without protesting. Anyway," Ben added, putting his arm around me, "my mother may have those folks in pretty good shape by now."

Ben's mother had indeed made what I thought were tremendous adaptations for a Southerner. She had met Barbara and Leland at our house and, when Leland was in Detroit, had invited him for dinner in their totally white suburb. I knew she had got into many arguments with the family patriarch, Uncle Francis Marion Cullom. As a member of the school board for fifty years, Uncle Francis, I had heard, fought integration until, at eighty, sheer age defeated him. He had retired from the school board, but according to what I had heard, was still arguing the perils of "race-mixing."

I finally decided to make the trip South. The children would each be away from us for the month of July and I did not want to be apart from them for an additional two weeks. Spike went off to DePauw University for his computer math course; Sarah spent six weeks at music camp and Noah chose a co-ed Y camp where, according to his friend Mike, the girls were pretty and the canoe trips "cool." I was glad they did not miss me as much as I missed them, but when they all came home, I was ready to follow them down South. I would, I suspected, feel like a Catholic at a Planned Parenthood convention, but at least we would be together. I packed my clothes and included every one of my stereotypes about Southerners. We traveled to what I considered hostile territory.

When Ben's cousins and their wives arrived at his parents' house, my heart lurched. The men looked exactly like those photographed holding shotguns and ropes and the matches to light burning crosses. The women were smartly dressed and attractive, but a roomful of southern drawls was frightening. Everytime the doorbell rang, I expected someone in a white sheet. When Uncle Francis Marion Cullom arrived, he proved to be a still-tall man, worn and weathered as the ancient cypress trees on his land. Ben's mother, I thought, began to look worried.

Uncle Francis asked to sit next to me and I smiled at him with the same nervous foreboding Richard Nixon might feel toward John Dean. In ten minutes, I was thoroughly charmed by this soft-voiced gentleman who called me "ma'am" and who, to my complete astonishment, began to talk of the "colahed man across the road who has a daughtah in Philadelphia."

It was Cousin Julia who introduced the topic of integration from across the room. Glancing shyly at me, she took a breath and said, "Ah know we've got a long way to go down heah in integratin' our schools, but we ah tryin'." I realized she looked as nervous of me as I felt of her.

Still, I had to ask the one question that would measure that "tryin'." I said, "Oh? What is the color proportion of the school Marion Lou goes to?" Marion Lou, her blond, pretty teen-age daughter, was the granddaughter of Uncle Francis. Even if he said "colahed" instead of "nigger," it did not seem likely that he would allow his granddaughter to attend the kind of school he had fought against so long.

Cousin Julia said apologetically, "Well, two yeahs ago, Marion Lou was the only white chile on the public school bus." Then, brightening, she added, "But theah's more whites this year, almost twenty-five percent white, ah guess."

I turned to Cousin Florence. Her husband was a successful tobacco broker, and she had just told me they were organizing a Junior League chapter in her small city. The Junior League and private schools, I believed, went together like cream and calories. I asked, "And your children's school?"

The public high school Cousin Florence's daughter attended was, she told me, about 75 percent black too. Again, there was an apologetic, but optimistic addition: "But Melinda's nursery school class is almost fifty-fifty!"

These two astonishing answers pushed another realization to the front of my mind; Ben's parents had built their new house directly across the street from a black family! I thought of my own Northern aunts, uncles and cousins. Every one of them lived in all-white neighborhoods and sent their children to all-white schools. I thought of our white "liberal" neighbors who took their children out of Willis School for private school.

It felt good to have bare facts brush away my own bigotry. I said, "Florence, Julia, you're not just *trying* down here, you're *doing*. Much better than we're doing up North!"

Cousin Julia's round pink face relaxed for the first time and she said, "Oh, my, ah'm *so* glad to heah you say that! We got to feelin' that segregation was all our fault! It kinda hurt our pride, you know?"

It was a wonderful vacation. I grew to love Uncle Francis Marion Cullom who had taught himself to say "colahed" after seventy years of saying "nigger," who had fought integration but now calmly accepted the choice his granddaughter had made. I listened, tremendously moved, as Marion Lou, sixteen years old, explained that it was she who had made the choice. "The South is mah home an' we cain't run away from our problems. Colahed and white have to learn to work together. In school, ah learned how colahed people really feel. Ah couldn't have broadened mah mind any othah way." Her father, who resembled Mississippi Sheriff Bull Connor, smiled fondly as Marion Lou expressed her feelings.

In the small nearby town where we shopped for groceries, I watched in the store, in the restaurant, in the library and saw the same unselfconscious mixture of blacks and whites that I saw in our far-from-typical Northern neighborhood—a mixture I did not see in most parts of Philadelphia where we Northerners congealed in all-white or all-black enclaves. On television in Southern Carolina, the local white candidates for political office were shown shaking hands with black voters and the newscasts covered more predominantly black events than I had ever seen on Philadelphia stations. Our black neighbor brought over a big basket of fresh figs and I brought a loaf of homemade bread back to her. I said, "Mrs. Adams, I didn't know things were so good down here!" She said, in the accents of her native New York City, "I always felt the South would change first." Two wonderful weeks of shedding my prejudice about the South were like watching spring begin again.

Not everything was perfect. Several other relatives did send their children to the new private schools that were sprouting in the South. The teen-age social life into which Spike, Noah and Sarah were happily whisked was as all-white as in any Northern suburb. The black teen-ager who worked beside Marion Lou preparing tobacco for auction had not been encouraged to take the college-required subjects in high school. I heard young whites call elderly blacks by their first names and receive a "Miss" or "Mister" in return. But Mrs. Jefferson had told me that, in our Northern neighborhood, most of the other families she cleaned for permitted their children to do the same.

Ben beamed at my discoveries and my newfound love for the South. He had always given me newspaper clippings about the increasing integration in Southern schools. I had read that there were five times as many integrated schools in Birmingham as in Chicago, almost twice as many in Nashville and Norfolk as in New York. But I had believed that only the big Southern cities had changed, that the small town South was still in the clutch of the Klan. Now Ben's relatives were teaching me how wrong I had been about the small-town South—just as our school had taught me I was wrong about the "liberal" North.

"You know, honey," I said to Ben one night as we sat on the porch, gazing out at trees festooned with Spanish moss, "I think the South has already lived through what the North is just beginning to face. The South has always expressed its racism openly, honestly and, lord knows, fully. Okay. Lots of white Northerners came down here, demonstrated and shamed the South into changing. Yet we Northerners never faced the fact that we were living equally segregated lives with invisible, but effective, Whites-Only signs. Before the North can change we're first going to have to admit the racism we denied for so long. The South never denied theirs. They just got on with the job."

Ben's I-told-you-so is always tender. And on August 22, we watched the Republican convention together. I watched black entertainer Sammy Davis, Jr., embrace (politically and physically) the president who had done so little to "bring us together." But I felt that I at least had been brought together with the half of my country I had once underrated. Ben's arm was tight around me when we said good-bye to everyone on September 3. When they all said, "Y'all come back, y'heah," I said a heartfelt, "Often!"

The optimism I felt in the South was to wilt slowly. We returned to Philadelphia to find that the schools would not open on schedule. For the third time in two years, the Philadelphia teachers' union had called a strike. Their contract with its $57.3 million wage package, signed only two years before, had expired. The public schools were already operating with a huge deficit and the school board felt it could not meet the union's new demands. I was not yet aware of the subtle undercurrents of the strike, but as the weeks passed, I was concerned that children who had already been cheated would lose even more.

Of our three children, Noah seemed most disappointed

(295)

that he would not begin ninth grade at the brand-new Baldwin Junior High with its ultramodern equipment. Although Noah's Iowa Test Scores had qualified him for the academically selective Central High, he had not worked hard enough to earn the necessary "all *A*'s and *B*'s" on his report card. He would not go to Central, but we believed he had learned an important lesson. Willis School's guidance counselor told him, "Your mother can fix it for you to go to Central. Just have her call the District Superintendent. He knows her." I refused.

"Noah, remember how you felt in mechanical drawing class? You said it was no fun getting good marks if Mr. Muchinski cheated in your favor? This would be cheating too. It's not right for you to go to Central unless you've worked hard enough to earn the grades."

Noah said, grinning, "Yeah. I know it. Just wanted to see what you'd say." He added, as if he meant it, that he was going to work hard at Baldwin and get into Central next year. Ben and I agreed that it would be fine if he did, but privately we were not concerned. Baldwin Junior High was the feeder school for Germantown High School. If Noah got the same excellent education Spike had gotten the year before, we would be pleased.

During the three-week strike (then the longest in Philadelphia's history), Sarah taught herself to type, Noah talked his way onto several teen-age television shows on our local stations and Spike became a volunteer at the Philadelphia McGovern headquarters.

Within a few days, Spike became a dedicated McGovern supporter and was given the surprisingly responsible job of sending tapes to radio stations around the state and recording statements by local candidates. I enjoyed watching Spike's pride in his new skills. I did not want to dampen his enthusiasm, but I had to point out that while McGovern strongly supported forced busing, he sent his own child out of Washington to a 97 percent white school in Maryland. I admitted that none of the other "liberal" presidential candidates—except "Scoop" Jackson—sent their children to Washington's public schools either. Could any of them project the genuine sincerity voters hoped to find? Spike looked at me soberly. He sighed. "Well," he finally decided, "he's still better than Nixon."

On September 29, 1972, the Philadelphia schools finally opened under a temporary agreement with the union. Spike began eleventh grade at Germantown High and worked for McGovern on weekends. Sarah entered her last year at Willis School and Noah started his ninth-grade classes at Baldwin Junior High.

We expected that Noah would have the same experiences at Baldwin as Spike had had at Germantown High. Germantown High had gone from 89 percent to 96 percent black that year, but except for Bernard Ludenheiser, Spike had had no problems as a minority student. (He had, in fact, been urged by his classmates to run for student council. Unfortunately, Spike was too absorbed in extra chemistry work and computer math to become the council's token white.) At Baldwin, Noah would be among three thousand ninth and tenth graders, 99 percent of them black. While the percentages by now meant nothing to us, it was sad to remember that Baldwin with its planetarium, lavish library and electronic equipment, had been planned as a model, well-balanced integrated school. When its location was chosen, the neighborhood around it was predominantly white; while the school was being built, unethical realtors had conducted a successful and profitable panic campaign. The whites had fled their small row houses and the area was now black. But the same panic selling had taken place around Germantown High many years before. When Noah began classes at Baldwin, I was unaware of the many differences between his school and Spike's.

Unlike Spike, from whom I always had had to pull information, Noah came home each day to paint me a vivid verbal picture of his school. It was "real cool-looking . . . everything brand new"; the school was divided into six "houses" and his housemaster was "a great guy." Some of his teachers, Noah said, were "okay"; some couldn't control the class and some didn't try. Yes, he saw T. D., Fish and Jimmy and other kids from Willis, but he didn't see them often—"Mom, that's a *big* school! Three thousand kids!"

Noah had begun making new friends. One was "Pint, a real little guy who tries to act tough with the gang kids. A real big guy, named BB, asked Pint to lend him a pencil. Pint cursed him out and got socked. I told Pint, 'You got a suicide complex or something? Any guy that big and bad-looking, y' make friends with!' " Noah did and reported later that BB was a nice guy. "But, Mom, I don't think his folks give him any money to buy school stuff. You can kinda tell."

After two weeks of school, a bright-voiced, young-sounding woman phoned me identifying herself as Miss Santilli, Noah's counselor. Noah, she said, had come to see her about getting into advanced classes "so that he can qualify for Central next year." I was delighted that Noah was serious about his promise to stop clowning.

Miss Santilli's young voice strained to speak as a background noise of voices competed with her. "We don't have advanced classes here," she said. Then she lowered her voice and spoke closer to the phone. "I don't know what a child like Noah is doing here. He should be in Central."

I was about to explain when she said, "Excuse me just a minute." I heard the clunk of the phone being placed on a hard surface and then her voice, "But it says right here on your roster—you're to go to physical science, not biology. Can't you read English?"

Just then a louder female voice rang out in the background, high-pitched and angry. "What the hell's the matter with you, boy? You're supposed to be in gym! Stupid! Move!"

Miss Santilli came back on the line. "Sorry to keep you waiting, but it's pretty wild in here, and this is my first year. Now, wouldn't you rather have Noah in Central?"

I told her, "Only if he earns it," and explained. I added that his older brother, Spike, was doing very well at Germantown High and we expected Noah to do well at Baldwin. Miss Santilli said, "Wow! I hope you know what it's like here and I heard Germantown High was even worse!"

From what I had heard through the phone, Germantown High sounded much better. I could not imagine the principal there allowing the chaos and adult cantankerousness I had heard at Baldwin. All I knew of Baldwin's principal was that he was white and that this was his first principalship. He would, I hoped, get his new school organized soon.

Noah, meanwhile, was acting as if he enjoyed school. Miss Santilli had finally arranged for him to have extra work assigned by his teachers and Noah began bringing home *A* papers. He also brought home the story of his new friend, Henry.

"Mom, that Henry is really somethin'. I never saw *anyone* try so hard." Noah explained that he had noticed Henry in English class. "I'd finished my work. It's kid stuff—spelling that we had in sixth grade. But I saw this real big kid, chewin' his pencil and writing real slow and frownin'. So I went over and asked if he wanted some help."

I asked, "But where was the teacher?" Noah said, "Oh, she just gave us some pages to do and she went some place. Anyway, Mom, I helped Henry and then he started to tell me the whole story of his life!"

Noah's open, easy-to-read face showed all his emotions as he talked about Henry—shock, sympathy and pride. Henry had confessed that he was sixteen years old and had cut classes most of his school life, that his parents were dead and he lived with two older brothers. "He said that last year his best friend got killed in a gang fight. That really shook him up and he decided he was gonna change. He said there was a good social worker in his neighborhood who could maybe have kept his friend from getting killed—but the money for the social worker ran out and he had to leave. Henry says

(299)

he wants to study real hard and catch up and go to college and be a social worker and then he'll work even if nobody pays him."

Noah, now five feet ten inches, heavily muscled and with a square outdoorsman face much like Ben's, shook his long blond hair back from his face and his eyes blinked back moisture. "Henry says he's gonna catch up and go to college if it takes him ten years. He says his brothers can't help him cuz they both work two jobs and anyway, they weren't too good in school. But Henry's in most of my classes, so I'm helpin' him and, Mom, I *never* saw anybody try so da . . . awfully hard."

For the next two weeks, Noah came home with stories of Henry's successes and casually handed me his own test papers. Noah also reported other incidents at school, all of which he turned into humorous anecdotes. That Tuesday, word had gone around that the white kids were going to get beat up. ("My gosh, there's only about twenty white kids in that whole school an' I had about a *hundred* black kids tellin' me they'd keep anybody from touchin' me! I spent the whole day thankin' kids who offered to be my bodyguards.")

On Monday, October 23, Noah came home to tell me that Henry had gotten a *B* in an algebra test. When I grabbed Noah's shoulders in my own delight for Henry, Noah winced. He said he'd fallen on the stairs that day. And he quickly asked if I'd found "that clipping you told me about yet." After he assured me he was "okay, just bruised," I gave him the clipping. It was an article about a young black man who was told he had an IQ of sixty-nine, decided one day he "didn't *feel* retarded" and, though he was in a reformatory for armed robbery, began to study. He was now, in September, 1972, carrying a straight *A* average in graduate school, planning to teach criminology in college. I had told Noah that Henry might feel encouraged if he knew that somebody farther behind than he had made it.

Noah read the newspaper article. "Yeah, wow! Henry'd like

that! I'll read it to him." Noah explained that "Henry doesn't read so good yet, but he's getting better."

On Wednesday, October 25, Noah reported that Henry had read the clipping himself "except for a couple of really hard words," but behind Noah's happiness for Henry, he looked troubled. Finally, he said, "Mom, I got patted down today." What was "patted down"? I asked.

Noah tried to treat the episode lightly, but he explained that "patted down" meant being searched for money. "Five kids surrounded me and one of 'em went through my jacket pockets. Then one other kid came up and said, 'Let him be,' and they split—went away. Wow! Was I glad they forgot to check my pants pocket! *That's* where I had my lunch money and trolley tokens."

Noah grinned, but the grin did not reach his eyes. He said, "Don't worry. It turned out okay." Did it? I thought Noah needed to talk about it; to deal, perhaps, with the same feelings of humiliation, fear and helplessness Spike had felt when Bernard Ludenheiser knocked him down.

Noah said, "Yeah, well, I was scared, but it would have been stupid if I'd have swung at them." What about his friends? "Aw, Mom, they're from a different gang and it woulda started a war if they'd have stepped in. Anyway, they weren't around and it turned out okay."

Perhaps it had after all, I told myself. Noah had kept his head and this experience might someday be lifesaving for him. Police strongly advise cooperating with robbers rather than risking your life. Ben was in high-crime Washington that week and I found myself wishing that Ben had had some practice in remaining calm in a situation like Noah's. There was little else I could do but rationalize. Noah insisted he had never seen this group of students before and, among three thousand kids, it would be hard to find them. "Don't worry about it, Mom," he said. "It turned out okay."

That evening, I telephoned Barbara Hamilton. We had never lost our close relationship during the years since they had moved to be nearer Leland's church. With our husbands, we were often together on weekends, but it was those three or four phone chats each week that strengthened the strong bond between us. For ten years, we had shared our large and small problems and it had become a joke between us that we each often exclaimed, "Well, am I glad I called *you!*" This was to be the first time I was not.

I called Barbara for reassurance and I did not get it. At first, we compared notes on our children's schools. Her son Jimmy went to a public high school in their neighborhood that had recently got bad publicity in the papers. According to Jimmy, the newspapers had greatly exaggerated. There were some "bad kids" who hung around certain corners; Jimmy simply avoided those corners. I agreed wholeheartedly with Barbara's statement that "children do not learn through being protected until they're eighteen . . . they have to learn gradually and by coping with reality." I told her of some of Noah's experiences, fully believing she would agree he was learning valuable lessons.

I felt an unusual irritation with Barbara when she paused for a moment and then said, "I don't know why, but something bothers me about Noah in that school. I've just got a funny feeling." "Funny feelings" I did not need. It was unlike Barbara to pass on rumors or gossip; why, of all times, would she make a vague statement like this?

Barbara added immediately, "I shouldn't have said that, I guess, but are you sure Noah is telling you everything?"

Of course, I was sure. Unlike Spike, Noah loved to talk about his experiences; his wide-open face had always made it difficult for him to hide his feelings and, I assured Barbara, he would have no reason to hold anything back.

"Oh, yes, he would, Lois. He knows how you and Ben feel about public school and he loves you."

I protested that Noah knew that the truth was important to me; if we had taught our children nothing else, it was that honesty was the only way to solve a problem. Barbara said,

"I hope you're right." When we ended our conversation, I felt angry at her for planting a foolish worry in my mind so late at night. I saw a light under Noah's door and decided to disprove Barbara's "funny feeling" so I could sleep comfortably.

Noah was reading in bed, his blond hair still dark from his shower and his bulky frame taking up most of the bed. I sat on the edge and said, laughingly, "Mrs. Hamilton thinks you aren't telling us how you really feel about Baldwin School."

Noah did not speak. He looked momentarily surprised and then he shook his head, silently, and then tears began to roll down his cheeks. I felt empty. Barbara had been right. There was something terribly wrong.

I said, "Noah, honey, don't ever tell someone only what you think they *want* to hear. People who love you want to hear what's true—no matter what it is."

Noah fought manfully against his tears. Amid blinks and gulps, he finally managed, "I didn't want you and Dad to think I was a cop-out."

At that moment, I was overwhelmed with pride in Noah's love and courage, but with anger at my own blindness. I said, "Oh, honey, we *know* you're not a cop-out. You couldn't be. If you're having problems we want to know."

Noah let out a huge sigh and began to talk about what he had held in so long. He had tried everything he could think of, he said. He had made friends with everyone possible. ("But there's three thousand kids in that school!") In his "house," it was okay, but on the way to or from the bus and to the gym was when the incidents happened. He had ignored the name-calling and the threats, but he had been spat upon, kicked, pushed down the stairs and punched. He had worked out different routes to the gym and the bus. ("So I just met *different* kids . . . like the kids who patted me down today.") And, Noah said bleakly, it was always different kids . . . "never the same kid twice."

"It's okay in my classes, Mom. Those kids are my friends,

but they're scattered all over when we leave. They're not around."

My stomach felt hard and cramped, but Noah had more to say and I wanted to appear calm so he could feel comfortable in telling me everything.

"And, well, I worry that I might lose my temper and hit one of those guys. Then I'd be hamburger in ten minutes. Half that school would jump me."

I asked about Warren, another white boy from Willis School, who was much smaller than Noah. "No, Mom, they don't bother him, only me."

Shocked and sick as I was about what Noah had hidden from us, I could think clearly enough to realize that small, slight Warren was no challenge to those hostile students. Big, husky, blond Noah was the natural lightning rod for every tough black kid who had to prove he was somebody; had to prove symbolically that he wasn't scared of "whitey."

Noah's blue-gray eyes filled suddenly with tears again. He gulped and looked down at his hands, pulling at the fabric of the blanket. "And today, Mom, when those guys surrounded me and searched me, I was scared. Those kids knew it. And if they know you're scared, it just gets worse."

I could be genuinely calm now because I had decided that Noah was not going back to Baldwin Junior High. We had believed that the rumors about Baldwin were as false as those about Germantown High and that Noah would be as comfortable in his school as was Spike. We had been wrong. I did not yet know why our sons' experiences were different, but I was planning to call St. Peter's Academy in the morning.

Then Noah swept my calm away. "Mom, you're right about telling the truth. I feel much better now and I think I can handle things at school tomorrow."

"Oh, no. You're not going back there, Noah. You've tried everything you could and we're proud of you, but I think you ought to go to another school."

Noah shook his head. "No, Mom, I want to go back there. I *gotta* try it again. I think I can handle it now. Please?"

Once more, a son of mine was asking me to have the courage to let him test his. I said, "No"; I said, "Let me think about it"; I said, "Let's decide in the morning." But I knew that by morning I had to be prepared to give Noah what I had given Spike after his attack by Bernard—the chance to face down his fright.

Back in my own room, I thought of phoning Ben in Washington, but I knew exactly what he would say and do. He would say I must let Noah go and he would sit up and worry as I was going to do.

I sat and smoked and stared into space. Spike's success at Germantown High had blinded me to the differences at Baldwin Junior High. Germantown now served eleventh and twelfth graders plus a handful of tenth graders in a special "magnet" social studies program. These students had nearly all passed the drop-out age and had *chosen* to stay in school; Baldwin's students were still victims—not of compulsory *education,* but of compulsory *attendance.* They were too young to drop out, too far behind to succeed. Yes, there were probably other Henrys there who, by some miracle, were working for a second chance, but how many others were like Josh Pitt, too ashamed of their illiteracy to get help, full of self-doubt, pride and anger.

Huddled in my chair, unhappy and dispirited, I realized that Baldwin Junior High was the terrible sum of all the mistakes, indifferences and racism I had seen accumulating over the years. It had been built, not in a stable, established black neighborhood like that served by Germantown High, but in a neighborhood newly emptied of whites where the new black families were strangers to each other, often desperately trying to meet the maintenance costs that realtors had minimized. I had seen the sad sequence as Mrs. Jefferson lived it: new house, new costs, two jobs for husband and wife, less time for the children. The children, new to the area, needed to prove themselves in whatever ways they could. Too many of these children had only one way to excel—through toughness and the courage to attack a big white kid like Noah.

I also recalled sitting next to a district school superintendent at a luncheon who said, "I'll deny it if you quote me, but the junior high concept was disproved years ago. This age group should not be isolated. They need the influence of the older mature seniors and they need four years in one school." But Baldwin Junior High had isolated this age group. After Central and Girls High had drained off the achievers, they had isolated the failures.

The stupidity had been compounded. Baldwin was equipped with costly frills—language labs, photo and automobile shops, closed-circuit television, an elaborate library—all as useful to illiterate students as a ten-speed bike to a crippled child. And to oversee this costly monument to bungling, a principal was chosen, not a black man with whom the children could identify, but a white man who had never been a principal before.

That night, I wished passionately that I could forget how many of those students had been hit and humiliated by the kinds of teachers I had known at Willis School. I knew too that, in the neighborhoods from which many of these children had come, the only white faces they saw were the policeman and the teacher, both symbols of white authority they had come to hate. These youngsters were old enough, big enough to hit back at those symbols. Noah was a handy target.

But although I had got my child into this, he would not let me get him out. Noah's pride and sibling rivalry were inextricably involved. Would it do any good, I wondered, to remind Noah that Spike had had only one, easily spotted white face to avoid while he had had a dozen attackers, each of whom could strike and disappear into the crowd? No, this was a foolish point to present. It would only make Noah more intent on surpassing Spike.

When morning finally arrived, I asked Noah, "May I drive you to school?" He softened his quick, firm No by explaining it wouldn't help. "I still gotta walk from the street and I gotta walk to gym class." Spike had already gone; Sarah was still dressing when Noah stood at the door, grinned and said, "Stay cool, Mom. I think it's gonna be okay today."

For the next six hours, I paid dearly for any pride I had ever felt in my principles. At three-thirty, I put on a coat and walked to the end of our driveway. Noah was coming along our street, limping. When I met him halfway down the block, he smiled weakly, "Don't worry. I'm just bruised. A bunch of kids threw me down the stairs." Then, "Mom, I guess I'm not gonna make it at that school."

Inside the house, Noah said, "Mom, I don't want to go to private school and I don't want to go to Turner High. Isn't there some school that's fifty-fifty?" I only wished there were. Turner High, at the edge of our district, was 82 percent white and Noah had met many of the Turner students at the skating rink. They were all, he insisted, "real bigots and they're all into drugs." (A friend of mine who worked there had described the drug problem: "Young kids walking around like zombies and the stealing that goes on there is horrible.")

Just then, Noah's "housemaster," a Mr. Ellwood, phoned. In a deep, rich, black voice, he said he knew what Noah had been going through and had tried to help. "In our house," he said, "all his classmates know him and like him. Outside . . . well, if it were just two or three students bothering him, I could handle it. I'll try anything you suggest, but I'll under- stand if he leaves. We'll all miss him here, but he's really tried." I told him about Noah's being thrown down the steps that day. "Yes," he said, "it's too bad things have to be this way. But right now, right here, that's how it is." The quiet despair in Mr. Ellwood's voice told me he knew, better than I, all the reasons why.

Mr. Ellwood asked where Noah would be going. I said I

did not know. "You might think about Saul High School," he said. "Not too many people know about it. It's an agricultural high school, but with a fine college prep curriculum." I thanked him for the suggestion and for everything he had tried to do.

The next morning, I phoned the principal of Baldwin Junior High to tell him we felt we had to take Noah out of his school. He asked no questions; expressed no regret. He said, "Oh. Well, the counselor for students whose names begin with S is absent today. Call back tomorrow."

I phoned the district office to explain why we felt Noah could not continue at Baldwin. Could he go to Saul High School? Dr. Kornreich, the Santa Claus-like superintendent who had once told me an integrating school area had been "written off," called me back in five minutes. "Ah, Lois, you *know* I'm always happy to help you. When would you like him to start?"

Noah was to begin at Saul High School on Monday. On Friday, Noah slept late and then rushed downstairs. "Mom, I forgot about Henry. What's gonna happen to him? Nobody helps him but me!"

I told Noah I would phone Miss Santilli who was Henry's counselor and his. Weeks before, I had asked her, at Noah's request, to try to get Henry into the "M" program, a special motivation program designed for underachievers with potential. She had tried to persuade Noah to join the program, but he felt (and I knew) that he did not need the trips to concerts and theaters, the tutoring, counseling and attention. Henry did. She had promised to check. So far, Henry had heard nothing.

Miss Santilli was glad Noah was leaving Baldwin. "This is no place for a child like him," she said. Henry? Oh, yes, she had checked Henry's records. He did not have the IQ the "M" program required.

Miss Santilli got my undiluted outrage. I told her about the young man in the newspaper article who had been labeled with a 69 IQ and was now a doctoral candidate; I demanded to know why none of the teachers, only Noah, had noticed how hard Henry was working and how completely alone. I shrieked into the phone, "Do you mean the motivation program only wants students who have always been motivated?"

"Gee, Mrs. Stalvey, I'm new here and those are the rules."

On October 30, 1972, Noah entered the school to which we finally had to flee. Ironically, it is the kind of school Noah's classmates at Baldwin need so much more. It has four hundred students, a staff of mature, experienced teachers, a curriculum that includes academics plus hours of physical work with plants and animals on acres of land. A boy can work up sweat and work out tensions, prepare for college or for a career in undercrowded professions. It is, I was appalled to learn, the only school of its kind in America. There are no plans for more.

At the same time that Noah left Baldwin School, the North had its own Little Rock and I thought of our Southern relatives. In the Canarsie section of New York City, police struggled to hold back a thousand jeering whites while twenty-eight black children entered a junior high. I wondered if any of the middle-class Jewish or Italian families of Canarsie had ever marched in the South.

On January 8, 1973, the Philadelphia teachers' union began another strike. This one would last a record two months. For me, it was the end of what few hopes I had for children like Henry, Josh, Almira, Poncho and Gus. Germantown High and Baldwin Junior High closed along with all the other secondary public schools. At Willis School, parent volunteers and the black teachers (along with a few white colleagues) kept classes going. Across Philadelphia, black teachers continued to work in predominantly black schools. Pickets (nearly all of them white) harassed them with obscenities and threats, slashed their tires and put sugar in their gas tanks. Telecasts of these professionals sticking out their tongues and defying police were depressing.

On February 16, a distinguished civic watchdog group, The Committee of 70, raised an even more depressing possibility. They had been told that most of the striking teachers were suburbanites "who have no stake in the city's schools beyond wanting to make a living from them and whose children, if they have any, go to school elsewhere. The implications of this are monstrous."

This accusation was never refuted. Instead, on February 18, Peter Binzen, a Philadelphia *Bulletin* reporter with a reputation for careful research, confirmed the fact that half of Philadelphia's thirteen thousand teachers live outside the city and that most of the nine thousand striking teachers were white. In addition he reported that not one of the negotiators on either side had children in the public schools—not the union officials, the school board negotiators, the school superintendent, the mayor, his cabinet nor sixteen members of the City Council. The implications were monstrous indeed.

On March 2, the strike was settled and again, the children lost. The city gave the union everything they had asked for— including the shortest teaching day in the nation.

On March 3, the superintendent of the Philadelphia schools talked of "teacher accountability" and urged parents and labor unions to cooperate in "weeding out incompetent employees." In a fine spirit of cooperation, the chief spokesman for the union replied immediately that the superintendent should resign. "He's the most expensive incompetent of them all."

Philadelphia's schools—like Detroit's, Boston's, Newark's and most other big cities—are close to bankruptcy. It is feared that if taxes are raised to meet union demands, more whites will run to the suburbs. If taxes are not raised, the mostly black big city schools will close. The children who got so little will get nothing at all.

epilogue

ON JUNE 28, 1973, SARAH WAS GRADUATED FROM THE SCHOOL where our children's education—and mine—began eleven years ago. I wish I were still naïve enough to count only the benefits to my children. There have been many. Spike, Noah and Sarah are unquestionably better prepared to cope with modern life than they would have been had we stayed in our Omaha suburb. If Sarah had grown up among suburban house-wives, her models would be limited. She might never have known woman judges, doctors, editors, college professors and lawyers. She may choose, as I did, motherhood bracketed by a profession. She has had a lifetime of liberated life-styles from which to make her choice. Spike's achievements in his big public high school have continued and increased. He has a confidence now that could only have come from conquering his handicap by himself, without special crutches, in a world where he must soon walk alone. If Noah continues to aim for a career in law and politics, the panorama of people he has known will free him from many blinding myths; he will never be handicapped by the artificial barriers of class or color.

As for my own education, it has brought me joy and fear —joy for my children and fear for what may be ahead. I am glad I am not now sitting in our suburban living room, flipping the pages of a newsmagazine, and believing the cities' problems do not affect my life. If I had not known the teachers, the administrators and the children, I might read Christopher

Jencks' report and naïvely believe his conclusion that education cannot change the future of children; I might accept the Jensen theory of inherited black ignorance. I might shrug my shoulders and feel these problems have nothing to do with me, that my children are secure. And I would be like Bluebeard's wife before looking into the forbidden room.

There was a time when I feared that America would create concentration camps for black Americans. The concentration camps I fear now are those we whites are creating for ourselves. If black children are "educated" for nothing but despair, our cities will soon be truly forbidden zones filled with the hopeless and the bitterly angry. South African apartheid was better planned than ours; they kept their cities in white hands and forced their blacks into the scattered suburbs. Even now, our concentration camps for whites have locks, guards and self-imposed curfews. It may soon be as impossible for people to leave their suburbs as it was for Noah to stay in Baldwin Junior High—and for the same reasons.

If, in this silent war, we lose our cities, we could lose our country. Cities are more than buildings and historical sites; they are where our young and our talented have cultivated and marketed their abilities, where minds cross-pollinate each other to bring forth a culture that enriches us all. If we whites are scattered and defending our isolated forts, united black cities could make us the butt of one of history's most ironic jokes. As the scattered tribes of native Americans did, we could lose our country to a small band of desperate and dedicated black people while we flee further and further into the wilderness.

The desperation is here and the dedication has begun. Black friends remind me that, since the 1954 Supreme Court decision, there is *more*, not less, segregation and most of it in the North. The big city schools, they say, are being bled "white" by white unions to a now-impending death. In anticipation of this, black schools like those of the Muslims have begun to form. Like the Catholic schools long ago, they are being formed, not to teach separatism, but to protect children from discrimination and to teach them pride. For the sake of children like Almira and Josh, like Gus and Poncho and Noah's friend, Henry, I hope these schools succeed. For the sake of my children and theirs, I am sorry white America offered no alternative.

Meanwhile, I try to hope and I grasp any small evidence I can find that promises this nightmare of separation may not come true. On Sarah's last day at Willis School, I thought I saw a glimpse of what could still be.

On the sidewalk outside the dull-red brick school, I watched a young white mother bend down to inspect her small son's drawings, as I had done so often during the eleven years as my children grew. I heard a noise. A young blond teacher had grabbed a small dark brown child and was shaking him, yelling while the child's face crumbled and his tears began to flow. My own reflexes started me moving toward her. Then I stopped. The young white mother had reached her first, had bent down and was wiping the little boy's eyes. The teacher had looked at her nervously and walked away into the crowd.

As I watched the teacher retreat, I noticed other white mothers with small children. Were there more than on that September day in 1962 when Spike's education and mine had begun? I think there were.

Perhaps it is still possible for integration to work in the only way it can ever work—if we white parents learn, along with our children, in schools we have come *to*, not run *from*.

It will take many strong, secure—and suspicious—parents to question "experts," to question why teachers are paid solely on their physical presence, why the school room is the only assembly line where the *product*, and not the producer, is blamed for its flaws.

Perhaps there are enough parents willing to try. Someone once said, "Men and nations act wisely only when all other alternatives have been exhausted."

MY THREE CHILDREN, NOW GROWN, HAVE TOLD ME WITH THEIR WORDS and their actions how valuable their education was for them. Sarah and Noah chose careers that involve working with children in trouble. (Spike chose a career where, he says, his hyperactivity is an asset. He is chef in a beautiful restaurant in Seattle.)

In 1979, when Noah was in Ithaca, New York, and Sarah was at the University of Florida, I left Philadelphia and chose Arizona, partly because it was equidistant from all three children. I expected that, with my children grown, the sadness of what I had learned about public education would no longer be part of my life.

I was wrong.

When I decided to teach a creative writing course one summer at Northern Arizona University in Flagstaff, I was asked to teach a course on racism based on my books.

Again, my WASP naïveté surfaced. "Is there racism in Flagstaff?" This beautiful campus, surrounded by pines and peaks and only miles from the enormous Navajo reservation, seemed so far from the problems of big cities.

It did not take long to learn that racism knows no geography.

Summer courses attract a potpourri of people. That first semester, I found a variety that surprised me. Privileged students from the suburbs of Phoenix and Tucson mixed with Navajo and Hopi students; the Middle East was well represented; African American students, mostly from football and basketball teams, added to the mixture. They would all, I knew, learn from each other.

I had, of course, heard about the nationwide practice of recruiting outstanding athletes no matter what their academic scores. And in the West, many of these young men come from Los Angeles high schools —in South Central L.A.—and are members of the Bloods and the Crips.

My students assured me that a truce prevailed at college. From the first year, my classes worked just as I had hoped. These young people actually formed friendships across the lines of color and class. Just as my children had learned about all people, so did my students. (It was interesting to me that so many upper-middle-class students very much wanted this experience.)

Like so many of the young people at Willis School, these young men and women from Crip and Blood territory responded to ordinary respect from an instructor.

But then I learned two things. The first was that just as "my" class at Willis School was being graduated into high school unable to read, many of these young athletes had made it all the way to college with second- and third-grade reading skills. Since my course was based on discussion and interaction, these young people could—and did—earn good grades, but how could they possibly manage in classes where reading was required? I could only imagine their frustrations. And I could only imagine what would happen to these young athletes if they did not achieve their dreams of playing in professional sports. When they talked with me, I could feel pain at their determination to beat the odds and make the pros. (Two actually did. One was shot to death when he went home to Crenshaw between seasons.)

The other example of the long reach of racism was how the bright minority students were counseled. Here in the West, Native American students were victims of the same kind of racist treatment as were African Americans. In both groups, I found that the brightest students were never encouraged to consider graduate school.

Students with 4.0 GPA's looked at me as if I were speaking a foreign language when I asked if they planned to get a Master's or a Ph.D. Once again, young people like my children were counseled and cosseted while students whose parents could not possibly counsel them were ignored.

The summers at NAU brought me some of the same experiences I endured at Willis School and, I kept reminding myself, these were the very last chances for young people who had miraculously made it this far.

I do not cherish being right. I wish I did not see evidence that my jeremiad at the end of this book is gradually coming true. Because of the angry young people in the cities, white people are indeed locking themselves away in gated communities. Millions of dollars are naïvely spent on belated attempts to conquer crime.

Perhaps someday we will realize that the criminals in the schools are not the children.

LOIS MARK STALVEY

Sedona, Arizona
January, 1997